SECURITY AND
SOUTHEAST ASIA

SECURITY AND SOUTHEAST ASIA

Domestic, Regional, and Global Issues

ALAN COLLINS

LYNNE
RIENNER
PUBLISHERS

BOULDER
LONDON

Published in the United States of America in 2003 by
Lynne Rienner Publishers, Inc.
1800 30th Street, Boulder, Colorado 80301
www.rienner.com

and in the United Kingdom by
Lynne Rienner Publishers, Inc.
3 Henrietta Street, Covent Garden, London WC2E 8LU

Library of Congress Cataloging-in-Publication Data
Collins, Alan, 1967–
  Security and Southeast Asia : domestic, regional, and global issues / Alan Collins.
  Includes bibliographical references and index.
  ISBN 1-58826-210-3 (hc. : alk. paper)
  ISBN 1-58826-235-9 (pbk. : alk. paper)
  1. Asia, Southeastern—Strategic aspects.   2. Asia, Southeastern—Defenses.   3. National
  security—Asia, Southeastern.   4. World politics—21st century.   I. Title.
  UA832.8C64   2003
  355'033059—dc21

                                                                              2003046723

British Cataloguing in Publication Data
A Cataloguing in Publication record for this book
is available from the British Library.

Printed and bound in the United States of America

The paper used in this publication meets the requirements
of the American National Standard for Permanence of
Paper for Printed Library Materials Z39.48-1992.

5   4   3   2   1

Contents

Preface

This book follows another I wrote on Southeast Asia back in 1999. In that book—*The Security Dilemmas of Southeast Asia*—I was concerned with developing the concept of the security dilemma, using Southeast Asia as a case study. Once it was completed, I was keen to cast my net wider to examine the variety of security issues that bedevil this region. I also wanted to engage in the debates taking place within the field of security studies itself, particularly with regard to the broadening and deepening of what the field encompasses. Finally, having written two books aimed specifically at an audience of specialists, I wanted to write something that would be accessible to undergraduates as well. This book is the result.

The book is not a state-by-state account of military doctrine (a traditional approach), nor does it cover all the nontraditional security issues, which include people-smuggling, international crime, and AIDS. I do, though, attempt to apply the concept of security in its varied manifestations to Southeast Asia and thereby to reveal not only the range of security matters in the region, but also the complexity of what security itself means.

When I was nearing the final draft of my previous book in early 1998, the wide-ranging impact of the Asian financial/economic crisis was just beginning to be appreciated. I was suddenly left having to time-restrict certain findings and to adjust others in the light of reactions to the crisis—the fall of Suharto and the notion of flexible engagement being prime examples—delaying the book by at least a year. And now again, a major event in the world, one with tragic consequences, has led me to adjust a book manuscript: September 11. I had always intended to conclude this book with illustrative case studies. The first case was, and still is, the South China Sea dispute. The second was to be East Timor, illustrating the failure of Indonesian nation building and providing an initial assessment of East Timor's nation-building approach. This has been replaced by a discussion of the "War on Terrorism," in which Southeast Asia is apparently the second front—as illustrated all too clearly by the bombing in Bali.

*   *   *

There are of course many people and institutions to thank for helping me to write this book; they have provided the financial, intellectual, and emotional support without which the work could not have been accomplished. I am again indebted to the British Academy and its Committee for South East Asian Studies for their financial support, which enabled me to spend ten weeks in Singapore in late 2002 as I was putting the finishing touches to the manuscript. While in Singapore, I was a visiting fellow at the Institute of Defence and Strategic Studies (IDSS) at Nanyang Technological University and used the library facilities at the Institute of Southeast Asian Studies (ISEAS). There are a number of people to thank at IDSS for their help. The entire staff made me feel welcome and created a supportive environment in which to work. A number deserve special thanks in this regard: Ralf Emmers and Tan See Seng, for commenting on earlier drafts and providing useful feedback; Helen Nesadurai and Evelyn Goh, for help on economic and environmental details, respectively; Yee Ming, for helping me locate numerous articles held in a multitude of databases; and Peter Ee, for helping to arrange all of the paperwork and accommodation. I am also grateful to Mark Hong for inviting me to attend the RUSI-IDSS conference on the "New Security Environment After 9/11." All in all I could not have wished to be in a better environment to complete the research.

I want to thank my own Department of Politics and International Relations at the University of Wales Swansea for providing an intellectual home and financial assistance. I am also indebted to the anonymous reviewer who provided insightful and thought-provoking comments that certainly helped to clarify issues in my mind and improve the text.

Two friends deserve special thanks: in the UK, Helen Brocklehurst, for always making me laugh, often unintentionally; and Patrik Wahlberg, for his companionship while in Singapore (our unnerving visit to Bintan a couple of weeks before the Bali bombing brought home the enormity of the tasks facing the Jakarta regime as it tries to resurrect Indonesia).

Finally, my thanks to my parents, who provided wonderful support during a time in my life that witnessed much change.

All of these people have had a role in making this book possible, and I am grateful for their time and patience.

Alan Collins

I

Introduction:
Security and Southeast Asia

This is a fascinating time to be studying security and the security of Southeast Asia. The idea of security, its assumptions for so long unquestioned, is now being examined. Scholars are asking questions about the nature of security itself. What does it mean to be secure? What is to be secured and what constitutes a threat? This has entailed both a broadening and deepening of what the study of security entails. The state has traditionally been the unit of analysis to be secured—the referent object of security—but it is not the only referent object. What of the international system itself, or indeed, societies within states such as ethnic groups? Perhaps the individual should be our referent object? Is security solely a military issue? Could security considerations also arise from environmental degradation, economic collapse, societal upheaval, or political illegitimacy?

The events taking place in Southeast Asia are likewise posing challenging questions. The financial crisis of 1997–1998 had not only an economic impact on the region, but also political ramifications, most spectacularly in Indonesia where it brought to an end the thirty-year rule of Suharto's New Order regime. Since 1997, other security issues have come to the fore. In the environment sector, the forest fires in Indonesia have created security problems, in terms of both health and lost tourist revenue, and led to diplomatic squabbles between states. The region is home to a host of other nontraditional security problems, such as drug trafficking, human trafficking (slavery), and organized crime. The Association of Southeast Asian Nations (ASEAN) has struggled to cope with this myriad of problems, leading many commentators to question its continuing viability. Not all of these subjects are covered in this book, but I will endeavor to locate a number of Southeast Asian security issues within the broadening and deepening of security that has emerged since the end of the Cold War.

This chapter has two objectives. The first is to introduce the development of security studies from its Cold War strategic-studies emphasis to the new approaches of critical security studies, securitization, and human security. The second objective is to introduce Southeast Asia as a security complex, providing a brief account of its history and a context for the material that the succeeding chapters examine.

The question of what constitutes a security issue, and indeed who or what is to be secured, had been little debated in the academic field prior to the publication of Barry Buzan's seminal work, *People, States and Fear,* in 1983.[1] This is not to say there were not a plethora of important and highly influential books on contemporary security issues, for there clearly were. The writings of Bernard Brodie, Thomas Schelling, and Albert Wohlstetter, for example, are crucial in understanding the direction of nuclear deterrence theory and U.S. nuclear strategy in particular during the Cold War. That this literature was so important in the security field reflected the dominance of military issues, especially those concerned with nuclear weapons. Consequently, security studies during the Cold War focused almost exclusively on military defense and deterrence, particularly the East-West conflict. Hence David Baldwin's statement that

> Security has not been an important analytical concept for most security studies scholars. During the Cold War, security studies was composed mostly of scholars interested in military statecraft. If military force was relevant to an issue, it was considered a security issue; and if military force was not relevant, that issue was consigned to the category of low politics. . . . [P]uzzlement as to how a central concept like security could be so ignored disappears with the realisation that military force, not security, has been the central concern for security studies.[2]

With the end of the Cold War and the military standoff between the superpowers, scholars have challenged the assumptions underlying security studies. In particular, the emphases placed on protecting state sovereignty and territorial integrity from an external military threat have been attacked for being too narrow. Indeed, those writers who had focused attention on the military aspect of security at the expense of other areas have been regarded as part of the security problem, not part of the solution.[3] *People, States and Fear* and even more so its successor, *Security: A New Framework for Analysis,* broadened the scope of security to encompass, in addition to the military dimension, such issues as economics, the environment, and society. In addition to broadening security to other sectors, there has also been a deepening of security. Who or what is to be secured—the referent object of security—has become a key issue in the security studies literature. Essentially, this deepening entails moving away from the state as the sole focus of security, or referent object, and embracing, among others, individuals and identity as possible alternative referents. This becomes particularly important when addressing security problems within states, where for instance a challenge to a group's ethnic identity may lie behind an incidence of violence.

In addition to the broadening and deepening of security, the field has also been challenged on one of its key assumptions: power and stability equates to security. In keeping with the normative turn in international relations theory, the assumptions of Realism that had underpinned the national security debates of the Cold War have been subjected to re-evaluation. One such approach is known as critical security studies (CSS).[4] CSS rejects the assumption that security is achieved through accumulation of power and instead argues that because states with similar notions of social justice and economic wealth do not go to war against one another, here lies the basis of security.[5] Drawing upon Michael Doyle's liberal peace theory—essentially, democracies do not go to war against one another—the critical security studies literature replaces power with emancipation.[6] Hence, as Ken Booth so forcefully argues, "Security and emancipation are two sides of the same coin. Emancipation, not power or order, produces true security. Emancipation, theoretically, is security."[7] Booth is claiming that security comes from the freeing (emancipation) of people from constraints. These constraints can be structural—the way in which the international system operates—as well as constraints created by the elite in power. Structural constraints would include an international trading system that favors developed nations, while constraints proposed and enforced by an elite would include discrimination against minority ethnic groups. The attainment of economic wealth and social justice, via the provision of education, the eradication of poverty, and freedom from political oppression, enables individuals and groups to acquire security. Like-minded states that provide economic and social well-being for their populations are able to form security communities and thus eliminate force as a means to solve problems. Thus for CSS, security comes from freeing people from poverty (want) and political oppression (fear), not by achieving stability or maintaining an order that reinforces constraints placed on the people.

The interest in expanding the referent of security to include individuals or groups within a state has become part of a recently named concept of security called human security. The first major statement on human security came in the 1994 *Human Development Report* from the United Nations Development Program (UNDP). The definition of human security is twofold: "first, safety from such chronic threats as hunger, disease and repression. And second, it means protection from sudden and harmful disruptions in the patterns of daily life—whether in homes, in jobs or in communities."[8] The second element is so broad as to encompass almost any discomfort in a person's life, but the first clearly echoes the CSS emphasis on emancipation.

The *Human Development Report* identifies seven specific elements that constitute human security: economic security (freedom from poverty); food security (access to food); health security (protection from disease and provision of health care); environmental security (protection from pollution and resource depletion); personal security (physical safety from torture, war, and criminal attacks); community security (survival of cultural identity); and political security (freedom from political oppression). Thus it is a mixture of two aspects: freedom from want and freedom from fear.[9] As noted below, these are not new concerns and indeed were appearing in security literature on the third world in the 1980s. The key issue with human security is that with the security referent becoming people (whether individuals or groups) as opposed to states, what constitutes security changes. Rather than the traditional notion that security emanates from achieving strategic stability for external defense or domestic order for internal stability, human security is achieved by changing a domestic order that causes insecurity for its people and an international order that condemns them to lifelong poverty.

Whether the concept of human security—and the CSS emphasis upon emancipation—entails a challenge to the discipline's statecentric approach is a moot point.[10] The former Australian foreign minister, Gareth Evans, when commenting upon cooperative and human security, claims they are "less likely to be inhibited by familiar . . . traditional state-centered security thinking."[11] Yet writing in 1999, Lloyd Axworthy, the Canadian foreign minister, was clear that while enhancing the security of the people was the primary objective, this was best accomplished by strengthening state security. He writes that "security between states remains the necessary condition for the security of the people."[12] This difference can also be seen in the academic literature. Barry Buzan, writing about human security, claims:

> States may not be a sufficient condition for individual security, and they may even be the main problem . . . But they are almost certainly a necessary condition for individual security because without the state it is not clear what other agency is to act on behalf of individuals.[13]

For Tan See Seng, however, human security discourse should not hold allegiance to the state as a necessity.[14] Human security should be focused on humans, not states.

In this text since the concern is with the security problems of states within Southeast Asia and the threat state elites pose to their own people, I have adopted the Buzan approach. Thus when the prime minister of Malaysia, Mahathir Mohamad, argues that the attainment of "national security is inseparable from political stability, economic success and social harmony," this is true only if that stability, success, and harmony are constituted by the population rather than constituted at their expense by the elite.[15] It will be noted below that in the context of third world security, the elite usually determines what constitutes security, and more often than not, political stability, economic success, and social harmony are sought to achieve "regime security," which the elite erroneously treats as synonymous with "national security." The question of which actors within a state have the power to determine what constitutes a security question is one addressed by the Copenhagen School.

Bill McSweeney uses the term *Copenhagen School* to refer to pioneering work conducted by, among others, Barry Buzan and Ole Wæver on the broadening and deepening of security.[16] With regard to the latter, it was the Copenhagen School that introduced society as a referent object (societal security) to complement the state. The Copenhagen School also has addressed the question of what is and is not a security issue, and this work has become known as securitization.[17]

Although a cumbersome term, securitization refers to a two-stage process that makes an issue a security issue. First, an actor (usually the elite) has to couch the issue as an existential threat. This does not automatically mean it has become a security issue. Wæver writes that a "discourse that takes the form of presenting something as an existential threat to a referent object does not by itself create securitization—this is a securitizing move, but the issue is securitized only if and when the audience accepts it as such."[18] Therefore—and this is the second stage—for an issue to be regarded as a security issue, the audience (usually the population) has to accept the elite's interpretation of events and recognize that extraordinary measures must be implemented. Securitization not only provides the definition of a security issue—an existential threat—it also examines which actors initiate the securitizing move and the need for the audience to accept this interpretation of events so that it becomes a security issue. Securitization therefore also reveals the power of the actor that initiates this move. While it is possible for the population to initiate the securitizing move, such as the people-power revolutions in Eastern Europe at the end of the Cold War or the *reformasi* movement in Indonesia and Malaysia, it is more common for the securitizing move to come from the elite. The elite, or government, is thus privileged in this respect. Hence Wæver's comment that to "study securitization is to study the power politics of a concept."[19] Wæver's work on securitization is, along with the CSS literature, a seminal piece in the security studies debates of the post–Cold War era.

A recent example of securitization took place in Indonesia in the aftermath of the terrorist attack on October 12, 2002, in Bali. In this attack over 180 people were killed when two bombs exploded in the Kuta beach district, destroying a number of buildings including the Sari nightclub. The Indonesian authorities immediately sought executive powers to detain suspected individuals without recourse to the rule of law. Justice Minister Yusril Ihza Mahendra made the securitizing move when he justified the need for such powers by stating: "Terrorism is an extraordinary and inhuman crime. Therefore, we need extraordinary laws to deal with it."[20] Although human rights activists expressed concern the government was adopting the draconian powers employed during President Suharto's dictatorship, they represented a minority voice. The main reaction from within Indonesia—the country's two main Muslim groups supported the decision—and from other states was to welcome the government's decisive action after months of procrastination. The audience thus accepted the securitizing actor's interpretation of events. That is, terrorism was recognized by the audience as a threat, thus requiring extraordinary measures from the elite to counter it.

Security studies has therefore thrown off the all-consuming element of military matters (what is better known as strategic studies) to encompass the myriad of issues that affect the security of states and individuals. This has not taken place without its dissenters who argue that broadening the scope of security will mean that it becomes a catchall concept that loses its "intellectual coherence."[21] Roland Paris notes this lack of coherence with regard to human security, which he derides as "so vague that it verges on meaninglessness."[22] This concern—that human security is both vague and also such a fundamental challenge to core traditional security assumptions that it risks becoming marginalized in policy circles dominated by traditional thinking—has led William Tow and Russell Trood to argue for a reconciliation between traditional thinkers and the human security agenda. They note that there "continues to be a large number of writers and practitioners for whom the key elements of the traditional security paradigm is as relevant today as at the height of the Cold War. In these circumstances, the challenge for the advocates of human security is to define and present their concept with rigour and clarity and to demonstrate how it might be operationalized in an international environment not readily conducive to radical reinterpretations of security."[23] Whether such reconciliation is possible is questionable, given the different underlying assumptions about what constitutes security, but as will be discussed later, it is not impossible.[24]

The work on securitization has also been critiqued, with Olav Knudsen arguing that by seeing security as a speech act, in which a privileged actor makes something a security issue by convincing others that it is, the issue becomes nothing more than something the actor fears. Knudsen's view is that this may discount "real" dangers that have an independent existence.[25] While Knudsen's critique is actually less about securitization and more about the move away from the state as the referent object of security, the point is well made that securitization makes an issue a security issue because it is presented as such, not because an actual threat exists.[26]

The field of security studies has therefore undergone some important changes in recent times. In addition to broadening security to encompass economics, the environment, and society, it has also deepened to ask what unit (the individual, the state, the international system) is to be secured. This has led to the questioning of key assumptions underpinning the study of security and has raised the prospect that security comes not from power or order, but from emancipation. A sophisticated approach has also developed for understanding why certain issues are regarded as security issues. The upshot is that the study of security has undergone an extensive period of examining its key concept (security), which has provided more questions than answers. This, though, is not a problem; Steve Smith is right to argue that the study of security "is in a far healthier state than [before], even if, no, *because*, it is less secure about its referent points, about the meaning of security and above all about its foundations [emphasis in original]."[27]

In the aftermath of the terrorist attacks on the World Trade Center and the Pentagon on September 11, 2001 (9/11), the security studies field has focused not surprisingly on the military threat posed by global

terrorism and the military response to that threat. The latter was evident
in the immediate months after 9/11 in the U.S. attack against al-Qaeda
in Afghanistan and, more broadly, its "war on terrorism" that U.S.
President George W. Bush has claimed will not stop "until every terrorist group of global reach has been found, stopped and defeated."[28] This
return to military matters is having two immediate effects in the field of
security studies, the first concerned with human security.

One response to global terrorism has been for the state elite to make
it harder for terrorists to operate by limiting civil liberties within their
country. This has immediate consequences for human security, with the
prospect of policies, measures, rules, and/or practices being adopted that
give the elite enormous coercive power vis-à-vis their populations, for
example, the ability to hold without charge an individual suspected of
subversion. This is a prime example of a threat to human security and is
captured in Booth's call to emancipate people from political oppression.
It should be noted that in some Southeast Asian states the coercive powers available to the elite—known as internal security acts (ISA)—are not
a new phenomenon. However, because of 9/11 these powers have been
consolidated. Hadi Soesastro notes, while before "September 11, there
was some talk about phasing out . . . the ISA [in Singapore and
Malaysia] . . . This agenda is likely to be postponed."[29] The impact of the
war on terrorism on Southeast Asian security is examined in Chapter 7.
The immediate consequence of 9/11 therefore is that attempts to shift the
security paradigm away from the state as the referent object, and military
matters as *the* existential threat, are likely to become frustrated.

The second consequence of 9/11 on the security studies field relates
to academic discourse. The danger is that the progress the field has
made in broadening and deepening will be stymied by those interested
in keeping security within the tight parameters established during the
Cold War. Richard Stubbs provides a forewarning of this in his review
of *The Many Faces of Asian Security*, which was published before 9/11
and embraces the broadening of the definition of security. Stubbs writes
that while "the book makes a significant contribution to the literature on
security in the Asia-Pacific region, its impact will be lessened some-
what by the fact that global security was changed dramatically by the
events of 11 September 2001. The definition of security has, in [Donald
K.] Emmerson's terms, once again been narrowed."[30] While 9/11 has
raised global terrorism to the top of the security agenda, the myriad of
security problems unearthed by broadening and deepening has not disappeared. It remains incumbent on academics working in the field to
comment upon them, even if the policymaking community is more con-

cerned with direct attacks on national security, as they were during the Cold War.

The broadening and deepening of security studies is a development of particular relevance to those interested in the security of third world states. For the most part, security studies, like much of the international relations literature, has assumed a Eurocentric view of the international system. The focus lay on the anarchic nature of the international system determining state interaction in the security field—epitomized by the security dilemma—and this was transplanted to other parts of the world, hence the focus on external threats to state survival. The security of Asia was seen through the lens of the superpower conflict, as the United States and the USSR sought allies in their global struggle. Any interest shown in a particular region was determined by its impact on the global balance of power. Hence Joseph Nye and Sean Lynn-Jones's comment in their 1988 survey of the security studies field that much "of the work in international security studies has neglected the regional political context of security problems. Many American scholars and policy-makers made recommendations for U.S. policy in the Vietnam War in almost complete ignorance of the politics of Southeast Asia."[31]

By the 1980s, however, a number of publications appeared that examined the security problems of the third world from its own perspective. One of the most prolific authors has been Mohammed Ayoob and his work on state making, which will be discussed later. Caroline Thomas was one of the first authors to explore the need to move toward state making and nation building and away from focusing on external threats to the state—military threats in particular—in order to appreciate third world security problems. She writes:

> [S]ecurity in the context of the Third World . . . does not simply refer to the military dimension, as is often assumed in the Western discussions of the concept, but to the whole range of dimensions of a state's existence which are already taken care of in the more-developed states . . . for example, the search for internal security of state through nation-building, the search for secure systems of food, health, money and trade.[32]

The significance of Thomas's "already taken care of in the more-developed states" comment cannot be underestimated. This reveals that the core of the security problems facing third world states stems from their early stage of state making and nation building, when the state and regime in power are seeking to consolidate their legitimacy. These problems have largely been resolved in the developed world, although the rise of internal violence within the former Yugoslavia and former Soviet Union in the post–Cold War era indicates that these issues are relevant to some of the security problems of what used to be called the second world. Indeed, it is the relevance of this third world security literature to the new security problems facing Europe that leads Amitav Acharya to argue that the "analysis of regional conflict in the contemporary security discourse can benefit from a framework that captures the significantly broader range of issues . . . that lie at the heart of insecurity and disorder in the Third World."[33] The security studies literature that seeks a broadening and deepening of security studies in the post–Cold War era is therefore much more relevant to the third world than its strategic studies predecessor, and vice versa. Hence Acharya's conclusion that "the end of the Cold War should serve as a catalyst for the coming of age of Third World security studies."[34]

In this book I focus on security issues in Southeast Asia, which entails an appreciation of the security problems of third world states. This assertion requires some clarification since it might be argued that because Southeast Asia includes at least one Asian newly industrialized economy (ANIE)—Singapore—and contains others on the verge of such a status, the term *third world* might appear inaccurate. However, the term is not purely an economic one relating to issues of underdevelopment, resource scarcity, and poverty but also to the primacy of internal threats to security and the dependence on external actors for security guarantees. The latter two are certainly evident in Southeast Asia, and indeed the poverty associated with the third world can also be seen— even before the 1997 economic crisis—in Indonesia, Thailand, and Vietnam, for example. The primacy of internal threats to state security, and especially regime security, however, most readily makes Southeast Asia a part of the third world. Internal threats to these states will be examined in Chapters 2 and 3.

The key to understanding the security issues in Southeast Asia is legitimacy; and the legitimacy in question concerns both the regimes in power and the state's borders. In the former case, legitimacy is dependent upon "whether citizens are loyal and willingly support state policies—whether they accept the authority of the state and believe existing institutions are in some sense appropriate."[35] The legitimacy of state borders is dependent upon the population's sense of loyalty and identity with what are often colonial creations. This issue of regime and state legitimacy lies at the heart of third world security problems; it is the lack of legitimacy that makes them weak states.

The concept of weak states was introduced to the literature in

People, States and Fear, and this term is particularly apt for the third world.[36] The defining characteristic of a weak state is the lack of sociopolitical cohesion within the state; it does not refer to its poor military or economic capacity. Thus while China has the economic growth and increasing military capability to be regarded by some observers as the next great threat to the West, the Chinese Communist Party's (CCP) concerns about secessionist demands from Tibet, Taiwan, and the western province of Xinjiang, combined with concern over its flagging legitimacy after the collapse of communism in Europe and the brutality the regime showed toward the student protestors at Tiananmen Square, add up to make China a weak state.[37] The lack of sociopolitical cohesion relates directly to the issue of legitimacy. Buzan acknowledges that many weak states can be found in the third world and that this "fact points to decolonization as one cause."[38]

The establishment of colonial states rarely resulted in the creation of a single nation-state but rather a territorial entity with many ethnic groups within it. Likewise, it was not uncommon for these states' borders to divide groups, thus producing within a state disparate groups of people that have more in common with people in neighboring states than they do with one another. For example, because of the location of the international border between Thailand and Malaysia, the southern states of Thailand are home to the Patani Malay. The Patani Malay are ethnically and religiously part of the Malay world, and thus the Muslim population identifies with the people of Malaysia more than with their fellow Thai citizens.[39] This divide occurred because of British colonial influence, and Clive Christie asserts the "division provides a classic example of an *ad hoc* colonial arrangement that has since hardened into a permanent international frontier. The British takeover of the four Malay states undoubtedly had the effect of triggering irredentist ambitions in Patani itself."[40] The international border between Indonesia and Papua New Guinea has likewise divided the Melanesian population of New Guinea, leading to irredentist demands from the peoples of West Papua (previously known as Irian Jaya/West Irian). Such divisions of ethnic groups can be witnessed not only in other areas of the third world, but they can also be seen in Europe, especially the former Yugoslavia, with Serbs living in the Krajina region of Croatia and Albanians living in the autonomous Serb province of Kosovo.

The elite in the decolonized states of the third world—Thailand was the only state in Southeast Asia not a colony—found themselves at the early stage of state making and nation building with a territorial entity that had contentious borders and a population of different ethnic groups that did not necessarily see themselves as part of, for example, an Indonesian or Malaysian nation. State making entails the elite, or regime in power, achieving political legitimacy among the populace as it extends the state's institutions and bureaucracies from the core to the periphery of the state. Through maintenance of law and order, taxation, and provision of goods and services, the state's institutions provide security and well-being for the population. If this is achieved and the population has an influence on the decisionmaking process, then the elite will be able to rule by consent and will be regarded as legitimate rulers. This relates directly to the earlier discussion on human security. If the population can influence the adoption of policies, including those related to security, then the people constitute the state's security policies. The attainment of legitimacy by the elite is thus a critical element in safeguarding human security.

Nation building entails the creation of common cultural traits among the populace, which in turn produces a sense of community and solidarity. In view of the different ethnic groups within these states, successful nation building usually involves a degree of acculturation where an overriding national identity is adopted that supplements the ethnic groups' traditional identities. In Great Britain a British identity complements the national identities of Wales, Scotland, and England. In the third world this acculturation is sometimes referred to as "unity in diversity." The question of nation building thus relates directly to the *Human Development Report*'s emphasis on community security, or what the Copenhagen School calls societal security. As with state making, the acculturation process will have legitimacy so long as the population determines the policies pursued.

Successful state making and nation building, however, is not common in the third world. The elite often represent only a few of the groups that constitute the state's population, and thus extending the state's institutions and bureaucracies to the peripheral communities can be interpreted as a threat to traditional power holders in these communities. The elite state-making approach can have the paradoxical effect of creating resistance to the regime in power and thus lessens not strengthens its legitimacy. If this state-making approach is complemented by a nation-building approach that bases the nation's identity around the cultural, religious, and linguistic properties of the elite's ethnic group, then extension of the state's influence is even more likely to be resisted. The elite in power increasingly appear to be a threat to the peripheral communities. The consequence of this approach to state making and nation building is that alternative sources will emerge to compete with the regime for the populace's loyalty. Should these alternative sources succeed, then the regime's legitimacy will be further eroded, and if this alternative source takes the form of a secessionist movement, the legitimacy of the state's borders will also be brought into question.

The tragedy for states and their populations is that the early stage in the state-making and nation-building process is marked by use of coercion and/or violence by the elite. The reason lies in the type of institutional machinery available to the elite when resistance to their state-making and nation-building policies arise. With the institutional machinery in its infancy and underdeveloped, often the only "national" tool available to the elite is the military. Thus, for example, if actors representing opposing groups within the state's population question the regime's legitimacy, the elite have few alternative tools other than the military with which to impose order and coerce rebellious elements into accepting the regime's rule. Violence orchestrated by the regime was most cruelly epitomized by the barbaric Pol Pot reign in Cambodia and can be still seen in the weak Southeast Asian states of Burma (renamed Myanmar by the military regime in 1989) and Indonesia. The use of coercion, though, creates a paradoxical situation in which the elite's actions, far from strengthening their legitimacy, undermine it. The more the elite uses the military to impose and maintain order, the more the military gain influence over the direction of policy, and thus the more likely that the regime will resort to military action. In all too many instances, the result is establishment of military rule, or as in the case of Indonesia, the military gains a political function.[41] Security is thus equated with maintaining order.

The tragedy of the situation becomes even more marked, according to Mohammed Ayoob, because of the current international climate in which third world elites are trying to state make and nation build; he refers to this as the third world's security predicament.[42] Ayoob notes that violence in the early stages of state making is nothing new and, referring to the work of Charles Tilly, states that the European experience of state making was "painfully slow and extraordinarily violent."[43] The creation of strong states in Europe followed the path of brutal state making proceeding to nation building. The internal violence associated with the third world is thus not abnormal but in accordance with the European experience. However, the circumstances in which third world elites are state making and nation building are quite different from those their European counterparts faced in the seventeenth and nineteenth centuries. These differences not only make state making and nation building more difficult, they also suggest that resorting to coercion is unlikely to be a successful policy.

There are essentially two critical differences between the European and third world state-making experiences. The first concerns the politicization of the third world population prior to the establishment of a strong state, and the second relates to the short time span the third world elite have to make their state strong.

Politicization of the population refers to the awareness among them of their social, economic, and political rights. A politically aware population is one that will desire political participation and demand an equitable distribution of the state's economic wealth. This was not evident in the European state-making experience where "state-makers constructed, then imposed, strong national governments before mass politics began," whereas in third world regimes, "these two processes tend to occur together."[44] Thus the elite are faced with demands, such as political pluralism and respect for human rights that were not prevalent in the European state-making enterprise. Ayoob therefore notes that state making is much harder to achieve. He writes:

> Satisfying popular demands can frequently run counter to the imperatives of state making, because state making, as the European experience has demonstrated, is a rather unsavoury task and often involves levels of coercion that are bound to be unacceptable to populations that have been influenced by notions of human rights (for groups and individuals), political participation, and social justice.[45]

The existence of a politicized population therefore reduces the likelihood of a regime achieving legitimacy by resorting to coercion. Far from suppressing the people's demands or removing an alternative source for their loyalty, the regime's actions merely highlight the discrepancy that exists between its rule and that achieved by the liberal democracies of the developed world.

Another factor that makes state making much harder to achieve concerns the length of time the elite have to accomplish it. European state making was achieved over a period of centuries, whereas the third world elite are attempting to achieve something similar as quickly as possible. The problem that arises is the violence that marked the European experience was interspersed with periods of calm. The elite could grow stronger as each opposition was eliminated one at a time, until the elite emerged as the only rulers. In the third world, the crises follow one another over such short time frames that the elite do not have the opportunity to strengthen their power base and achieve legitimacy. Ayoob writes:

> When spread over a period of time and essentially localized regionally and socially, state-induced violence and counterviolence could give the appearance of a succession of manageable crises in the drawn-out process of state building.
>
> However, given the short amount of time at the disposal of state makers in the Third World and the consequent acceleration in their state-making efforts, crises erupt simultaneously, become unmanageable as they overload the political and military capabilities of the state, and lead to a cumulation of crises that further erodes the legitimacy of the fragile post-colonial state.[46]

The violence that marked the European experience is thus not a template the third world can use to successfully state make. The domestic demands of the population and the international environment in which the third world elite are state making require alternative approaches: respect for human rights and the adoption of democracy. In Booth's terms, internal security must come from emancipation, not oppression.

Although Ayoob is not convinced that emancipation is a useful security tool for the third world, he nevertheless recognizes that the different circumstances facing the third world elite make these alternatives essential to successful state and nation building:

> In the climate of these changed domestic and international attitudes, the move toward democratization is no longer merely a laudable goal for states in the Third World; it has become a political precondition for establishing legitimate state structures and regimes that enjoy the acquiescence, if not the enthusiastic support, of their populations.[47]

In other words, the attainment of state security can only be achieved in conjunction with and not at the expense of human security. The success and the failure of the states of Southeast Asia to state make and nation build by strengthening their legitimacy form the first two chapters of the book. Chapter 2 examines the challenge of state making and nation building where the state is home to a diverse set of ethnic groups. Chapter 3 explores responses of the region's regimes to political ideologies that have challenged their legitimacy.

Southeast Asia

The security concerns of Southeast Asian states are not solely concerned with internal threats; they also keep a watching brief on their neighbors. The security dynamics that operate among the eleven states of the region have produced a Southeast Asian security complex—one that exhibits both amity and enmity.[48]

The term *security complex* was coined by Barry Buzan to refer to a region where the interdependence between the states is sufficiently intense that their national security concerns cannot be analyzed or resolved separately from others within the region. Buzan has revisited security complex theory and expounded it; its previous incarnation is now referred to as Classical Security Complex Theory (CSCT).[49] The development of security complex theory has moved it away from a sole focus on traditional security matters, known as the political-military sector, to include additional security concerns and additional international actors. In *Security: A New Framework for Analysis,* two different types of security complexes are introduced.[50]

The first type of security complex is referred to as homogeneous. This complex maintains the focus on specific sectors found in CSCT. Where the sector under examination is the political-military nature of states' relations it is no different from CSCT, but the adoption of a different sector would change not only the nature of the security issue under examination but also the actors involved. For example, a societal security complex would examine issues of identity reproduction and comprise identity-based units.

The second type of security complex abandons the separate sector approach and examines the interaction within a region among a number of different actors within different sectors, producing a holistic picture of the region's interactions. This type of security complex is known as heterogeneous. The advantage of the heterogeneous security complex is that it provides a comprehensive picture of the region's security, and the analyst can more easily appreciate the impact one sector has on another. The homogeneous security complex enables one sector at a time to be examined in great depth but could fail to highlight the links between sectors. While it may not provide as comprehensive a picture of the region's security as the heterogeneous version, the homogeneous security complex allows a comparison between sectors. Buzan et al. are quick to note that neither is superior to the other. Regardless of whether the security complexes are classical, homogenous, or heterogeneous, the key point about them is that those actors within a security complex have closer relations—whether friendly or adversarial—with one another than they do with actors outside the complex.

To refer to Southeast Asia as a security complex entails an appreciation of the region's history and the interaction among the actors. The Southeast Asian complex has traditionally been divided into two subcomplexes: the Malay Archipelago security complex and the Indochina security complex.[51] The former is dominated by the security relationships between Malaysia-Singapore-Indonesia, while the latter revolves around the Thai-Vietnamese struggle for domination of Laos and Cambodia.

The struggle between Thailand and Vietnam for overlordship of continental Southeast Asia can be traced back to the fourteenth century, when first the Thai kingdom in Ayutthaya and then the Vietnamese successfully challenged the Khmer (Cambodian) empire. By the eighteenth century, the Laotian kingdom at Lang Chang had disintegrated, and Laos joined Cambodia as a buffer between Thailand and Vietnam. Alagappa asserts that if it had not been for French colonial intervention, Cambodia and Laos would probably have ceased to exist.[52] In addition to the Thai-Vietnamese struggle for domination, the Thais also fought with their Burmese neighbors to the west, eventually defeating them in 1785 after three centuries of warfare. This historical pattern of relationships has continued to the present day. The Vietnamese invasion of Cambodia in December 1978, and the establishment of a puppet regime there during the 1980s, were countered by Thailand via bilateral means—alignment with China and the United States—and multilateral through ASEAN. The Burmese-Thai border remains a source of tension, with Burmese troops regularly infringing on Thai territory in their fight against opposition ethnic groups that straddle the border. While Thai-Vietnamese relations improved in the 1990s, beginning with Chatichai Choonhavan—Thailand's first elected prime minister for twelve years—announcing his intention to turn Indochina from a battlefield into a trading market, this relationship nevertheless remains plagued by suspicion.

The states that comprise the Malay Archipelago security complex do not have the same intensity of historical interaction of their continental counterparts. The Sri Vijaya empire and its replacement, the Majapahit empire, were dominant over the islands of present-day Indonesia, while other contemporary states were either nonexistent (Singapore) or peripheral (Brunei) to the international politics of maritime Southeast Asia. The security dynamics of this complex arose from decolonization. The two key security issues in this complex concern the disparity in size between Indonesia and its neighbors, plus Jakarta's desire to achieve regional leadership. The other issue concerns Singapore's sense of vulnerability and its troublesome relationship with Malaysia. Other security issues include the Philippines' claim to Malaysia's Sabah province and Brunei's sense of vulnerability. At present, concern is focused on the possibility of Indonesia either imploding, like Yugoslavia, or a power seizure by the military and a return to an assertive Sukarno-style leadership.

While the security relationships within each complex have been dominant, some security issues have transcended these subcomplexes, including border disputes, such as that between Thailand and Malaysia, or a wider interest in regional stability, such as Indonesia's interest in and activity during the Vietnamese occupation of Cambodia in the 1980s. Indeed, as security issues in the 1990s have evolved, it has become increasingly possible to refer to Southeast Asia as one security complex. The enlargement of ASEAN to include ten Southeast Asian states, the regional impact of the economic crisis and its attendant political consequences, the environmental effects of the forest fires, the territorial disputes in the South China Sea, the emergence of China as a possible hegemon, and the regional impact of terrorism have all linked the states' security concerns sufficiently closely that in a number of sectors they cannot be analyzed and solved separately from one another.

The interstate security relations of Southeast Asia are examined in Chapters 4 to 6. Chapter 4 continues the broadening of security adopted in Chapters 2 and 3 to examine the region's environmental and economic security issues, as well as its traditional military security issues. Although the primary emphasis within this chapter is the state as the referent object, it is not the only one, and so a degree of deepening of security does take place. In Chapters 5 and 6 the holistic or comprehensive nature of security is maintained; however, here the traditional notion of security emanating from stability takes center stage. These two chapters focus on the management of state relations within Southeast Asia by ASEAN. Adopting a heterogeneous security complex approach, the chapters examine the interaction between economic and security relations among ASEAN members (Chapter 5) and between ASEAN and external powers (Chapter 6). The final chapter highlights the multifarious security issues that exist in two Southeast Asian security concerns: the South China Sea dispute and Southeast Asia as the second front in the war on terrorism.

Notes

1. The most notable exception to this was Arnold Wolfers, *Discord and Collaboration: Essays on International Politics* (Baltimore: Johns Hopkins University Press, 1962), Ch. 10. A second edition of Barry Buzan's book was published in 1991 and renamed, *People, States and Fear: An Agenda for International Security Studies in the Post–Cold War Era*, 2nd ed. (Boulder: Lynne Rienner and London: Harvester Wheatsheaf, 1991).

2. David Baldwin, "The Concept of Security," *Review of International Studies* 23/1 (January 1997), p. 9.

3. Ken Booth made this reference to problem rather than solution when he wrote that those "strategists and organisations that do not try to become part of the solution will increasingly become part of the problem." In essence, Booth is correctly arguing that the Realist assumptions that underpin traditional strategic studies produce an environment that leads to the pursuit of self-defeating policies. To escape the security dilemmas of the Cold War new thinking is required. Colin Gray acknowledges his "problem" status when he writes: "If Professor Booth and other right-thinking folk are correct, then it may well be that people like me, who like to flatter ourselves with the belief that we are part of the solution, turn out to be part of the problem." For Booth quote, see Ken Booth, "War, Security and Strategy: Towards a Doctrine for Stable Peace," in Ken Booth (ed.), *New Thinking About Strategy and International Security* (London: HarperCollins Academic, 1991), p. 372. For Gray, see Colin S. Gray, *Modern Strategy* (Oxford: Oxford University Press, 1999), p. xi.

4. There are a range of different approaches, including feminism and poststructuralism. For a brief overview see Steve Smith, "The Increasing Insecurity of Security Studies: Conceptualizing Security in the Last Twenty Years," in Stuart Croft and Terry Terriff (eds.), *Critical Reflections on Security and Change* (London: Frank Cass, 2000), pp. 72–101. For an account of critical security studies and the Copenhagen School, which are two approaches adopted here, see David Mutimer, "Beyond Strategy: Critical Thinking and the New Security Studies," in Craig A. Snyder (ed.), *Contemporary Security and Strategy* (London: Macmillan, 1999), pp. 75–101.

5. See Keith Krause and Michael C. Williams, *Critical Security Studies: Concepts and Cases* (London: University College of London Press, 1997). Also see Richard Wyn Jones, "'Travel Without Maps': Thinking About Security After the Cold War," in M. Jane Davis (ed.), *Security Issues in the Post–Cold War World* (Cheltenham, UK: Edward Elgar, 1996), pp. 196–218. For an account of the differences between the critical security authors, see Smith, "The Increasing Insecurity of Security Studies," pp. 88–90.

6. Michael Doyle, "Liberalism and World Politics," *American Political Science Review* 80/4 (December 1986), pp. 1151–1169.

7. Ken Booth, "Security and Emancipation," *Review of International Studies* 17/4 (October 1991), p. 319. Booth privileges the individual over the state as the referent object.

8. United Nations Development Program, *Human Development Report, 1994* (New York: Oxford University Press, 1994), p. 23.

9. Amitav Acharya, "Human Security: East Versus West?" IDSS

Working Paper 17 (Singapore: Institute of Defence and Strategic Studies, September 2001).

10. For an exchange on this particular issue, see Alex J. Bellamy and Matt McDonald, "The Utility of Human Security: Which Humans? What Security? A Reply to Thomas & Tow," *Security Dialogue* 33/3 (September 2002), pp. 373–377; Nicholas Thomas and William T. Tow, "Gaining Security by Trashing the State? A Reply to Bellamy & McDonald," *Security Dialogue* 33/3 (September 2002), pp. 379–382.

11. Gareth Evans, "Cooperative Security and Intrastate Conflict," *Foreign Policy* 96 (Fall 1994), p. 7.

12. William T. Tow, "Altenative Security Models: Implications for ASEAN," in Andrew T. H. Tan and J. D. Kenneth Boutin (eds.), *Non-Traditional Security Issues in Southeast Asia* (Singapore: Institute of Defence and Strategic Studies, 2001), p. 266.

13. Tan See Seng, "Human Security: Discourse, Statecraft, Emancipation," IDSS Working Paper 11 (Singapore: Institute of Defence and Strategic Studies, May 2001), p. 15.

14. Ibid., p. 21.

15. Anthony Burke, "Caught Between National and Human Security: Knowledge and Power in Post-crisis Asia," *Pacifica Review* 13/3 (October 2001), p. 218.

16. The three key texts from the Copenhagen School are: Barry Buzan, Morten Kelstrup, Pierre Lemaitre, Elzbieta Tromer, and Ole Wæver, *The European Security Order Recast* (London: Pinter, 1990); Ole Wæver, Barry Buzan, Morten Kelstrup, and Pierre Lemaitre, *Identity, Migration and the New Security Agenda in Europe* (London: Pinter, 1993); and Barry Buzan, Ole Wæver, and Jaap de Wilde, *Security: A New Framework for Analysis* (Boulder: Lynne Rienner, 1998). For the reference to the Copenhagen School, see Bill McSweeny, "Identity and Security: Buzan and the Copenhagen School," *Review of International Studies* 22/1 (January 1996), pp. 81–93.

17. Barry Buzan et al., *Security: A New Framework for Analysis*, Ch. 2.

18. Ibid., p. 25.

19. Ibid., p. 32.

20. Robert Go, "Jakarta to give security forces more teeth," *The Straits Times*, 19 October 2002.

21. The best-known advocate of retaining a narrow, military definition is Stephen Walt; see Stephen M. Walt, "The Renaissance of Security Studies," *International Studies Quarterly* 35/2 (1991), pp. 211–239.

22. Roland Paris, "Human Security: Paradigm Shift or Hot Air?" *International Security* 26/2 (Fall 2001), pp. 87–102. For a quantitative definition of human security, see Gary King and Christopher J. L. Murray, "Rethinking Human Security," *Political Science Quarterly* 116/4 (2001–2002), pp. 585–610.

23. William T. Tow and Russell Trood, "Linkages Between Traditional Security and Human Security," in William T. Tow, Ramesh Thakur, and In-Taek Hyun (eds.), *Asia's Emerging Regional Order: Reconciling Traditional and Human Security* (Tokyo: The United Nations University Press, 2000), p. 14. Also see Nicholas Thomas and William T. Tow, "The Utility of Human

Security: Sovereignty and Humanitarian Intervention," *Security Dialogue* 33/2 (June 2002), pp. 177–192.

24. For an excellent discussion of whether they can be reconciled, see Burke, "Caught Between National and Human Security," pp. 215–239.

25. Olav F. Knudsen, "Post-Copenhagen Security Studies: Desecuritizing Securitization," *Security Dialogue* 32/3 (September 2001), pp. 355-368.

26. For a critique of Knudsen, see Lloyd Pettiford, "When Is a Realist Not a Realist? Stories Knudsen Doesn't Tell," *Security Dialogue* 32/3 (September 2001), pp. 369–374.

27. Smith, "The Increasing Insecurity of Security Studies," p. 97.

28. "Bush reinforces anti-terror pledge," *BBC News*, 26 January 2001. Internet site: http://news.bbc.co.uk/1/hi/world/americas/1784099.stm.

29. Hadi Soesastro, "Southeast Asia and Global Terrorism: Implications on State Security and Human Security," *Indonesian Quarterly* 30/1 (2002), p. 35.

30. Richard Stubbs, "The Many Faces of Asian Security: Edited by Sheldon W. Simon," *Contemporary Southeast Asia* 24/1 (April 2002), pp. 178–179.

31. Jospeh S. Nye, Jr., and Sean M. Lynn-Jones, "International Security Studies: A Report of a Conference on the State of the Field," *International Security* 12/4 (Spring 1988), p. 23.

32. Caroline Thomas, *In Search of Security: The Third World in International Relations* (Boulder: Lynne Rienner, 1987), p. 1.

33. Amitav Acharya, "The Periphery as the Core: The Third World and Security Studies," in Keith Krause and Michael C. Williams (eds.), *Critical Security Studies: Concepts and Cases* (London: University College of London Press, 1997), p. 318.

34. Ibid.

35. Robert L. Rothstein, "The 'Security Dilemma' and the 'Poverty Trap' in the Third World," *The Jerusalem Journal of International Relations* 8/4 (1986), p. 16.

36. Buzan, *People, States and Fear*, pp. 96–107. Weak states have also been referred to as quasi states; see Robert H. Jackson, *Quasi-states: Sovereignty, International Relations and the Third World* (Cambridge: Cambridge University Press, 1993).

37. The key commentators who view China as a future threat are in the Pentagon, hence the U.S. military's shift of emphasis toward the Pacific Rim. See Thomas E. Ricks, "Asia moves to forefront of Pentagon planning," *The Washington Post/Guardian Weekly*, 1 June 2000. Also see Murray Hiebert, "What Threat?" *Far Eastern Economic Review*, 25 July 2002, p. 16.

38. Buzan, *People, States and Fear*, p. 98.

39. For more on the Patani Malay, see Clive J. Christie, *A Modern History of South East Asia: Decolonization, Nationalism and Separatism* (London: Tauris Academic, 1996), Ch. 9.

40. Ibid., p. 175. Acts of violence by Patani separatists, while infrequent, still occur. See Edward Tang, "Thai bombs and arson linked to separatist movement," *The Straits Times*, 31 October 2002.

41. Excellent coverage is given to the self-defeating nature of regime-

orchestrated violence in Brian L. Job, "The Insecurity Dilemma: National, Regime, and State Securities in the Third World," in Brian L. Job (ed.), *The Insecurity Dilemma: National Security of Third World States* (Boulder: Lynne Rienner, 1992), pp. 11–35. Also see T. David Mason and Dale A. Krane, "The Political Economy of Death Squads: Toward a Theory of the Impact of State-Sanctioned Terror," *International Studies Quarterly* 33/2 (June 1989), pp. 175–198.

42. Mohammed Ayoob, *The Third World Security Predicament: State Making, Regional Conflict, and the International System* (Boulder: Lynne Rienner, 1995).

43. Ibid., p. 28.

44. Charles Tilly, "Reflections on the History of European State-Making," in Charles Tilly (ed.), *The Formation of National States in Western Europe* (Princeton: Princeton University Press, 1975), p. 69.

45. Ayoob, *The Third World Security Predicament*, p. 40.

46. Ibid., pp. 32–33.

47. For Ayoob's view of emancipation as a security tool, see ibid., pp. 10–11; for quotation, see ibid., p. 179.

48. The eleven states of Southeast Asia are: Brunei, Burma (also known as Myanmar), Cambodia, Indonesia, Laos, Malaysia, Singapore, Thailand, Vietnam, the Philippines, and the latest, East Timor, which gained its sovereign independence on May 20, 2002.

49. References to CSCT, homogeneous, and heterogeneous security complexes can be found in Buzan, Wæver, and de Wilde, *Security: A New Framework for Analysis*, pp. 10–20.

50. For the latest work by Barry Buzan on security complex theory, see Barry Buzan and Ole Wæver, *Regions and Powers: The Structure of International Security* (Cambridge: Cambridge University Press, 2003). I am grateful to Amitav Acharya for bringing this work to my attention and to Barry Buzan for offering to show me the completed chapters, since it had not been published when I submitted this manuscript. Unfortunately, I did not have time to incorporate it.

51. Barry Buzan first referred to Southeast Asia as a security complex in 1988. By 1991, Muthiah Alagappa had subdivided Southeast Asia into five/six security complexes, but by 1998, he was referring to the region as maritime and continental, which corresponds to the Malay Archipelago and Indochina references of N. Ganesan. See Barry Buzan, "The Southeast Asian Security Complex," *Contemporary Southeast Asia* 10/1 (June 1988); Muthiah Alagappa, "The Dynamics of International Security in Southeast Asia: Change and Continuity," *Australian Journal of International Affairs* 45/1 (May 1991); Muthiah Alagappa, "International Politics in Asia: The Historical Context," in Muthiah Alagappa (ed.), *Asian Security Practice: Material and Ideational Influences* (Stanford: Stanford University Press, 1998); and N. Ganesan, "Bilateral Tensions in Post–Cold War ASEAN," Pacific Strategic Papers 9 (Singapore: Institute of Southeast Asian Studies, 1999), pp. 7–9.

52. Alagappa, "International Politics in Asia," p. 77.

2

Societal Security and Ethnic Tensions

This chapter is the first of two that concentrate on security threats in Southeast Asia that emanate from within the state. In the postcolonial period, the region's states adopted policies intended to help create strong nation-states. The internal challenge arises because these states are home to diverse ethnic populations that have resisted these state- and nation-building approaches. In this chapter, Burma (also known as Myanmar), Indonesia, and Malaysia are the case studies examined. First, however, it is necessary to determine the criteria for judging the legitimacy of a nation-state.

Legitimacy and Identity

A nation-state is a community of people who live within established borders. The nation is itself constituted by the peoples' shared memories and a desire to live together and perpetuate their commonalties for future generations. It is, in Benedict Anderson's renowned phrase, an imagined community, since the individuals never know most of their fellow members (hence it is imagined) but are nevertheless willing to fight for and die for one another (hence community).[1] The legitimacy a nation-state acquires thus comes from the recognition among the people of that territory that (1) they share a rich heritage of memories and thus form a nation, and (2) the state's boundary coincides with the nation's. If this identification with the state and others in the population is achieved, then the nation-state has legitimacy and can be considered strong.

Establishing shared norms and values (a shared identity) is thus

crucial to the creation of legitimacy for the nation and state. The referent object, therefore, for ethnic security problems is identity. Identity
security lies at the heart of the Copenhagen School's notion of societal
security, and it is particularly useful in understanding the dynamics
behind ethnic security problems.[2] Barry Buzan writes:

> [S]ocietal identity can be threatened in ways ranging from the sup-
> pression of its expression to interference with its ability to reproduce
> . . . The reproduction of a society can be threatened by sustained
> application of repressive measures against the expression of its identi-
> ty. If the institutions that reproduce language and culture are forbid-
> den to operate, the identity cannot be transmitted effectively from one
> generation to the next.[3]

Hence refusing to allow regional languages to be taught in schools or
banning cultural events are means by which an identity can be threatened. The elite of the dominant ethnic group often deliberately instigate
such challenges because they are seeking to establish a national identity
in accordance with their own ethnic identity. The advantage of focusing
on identity security is that it enables us to examine "soft" security matters, such as providing for the reproduction of language and culture
through, for instance, education, rather than being solely concerned
with the use of force by and against ethnic groups. This will allow an
examination of the sources of the ethnic security challenge, instead of
focusing only upon the violence that is its symptom.

Identities can also be threatened in less obvious, even inadvertent
ways. If an ethnic identity becomes associated with a low-class status
within society, then it may struggle to survive as the younger generation
is attracted by an identity perceived to be more advanced. For example,
Dutch colonial rule in Sumatra facilitated the spread of Islam among the
Southern Batak population because it was seen as superior to the
Batak's religion and way of life. Bernhard Dahm writes:

> It was the way of life and the proud behaviour of the Malays who ran
> part of the lower colonial administration that impressed the Bataks . . .
> The expression *masuk Melayu,* meaning "to become a Malay," was a
> synonym for entering Islam. It also meant, however, to clean oneself
> of the negative aspects of "Batakness." And this is what many Bataks
> in their southern countries wanted to do, after finding out about their
> very low reputation.[4]

This does not mean, however, that all aspects of the minority's identity
are lost forever, and indeed the Batak identity continues to exist in

Sumatra. Although ethnic conflict need not arise, in this instance the possibility remains that it will, especially if the newcomers face discrimination from the more advanced group. For example, in Thailand during the 1960s and 1970s, the migration of workers to Bangkok from the Northeast increased. The migrant workers admired the Central Thai community, but the Central Thais regarded the migrants as unsophisticated and uncultured. Migrant workers returning to the Northeast reported the Central Thais were unfriendly, discriminated against people from the Northeast, and thought them inferior. This created an enhanced awareness of the similarities among Northeastern peoples, and in the 1960s a common "Isan" ethnic identity emerged.[5] From the mid-1960s to the early 1980s, there was an insurrection in the Northeast led by the Communist Party of Thailand (CPT), and this gained support from the local Isan populace.[6]

Therefore, either because of rejection from the dominant group or refusal to accept their identity as subordinate, the minority group may seek to revive and/or safeguard its identity. Michael Hechter writes, "[T]here exists the probability that the disadvantaged group will, in time, reactively assert its own culture as equal or superior to that of the relatively advantaged core. This may help it conceive of itself as a separate 'nation' and seek independence."[7] This reaction to the "advantaged core" will be seen in the case study of Indonesia with the core Javanese group and Indonesia's Outer Islands of East Timor, Aceh and Irian Jaya. For now, the issue at hand is that a threat to an identity's security (its ability to reproduce) can arise as a deliberate policy of the elite and as an unintended consequence of the state's development program.

The success or lack of it of the various state-making and nation-building policies pursued by the governing elite will be evidenced by the incidence of resistance and violence these policies generate from the populace. The attempt to establish shared norms and values among an ethnically diverse population is usually through the assimilation of minority groups into the dominant one or the acculturation (or adaptation) of the main ethnic group to include elements of the minority communities.

The assimilation approach requires imposing the main (or hegemonic) group's identity on the peripheral or minority groups. The establishment of a monoethnic population indicates they share the same norms and values, and thus a strong nation-state is created. However, where assimilation is imposed, this may be resisted and, if it is, could have the paradoxical effect of strengthening the minority's identity as the ethnic group battles to maintain its distinctiveness. The accultura-

tion approach requires willingness in the hegemonic group to acknowledge elements of the minority group's identity and willingness of the
minority group to embrace an additional identity. In some cases acculturation is a conscious policy of the elite, while in others it arises as the
minority group seeks to adopt elements of the other group's identity
because they see it as more advanced. The key with acculturation is that
the new identity need not replace the ethnic group's current one. When
acculturation is a nation-building policy pursued by a hegemonic group,
the maintenance of traditional identity is achieved by establishing an
overarching identity that complements the local ethnic identity. This
attempt to achieve a sense of national identity while maintaining the
ethnic mix of the population is captured in the mantra, "unity in diversity."

Whether through assimilation or acculturation, identities do change.
Indeed, the cultural history of Southeast Asia reveals the fluidity of ethnic identity as it adapts to and adopt different influences. The first ethnic group was the Proto-Malays that arrived ca. 3500 B.C., and they
were subsequently followed by the Deutero-Malays who arrived ca. 300
B.C. The Deutero-Malays became the dominant group, with very few of
the Proto-Malays resisting the loss of their culture. Those who did were
the ancestors of the Bataks of Sumatra, Dayaks of Borneo, and the
Alfurs of the Celebes and Moluccas. This indigenous Malay culture was
subsequently influenced by the arrival of Chinese and even more so,
Indian culture. SarDesai writes that "the absorptive, syncretic quality of
Indian culture, itself enriched by numerous strands imported by series
of invaders of the Indian subcontinent, succeeded in striking roots in the
Southeast Asian region, which adopted the alien cultural traits without
in the process losing its identity."[8] The issue for identity security therefore is not change in itself, but whether this change is resisted.

The history of European nation building and state making, as noted
in the previous chapter, reveals that the establishment of shared memories and recognition of state boundaries, which provides the nation-state
with legitimacy, can be both a long time coming and marked by high
levels of violence. It was noted, however, that the circumstances in
which third world states are state making and nation building are different and that repeating the European experience is unlikely to achieve a
strong nation-state. However, as will be seen in the cases of both Burma
and Indonesia, the ruling elites have resorted to the use of force in their
attempts to create a strong nation-state. In other words, ethnic conflict
has arisen because the minority groups have resisted change.

This chapter is divided into two sections. The first examines the state- and nation-building policies the Burmese and Indonesian authorities have implemented toward minority ethnic groups in their territory. In both countries these minority groups live in the border regions, and thus these case studies highlight the ethnic tension that arises when the center extends its control over the state's periphery. In the Burmese case, the approach has been one of assimilation, while in Indonesia it has been acculturation.

The second section examines the ethnic security problems that have arisen from the presence of sizable Chinese minorities in some Southeast Asian states. Here the problem is not the extension of the center's control over a different community but the impact of the Chinese on the nation's identity. Malaysia and Indonesia are the case studies used. In Indonesia the authorities have sought to assimilate its Chinese population, while in Malaysia the approach has been one of acculturation.

Center-Periphery Ethnic Tension

Assimilation: Burma's Monoethnic Approach

The establishment of a monoethnic state is achieved through assimilating a diverse population into one that shares a single national identity. This approach usually occurs where the hegemonic group has control over the state machinery and uses this to safeguard and impose its own values on other groups within the state's boundaries. While this may create strong national identity, it is just as likely to create resentment in the peripheral communities as their identity is challenged. Our case study for this approach is Burma, also known as Myanmar.[9]

Burma has suffered from civil war since it became independent in 1948, with the fighting taking place between the hegemonic Burman (also known as Bama/Bamar) group and numerous ethnic minorities that live in the border regions. The main minority groups are the Karen, Shan, Araknese, Kachin, Chin, and Mon; together with the Burman they constitute the Burmese population.[10] The Burman dominate the central government, which since 1962 has been a military one, and they have pursued a policy of assimilating the Burmese population into the Burman group. The peripheral communities resisted this attempt to eradicate their identities and began an armed struggle against the central government. The fighting continued until 1992, when the military regime (at that time known as the State, Law and Order Restoration

Council, SLORC) adjusted their strategy from assimilation by war to assimilation via more peaceful methods. These methods included the signing of cease-fires and "steadfast" agreements with the different ethnic minorities, which enabled the government to divide and eventually defeat militarily the main opposition groups, namely the Shan and Karen. Fighting continues against the central government, but since the fall of the Karen main base at Manerplaw in 1995, there has been no resident group capable of militarily overturning the central government's control of Burma.

The central military government does not use the term *assimilation* to explain its nation- and state-building approach, but I argue here that because this is its method, the unrest will continue. In other words, although the military regime (now called the State Peace and Development Council, SPDC) has won on the battlefield, it will fail to secure peace and a strong Burmese nation because the elite constitute a threat to the societal security of the state's minority communities.

The label *monoethnic state* might appear initially to sit uneasily with Burma, given the state's declared interest in unity in diversity that was manifest in its 1947 and 1974 constitutions. In both of these, political authority was granted to the ethnic minorities. In the 1947 constitution, the Shan and Kayah states were given the right to secede after ten years, while the 1974 constitution divided Burma administratively into seven "states." Yet, as David Brown asserts, "it is not the formal provisions of the constitutions and the enacted laws which ensure that state penetration has involved a progressive centralization and Burmanization, but rather the dominance of Burmans in the state élites, and their assumption of Burman cultural superiority."[11] It is this domination by the Burmans of Burma's development that makes the monoethnic state label fit Burma. Hence David Steinberg's statement:

> Minority cultures and languages are relegated to one's home and cannot be used for other than local purposes. Education is in Burm[an]; the symbols of the state and deployment of power are Burman . . . "The Burmese Way to Socialism" might more accurately be termed the "The Burman Way to Socialism," because it reflects Burman cultural, political, and nationalistic norms.[12]

The first government of Burma was dominated by the Anti-Fascist People's Freedom League (AFPFL), which although initially an umbrella organization consisting of various groups, had by 1948 become dominated by Burmans.[13] The AFPFL's victories in the 1951 and 1956 national elections meant that the non-Burman groups fell under the political control of a Burman-dominated central government. In 1952, it was decided that all government business was to be conducted in the Burman language, Burmese history would be taught from the perspective of Burman nationalism, and the sole language used in education would be Burman. David Brown writes that "the call for assimilation into a new Burmese culture became in effect a call for assimilation into Burman culture."[14] This was further exacerbated when the military regime was imposed in 1962. Josef Silverstein notes that "[w]hile the military leaders, like their civilian predecessors, spoke in ways that seemed to lend support to the ideal of unity in diversity, they pursued a variety of policies that led to the assimilation of peoples into a common culture and a common loyalty. Thus they emphasized the nationalization of the society and the Burmanization of its culture."[15] The result of these policies was not the establishment of a strong nation-state but the paradoxical effect of weakening the state, as the minority ethnic groups reacted aggressively to the assimilation attempt. Because the assimilation threatened the minority groups' elites, they were able to pose the Burmanization of Burma as a threat to the ethnic group's identity or its societal security. Hence Silverstein's claim that "[w]hat moved them were their common fears of Burmanization, loss of cultural identity, interference in their affairs by the national government and a belief that the Burmans were creating an internal colonial system in which they would not share the wealth of the country."[16]

Resistance to the central government's assimilation approach became military in nature when it was evident the ethnic communities would not have autonomy. The first military clashes between the Shan and the Burmese army occurred in 1959, while hostility between the Karen and Burmans predates British colonial rule. After it became evident the Burmans would dominate postcolonial Burma, the Karen responded with the creation of the Karen National Union (KNU) on February 5, 1947. The KNU has its own military wing, the Karen National Liberation Army (KNLA), as well as defense militia organized in the Karen National Defense Organization (KNDO).[17] A number of other ethnic minority groups also resorted to violence against the Burman central government, although until 1976, there was little unity among the groups fighting the Burmans. They did form temporary alliances, such as with the Burma Communist Party, in order to acquire Chinese weapons, but since some wanted independence from Burma and others wanted to stay within a weak federation, there was little coordination of their actions. In 1976, however, several of the minorities formed a military alliance known as the National Democratic Front (NDF). If the Burmese army attacked one member of the NDF, then others would provide assistance. By 1984, the NDF had adopted a common political program. All members sought to remain part of Burma on the basis of a new federation. While NDF membership fluctuated as groups left and rejoined and fighting did occasionally break out among NDF members—as occurred between the Karen and Mon in 1988—the NDF survived because it ultimately benefited the minorities to remain united.

By 1992, the civil war, which had fluctuated in intensity since 1948, had become essentially unwinnable. The SLORC government, despite a concerted effort between 1988 and 1992, had failed to defeat the KNU. The SLORC thus adjusted its nation-building strategy but not its assimilation approach. The strategy now was to broker "steadfast" agreements with the separate ethnic communities. These agreements struck a bargain in which the SLORC government would provide rice to the border regions, bring development projects to the area via the 1989 Border Areas Development Program, and allow the minority groups to keep their weapons and nominal control over their areas and be free to engage in trade, which included drug trafficking, in exchange for halting the war against the SLORC and turning their weapons on the other ethnic groups. The military regime had tried such tactics previously, but this time the promise of food, development projects, and some administrative control over their territory made the agreements attractive to the ethnic minorities.

The SLORC was successful in gaining steadfast agreements with the Wa, the Palaung State Liberation Party (PSLP), and the Pa-O National Organization (PNO). The SLORC extracted an agreement from the Wa to fight the drug baron Khun Sa and his Mong Tai Army. The unity of the Shan State Progress Party (SSPP) collapsed when the majority of the Shan fighting forces refused to follow their leaders' decision to accept the SLORC agreement and joined forces with the Mong Tai Army. By 1996, sixteen groups had signed agreements with the SLORC including the Karenni National Progressive Party (KNPP), the New Mon State Party (NMSP), and Khun Sa's Mong Tai Army. The KNU, which had held out longest against the central government, suffered a devastating defeat in 1995 because dissension broke out among the Karen when Buddhist Karens revolted against their Christian leaders.

With the exception of the Wa, however, who through the narcotics trade have benefited economically from their agreement with Rangoon, the other minorities have seen little economic benefit. Indeed, all these agreements appear to have effectively enabled the military government to deploy its forces in the border regions to such an extent that a successful uprising is now highly unlikely. The civil war is not finished since some forces continue to harass the Burmese army, as evidenced by the continuing clash between the Burmese army and the Shan State Army (SSA) during 2001 and 2002, but there is no longer an opposition force that can defeat the military regime.[18] Tensions in Burma continue not only because the steadfast agreements fail to address the economic, political, and constitutional issues that concern the minorities but also because the Burmanization of Burma goes on.

In June 1989, the SLORC government changed the country's name from Burma to Myanmar Naing Ngan (Union of Myanmar) through the "Adaptation of Expression Law." The elite argue that Myanmar is an all-encompassing name that incorporates all the nation's people; however, it is derived from Myanma, which is closely associated with the language of the Burman ethnic majority. This name change law was not limited just to the country but was used for the names of places (e.g., Rangoon is now called Yangon) and to change the language of historical documents. The latter is particularly insidious since, as Gustaaf Houtman notes, the "regime is using Myanmar to crowd out all alternative concepts of unity that various ethnic groups and foreign languages might have expressed throughout history."[19] This is a continuation of the Burmanization of Burma. Houtman quite emphatically writes, "Myanmafication is in fact the unambiguous Burmanisation of place names, the attempt to make all place names conform to Burman pronunciation overriding all other grass-root variation[s] in the many languages present in Burma. It therefore should be read as the attempt to Burmanise Burma—it is Myanmafication."[20]

Mikael Gravers concurs when he notes that since 1992, the military regime has classified the minorities into 135 national races, which have local autonomy at the district level but are still controlled by regional representatives of the central government. Gravers notes that the junta's classification has led certain groups to be classified in more than one race and others not to be classified in their own race. Thus the Pa-o are listed as belonging to both the Shan and the Karen national races, while the Kayah are not included among the twelve groups that constitute the Karen. He concludes that the "regime uses ethnicity and ethnic differences politically to disguise its programme of 'Myanmarisation,' or 'Burmanisation,' where Burman culture, language and the Burman way of Buddhism are absolutely hegemonic. The device seems to be: rule, classify and divide."[21] The government's references to 135 national races therefore should not be taken as an indication that it wants to establish a multiethnic nation-state. This contradiction in the regime's position can be clearly seen in the following paradoxical statement in a press release from the Myanmar Embassy in London in April 2000. It read: "The people and the Government of the Union of Myanmar bear no ill-will against . . . its own 135 ethnic brethren who have lived together as a Kingdom for many centuries and the assimilation of the peoples over time has become so complete that so called ethnic differences are now barely discernible."[22] The strategy of how to assimilate the minority communities may have changed, but the goal of establishing a monoethnic nation has not.

If the solution to Burma's internal security problems lies in defending the identity of the country's ethnic minorities and, in so doing, establishing a strong multiethnic nation-state, what chance of peace is there with a military government determined to impose a Burman identity on the population? There are reasons to be hopeful for positive change, although optimism should be tempered.

On 8 August 1988 hundreds of thousands of students took to the streets in a peaceful protest against the ruling military regime. The regime responded by brutally suppressing the prodemocracy demonstraors, killing over ten thousand students. However, out of the massacre, colloquially referred to as 8-8-88, a positive development arose. After the crackdown on prodemocracy demonstrators (mainly Burman students), over ten thousand students fled Rangoon to the border regions and joined the ethnic groups in resisting the central government. Later that year on November 19, the disaffected Burmans and ethnic minorities established the Democratic Alliance of Burma (DAB). Silverstein states that DAB represented the "coming together of Burmans and minorities on the basis of genuine equality . . . In the past, equality between Burmans and the minorities had been stated in constitutional documents but never carried out in practice."[23] The DAB's goals represented for the first time in Burma an attempt to establish a multiethnic state in which all groups were to participate and "were genuinely Burma-centred rather than Burman or regional."[24]

Since 1988, Burma has been engaged in a long, drawn-out process of establishing another constitution. The military want a constitution that gives them a role in the legislature so that they can determine who becomes president, a position that under their proposals will have much power.[25] The discussions on constitutional change take place in the National Convention (NC), but the slow pace of progress is an indication that the military government has little interest in replacing their regime. Indeed, the NC has been in recess since April 1996. According to Tin Maung Maung Than, the reason for the stalled progress on a new

constitution relates to the ethnic minorities. He writes that the main reason why the NC has been recess is the inability to reach a "consensus
on the issue of autonomy for national races," and therefore it "seems
that the process is constrained by the sensitive issue of ethnic autonomy."[26]

In the May 1990 national election, the National League for
Democracy (NLD) led by Aung San Suu Kyi won an overwhelming
victory, and the DAB called for the immediate transfer of power from
the SLORC to the NLD. However, the military regime refused to trans-
fer power and began to intimidate, arrest, and imprison NLD members.
In the face of continued military rule, the NLD and DAB formed an
alternative government that came into effect on December 18, 1990: the
National Coalition Government of the Union of Burma (NCGUB). In
addition, they also formed a policymaking council, known first as the
Democratic Front of Burma (DFB) and subsequently renamed in
February 1991 the Anti-Military Dictatorship Solidarity Committee
(ADNSC); which was responsible for strengthening unity between the
peoples of Burma's heartland and border regions. Silverstein notes "that
it represented only the second time (the first had been the 12 February
1947 Panglong Agreement between U Aung San and the Chin, Kachin,
and Shan traditional chiefs) when recognised Burman leaders and representatives of the minorities had agreed to work together for common
ends in a united Burma."[27]

The DAB began drafting a constitution, and unlike the military
regime's version, their draft proposals, Silverstein notes, "were the
product of a real partnership which had been established between
Burmans and minorities."[28] The DAB recognized that peace in Burma
relied upon safeguarding the identities of the minorities within a federal
system, hence Silverstein's assertion that they "were determined to
ensure that the peoples of Burma would be able to protect their local
cultures and traditions, and govern themselves in all matters not specifically related to the national government."[29]

The positive outcome from the military's brutal show of force in
1988 is the creation of an alternative government (NCGUB), which represents the interests of all Burma's ethnic groups and one that recognizes that at the heart of Burma's ethnic civil war is the issue of identity.
Since 1993, however, the NCGUB leaders have been in exile in New
York, and although the opposition established an alternative parliament
in 1998 (the Committee Representing the People's Parliament), with the
defeat of the Karen at Manerplaw in 1995 few avenues remain to force
change on the military regime. Nevertheless, Burma's internal ethnic
problems, and hence Burma's internal security problem, will be

resolved only when the identities of Burma's minorities are protected. This can occur only within a federal system where autonomy is granted to each group; it certainly will not come from a program of Burmanization (or Myanmafication) that attempts to impose a monoethnic identity on Burma. For Burma to emerge as a strong nation-state, its multiethnic character must be acknowledged. The opposition movements, such as the NCGUB and the NLD, hold out the promise that Burma's internal security problems can be overcome and a strong nation-state can be achieved.

Since October 2000, the SPDC and NLD have been engaged in a dialogue on national reconciliation. The most high-profile outcome of these talks was the release from house arrest of Suu Kyi on May 6, 2002, but the talks have stalled and questions have been raised regarding the seriousness of the SPDC's commitment to democratic reform.[30] Although the ethnic minorities' voices are not directly represented— they are calling for tripartite talks—at least for the moment there is confidence that the NLD will represent their interests.[31]

Acculturation: Indonesia and Internal Colonialism

The ethnic security problems of Burma arose not just because the central governing Burman group challenged the identities of the peripheral border groups, but also because this challenge was political—that is, the political autonomy of the ethnic groups was challenged by the central government. In Indonesia there has also been an attempt to state make and nation build by imposing control from Jakarta. Like Burma, this centralization of control, referred to by the peripheral communities as Javanization after the dominant ethnic group (Javanese), is a source of the ethnic conflict in Indonesia. Hence Selo Soemardjan's statement that "[y]ou have a dichotomy between Javanese and non-Javanese areas, which is very strong. Because of that, it can easily develop into conflict. The provinces feel colonized by the government of Java."[32] One of the most tangible signs of this colonization or control has been the migration—sometimes official, which is known as transmigration, and sometimes not—of Javanese and other ethnic groups to the Outer Islands. This has led to ethnic violence directed against the central government, as well as conflict between the migrant and indigenous peoples, the latter graphically illustrated by the decapitation of Madurese migrants in Kalimantan.[33] Indonesia has also witnessed since 2000 a surge of communal violence between the Muslim and Christian communities in the Moluccas, in eastern Indonesia. However, this outbreak of violence is not caused by migrants or tension between Javanese and non-Javanese groups. The causes lie in political competition at the local level between the two religious groups, which was exacerbated when Muslim fighters from Laskar Jihad arrived in May 2000.[34]

Unlike Burma, Indonesia's nation-building and state-making approach toward its peripheral communities has not been one of assimilation. Instead, it has sought to create a sense of Indonesian identity while also maintaining the country's diverse ethnicity. This acculturation approach can be seen in the recognition of the country's ethnic differences in the arts. The Jakarta Arts Center supports regional performers and artists and also a theme park—"Beautiful Indonesia in Miniature"—that represents the diversity of Indonesia's architecture from one end of the archipelago to the other. It is, as William Liddle explains, "a politically safe response to the desire of local groups to maintain their unique and separate identities."[35] However, Jakarta's lack of cultural sensitivity in implementing its nation-building and state-making policies has often given a hollow ring to its claim of wanting to create "unity in diversity." Indeed, its economic development programs paradoxically have alienated the peripheral communities from Java, not bred a sense of belonging to Indonesia. The acculturation approach has failed.

It should be noted that it is contentious to regard Indonesia's nation-building approach as an example of acculturation. For some, the elite in Java have been engaged in assimilation as they have sought to eradicate the identity of the peripheral communities in the Outer Islands. Hence Marcus Colchester's interpretation of transmigration as "a political programme designed to extend government control over the peripheral islands through the elimination of ethnic diversity. Transmigration has become one of government's key means for assimilating tribal people."[36] The assimilation argument can also be seen in Peter Carey's description of Indonesia's occupation of East Timor. Carey writes that the occupation was the "slow death of a society and a culture. In brief, a form of ethnocide designed to undermine local values and replace them with an alien 'Indonesian-ness,' the national values of a Muslim Javanese colonial power."[37] The Indonesian occupation of East Timor undoubtedly witnessed horrendous acts of violence against the East Timorese; however, is it evident that this was part of an assimilation policy designed to eradicate the Timorese identity? Or was the violence and appalling abuse of East Timorese human rights the consequence of both a perpetual anti-insurgency war against guerrilla fighters and the implementation of a neocolonial economic model? As will be seen in the East Timor case study, part of the hostility directed against Javanese control arose from the failure of Jakarta to provide economic opportunities for the younger generation in East Timor to benefit from being part of Indonesia. Had these opportunities been made available, then prointegrationist sentiment may arguably have grown.

The problems between the Outer Islands (peripheral communities) and Java (the center) are not the only type of ethnic problem in Indonesia. The country also suffers from tension between the indigenous *pribumi* and non-*pribumi*, such as the Sino-Indonesian population; this will be examined below. In order to appreciate why Indonesia has suffered from societal security problems, it is necessary to combine the perceived threats to identities and to economic prosperity. This combination is known as internal colonialism, and I use it to examine Indonesia's ethnic security problems in its Outer Islands.

The key proposition of internal colonialism is that the center or core region of the state dominates the periphery politically and exploits it materially. The state's economic development is thus achieved at the expense of the peripheral region. Exploitation of the peripheral region in turn develops a reactive ethnic consciousness that is articulated in the desire for autonomy or even secession. The internal colonial model therefore posits a circumstance in which the core group safeguards its superordinate position by monopolizing political and economic positions of power, while the peripheral communities conversely are denied access to these positions. Thus the division of labor is drawn along ethnic lines. Far from seeking to assimilate the peripheral communities, the core (hegemonic) group seeks to maintain a distinction. With the core group enhancing its economic wealth through implementing economic policies that exploit the peripheral communities, the people in these regions are likely to see themselves as discriminated against because of their ethnicity. Rather than achieving a convergence or acculturation of identities through increased economic, political, and social interaction, the internal colonial model inhibits ethnic acculturation and the development of a strong national identity.

Thus in Indonesia the economic model adopted by the central Javanese has undermined the nation-building approach of acculturation. While local identities have been maintained, this has not been complemented with a sense of "Indonesian-ness" because by discriminating against the peripheral communities on the basis of their local identities, the economic model has bred resentment toward Java. In addition to economic grievances felt by the peripheral communities, ethnic unrest in the Outer Islands has occurred because of the manner in which the three main candidates for secession (Aceh, Irian Jaya, and East Timor) were incorporated into the Indonesian state. In all three cases the Armed Forces of the Republic of Indonesia (Angkatan Bersenjata Republik Indonesia, ABRI) successfully defeated the initial opponents of Indonesian rule, yet in all three the desire for secession remained strong. While the oppressive measures used by ABRI have ensured a continuing resentment toward Jakarta, the key failure of Indonesia's state-making and nation-building approach can be seen in its exploitative economic development programs.

Prior to World War II, Indonesia had been a Dutch colony, but after the defeat of the Japanese, Indonesian nationalists declared independence. The Dutch rejected this but after a failed attempt to regain control, the Republic of Indonesia was announced on December 27, 1949. The first president of Indonesia was the founder of the Indonesian Nationalist Party, General Sukarno. Although Indonesia started as a parliamentary democracy, in July 1959 Sukarno replaced it with an authoritarian system called "Guided Democracy." Not until 1999 did Indonesia again have a democratically elected president. On September 30, 1965, the Indonesian Communist Party (PKI) ended Sukarno's rule in an abortive coup. The military, acting under the leadership of General Suharto, defeated the coup attempt and banned the PKI. Confusion remains over Sukarno's ouster; it has been argued that it was actually engineered by the military so that the influence of communism could be nullified.[38]

The reign of Suharto and his New Order regime lasted until 1998. While this period saw great economic improvement for Indonesia— Suharto was dubbed the "father of development"—it also strengthened authoritarian rule and codified the military's role in Indonesian politics. ABRI possessed a dual function (*dwi fungsi*), which meant that it had responsibility for protecting Indonesia not only from external threats but also from internal ones. The internal security role enabled the military to be represented in politics, but it also brought widespread abuse of human rights. The military are still represented in Indonesian politics in the People's Consultative Assembly (Majelis Permusyawaratan Rakyat, MPR).

In 1998, the Suharto regime collapsed and his vice-president, B. J. Habibie, replaced him. Habibie's government was a transition one during which time Indonesia prepared for democratic elections. In 1999, free elections were held for the national legislature (Dewan Perwakilan Rakyat, DPR), and the MPR chose a new president and vice-president:

Abdurrahman Wahid and Megawati Sukarnoputri, the daughter of Sukarno, respectively. In July 2001, Wahid was impeached on grounds of corruption and incompetence, and Megawati became president. After four administrations in four years, it is widely expected that Indonesia will now enjoy a period of political stability, with Megawati likely to remain president until the next elections in 2004. This stability does not necessarily indicate a strengthening of democracy (examined in Chapter 3) or societal stability, as Indonesia's faltering economy raises the prospect of Jakarta ruling over a failed state. Indonesia has also fallen victim to terrorism (see Chapter 7) and despite a ceasefire agreement with the Acehnese in December 2002, a military solution in the rebellious provinces of Aceh and West Papua remains a distinct possibility. We now turn to the Outer Islands.

On August 30, 1999, in a referendum organized and conducted by the UN Mission in East Timor (UNAMET), 78.5 percent of East Timorese voted for independence from rather than autonomy within Indonesia. It was an overwhelming rejection of Jakarta's state-making and nation-building approach that had been in effect since Indonesia invaded East Timor in 1975. The loss of East Timor has raised fears in Jakarta that other provinces, notably Aceh and West Papua, will follow. At the beginning of the twenty-first century, therefore, the archipelago state of Indonesia is faced with the prospect of an exodus that would result not only in the loss of considerable territory but would also have a deleterious impact on Indonesia's economy. Why then did the East Timorese vote for independence, and is such an outcome likely in Aceh and West Papua?

East Timor. Unlike the rest of Indonesia, East Timor was not a Dutch colony, but Portuguese. In 1974, when the "Carnation Revolution" brought down the fascist Caetano regime in Portugal, independence for East Timor became a possibility. This raised a security problem for Jakarta because the armed forces believed that East Timor would become a base for communism. When the two main political parties in East Timor—the Timorese Democratic Party (UDT) and the Revolutionary Front for an Independent East Timor (FRETILIN)— failed to form a coalition government after the Portuguese withdrew, civil war broke out. Although FRETILIN proved victorious, the unrest provided the Indonesian military with an excuse to intervene. Invited in by the defeated East Timorese parties, ABRI invaded Dili, the capital, on December 7, 1975. East Timor was declared the 27th province of Indonesia on July 17, 1976, although ABRI was not successful in defeating the guerrilla fighters of FRETILIN until the early 1980s. Not until the Suharto regime collapsed in 1998 were steps taken by then President Habibie toward giving the East Timorese the choice of independence from or autonomy within Indonesia. Why then did they so overwhelmingly choose the former, given that Indonesia's integration approach toward East Timor was to promote development in the province? After all, such an approach, by improving the standard of living for the East Timorese, should have meant they welcomed membership in the Indonesian state.

East Timor received, on a per capita basis, the largest amount of Indonesian development finance. In comparison to the infrastructure established under Portuguese rule, the investment by Indonesia is impressive. The Portuguese built 47 elementary schools, two middle schools, and one high school, and with integration into Indonesia the numbers rose to 579 elementary schools, 90 middle schools, 39 high schools, and three colleges. In addition, transportation links were greatly improved with the building of 536 kilometers of paved roads.[39] However, contrary to expectations in Indonesia, where it was thought that a better-educated workforce fluent in Indonesian would bolster integrationist sentiment, resistance actually rose as East Timorese nationalism grew stronger among the younger generation.

The reasons for this and ultimately for the failure of the Indonesian government to successfully integrate East Timor into the Indonesian state were twofold. The first was the horrifying violence conducted against the East Timorese by the Indonesian army. Peter Carey writes that "at least a third of the pre-1975 population [was] murdered by the Indonesian army or perished as the result of war-induced famine and disease." The military occupation, Carey notes, was "as oppressive as any witnessed in post-war history."[40] It is estimated that over two hundred thousand people died in the aftermath of the invasion and subsequent famine.

The Indonesian army had expected a quick victory after it invaded in late 1975, and although it declared East Timor a province of Indonesia in July 1976, the army was still engaged in guerrilla warfare against FRETILIN. FRETILIN's success in frustrating the Indonesian army led to a change of Indonesian strategy in 1977; the army began a policy of encirclement and resettlement. Villages were surrounded by the military, FRETILIN sympathizers were killed, and the villagers were transported to newly created strategic camps. In 1978, the entire population of Arsabai, a village near the Indonesian border, was killed for supporting FRETILIN. Those transported to the camps were prevented from leaving, and because they could not cultivate or harvest the land, starvation became widespread. The encirclement campaign succeeded in quelling the resistance, and by 1980, the army was able to close its East Timor military command.[41] However, while resistance did not survive as a military force—by the mid 1990s the number of guerrilla fighters was estimated at two hundred—it continued throughout Indonesia's occupation in the guise of unarmed civil protest. The brutality of ABRI also continued.

In 1989, Xanana Gusmão relinquished his position as FRETILIN leader and formed the National Council of Maubere Resistance (CNRM). The CNRM acted as an umbrella organization that coordinated and encouraged nonviolent civil protest among the East Timorese regardless of their political affiliation. In October 1991, a parliamentary delegation from Portugal was due to visit East Timor and the CNRM began preparations for a demonstration. Anticipating a protest, the military cancelled the visit, but scuffles broke out between anti and prointegration youths, which led to the death of one youth on both sides. The CNRM planned a peaceful protest at the memorial mass on November 12 at Santa Cruz for the fallen anti-integration youth. When the crowd, numbering some two thousand people, reached the cemetery, truckloads of soldiers arrived. Some in the crowd were waving the FRETILIN flag and chanting "Long Live East Timor"; the soldiers opened fire and with the crowd hemmed in by the high walls of the cemetery, many had no chance of survival. Although Indonesian official figures put the death toll at 50, an independent report listed 271 killed, 250 missing, and 382 wounded. The Santa Cruz massacre—also known as the Dili massacre—gained widespread international coverage because of the presence of foreign journalists. It was not just the brutality of the army's actions that alienated the people, it was also the impunity with which the army could act. Not one of the soldiers was charged with homicide, while thirteen civilians were sentenced to life imprisonment for their participation in the peaceful protest. The military treated East Timor as a fiefdom, and with no respect for the rule of law or establishment of effective civilian institutions, it is hardly surprising that the East Timorese regarded ABRI as an occupation force of a neighboring, colonial power.

The second reason why Indonesia's nation-building and state-making approach failed is because the development programs that were initiated favored migrant communities rather than the indigenous East Timorese. The educational facilities Indonesia established created an educated workforce, but this workforce then discovered that few job opportunities were available to them. Javanese immigrants filled civil service positions, which if filled by East Timorese would have enhanced the chance of successful integration. Migrants settling in East Timor either as part of Jakarta's transmigration program or just "spontaneously" emigrating there, dominated businesses; a 1989 study of Dili traders found that only 20 percent were local people. The combination of few jobs—whereas 21 percent had gotten jobs in 1983, this had fallen to 3.4 percent of an estimated 4,707 job seekers in 1987—and the growing number of immigrants created a rising level of social tension. The resentment toward the non-Timorese, who were known as Battalion 702 (those who start work at 7:00, bring zero benefit to the local economy, and go home at 2:00), eventually led to the riots and destruction of shops that occurred in 1994 and 1995 between the indigenous people and immigrants.

The combination of a heavy-handed approach by ABRI and the failure of the development programs to filter through to the East Timorese ensured that Indonesia's nation-building and state-making approach was unsuccessful. Stephen Sherlock captures the problem succinctly when he writes:

> The educated unemployed at the forefront of urban unrest are precisely the people who could, if given openings in business and government, provide the leadership for integrationist sentiment in East Timor. Instead, domination by military and civilian outsiders has squeezed out opportunities for the emergence of an East Timorese business class or an administrative and political elite with a stake in Indonesian rule.[42]

The result, as Chisako Fukuda asserts, is that the Indonesians "were not much different from the Portuguese colonisers who had robbed them of their economic livelihood and culture."[43] Jakarta remained in the eyes of the East Timorese the capital of a colonial power that had occupied their land since 1975, had abused them physically, and exploited them economically. Despite the attempts of prointegrationists to intimidate voters leading up to the referendum in 1999, the turnout was 98 percent, a testimony to the people's desire to be rid of Indonesian rule. The vote did not herald an immediate improvement in the lives of the East Timorese, however; indeed in the following weeks the Indonesian military via their proxy prointegrationist gangs wreaked havoc in East Timor. More than three-quarters of the 890,000 residents were displaced, main cities and towns were laid waste, 70 percent of the physical infrastructure was destroyed, and although figures remain to be determined, Bishop Carlos Felipe Ximenes Belo, the 1996 Nobel Peace laureate, estimates that 10,000 were killed. Some 250,000 fled to Indonesian West Timor where they were held in camps reminiscent of those established during the encirclement strategy. Not until June 2001 were the refugees allowed to decide for themselves if they wanted to return to East Timor.[44] The violence was brought to an end when an international peacekeeping force led by the Australians (INTERFET) arrived on September 20, 1999. East Timor was then administered by the UN Transitional Administration in East Timor (UNTAET), which had the responsibility for preparing East Timor for self-government.[45] In May 2002, East Timor gained its independence and elected former resistance leader, Jose Alexandre "Xanana" Gusmão, as its new president.[46]

Aceh.   The East Timor referendum breathed new life into the demand for independence from two other restless regions in Indonesia. One of these is Aceh, located in the northern tip of Sumatra. The status of Aceh is quite different from East Timor, however, and the likelihood of the Acehnese gaining a referendum is slight. Unlike East Timor, Aceh was a part of Indonesia when it gained independence from the Dutch, and thus it is universally recognized as part of Indonesia. Although conflict occurred between Aceh and the central government in Jakarta during the 1950s, not until 1976 was the goal of independence adopted and the Free Aceh Movement (Gerakan Aceh Merdeka, GAM) established. This desire for independence grew, and in November 1999, half a million people took part in a proindependence rally in Banda Aceh, the provincial capital. After the fall of Suharto, calls for secession and demand for an East Timor-style referendum grew. When Jakarta rejected these demands, the region became wracked by violence. Although in 2000 a cease-fire was agreed upon between the Indonesian National Forces (which in 1999 changed its acronym from ABRI to TNI, its pre-1962 title) and GAM, the killings continued. It is estimated that as many people died between the fall of Suharto and the summer of 2001 as died between 1989 and 1998.[47] Since 2000, peace talks have been held in Geneva, and a cease-fire agreement was signed in December 2002. Although the December agreement amounted to more than just a cease-fire, outstanding issues remain, the most evident being the discrepancy between GAM's desire for independence and Jakarta's offer of autonomy.[48] This discrepancy eventually proved insurmountable and the cease-fire collapsed in May 2003.

The failure of Indonesia's nation-building and state-making approach is so stark in Aceh because the goal of independence adopted by the Acehnese was a direct consequence of Indonesian rule. The tension and subsequent conflict that ensued between 1953 and 1957, when Duad Beureueh declared Aceh an Islamic state, was not over secession but rather the status of Aceh within Indonesia. The elite in Aceh had expected their region to be a province of Indonesia when independence from the Dutch was achieved, but instead it was incorporated into the North Sumatra province. It was also evident to the Acehnese leaders that whereas they wanted Indonesia to be an Islamic state, the Indonesian president, Sukarno, wanted a secular state based around the principles of Pancasila.[49] Although a cease-fire was agreed to in 1957, Jakarta could not suppress the rebellion, and thus Aceh was given separate province status in 1959. Two years later it was given a "special region" status and promised autonomy in the areas of religion, customary law and education, and in 1962, Daud Beureueh ended the rebellion when Aceh was given the authority to implement elements of Islamic law. The key point is that this period of Aceh resistance to Jakarta was over Aceh's status within Indonesia, not independence from it. Hence Brown's assertion that the insurrections since the establishment of GAM "are . . . unique in Aceh's history, in that they are the first articulation of political opposition which asserts a secessionist rather than a regionalist goal."[50]

Why then did the Acehnese adopt the goal of independence? Like East Timor, the answer can be found in the economic development program implemented from Jakarta and the activities of the military. From the mid-1970s until the late 1980s, Aceh developed from being of little economic importance to Indonesia to becoming one of its richest areas, with the fastest growth rate.[51] The catalyst was the discovery of liquid natural gas and oil; during the 1980s Aceh contributed annually between U.S.$2 and $3 billion of the national revenue, making it the fourth largest contributor. Aceh itself gained little from this economic wealth because the 1945 Indonesian constitution stipulates that all the country's natural resources belong to the state. Where Aceh might have gained was through a sizable subsidy from Jakarta, but this was not forthcoming. Indeed, Aceh received only $82 million annually to fund its economic development. The result has been the perception in Aceh of its relative regional deprivation. Priyambudi Sulistiyanto writes that "Aceh could be a prosperous region similar to the small but wealthy kingdoms of Kuwait and Brunei, but it remains, instead, one of

Indonesia's less-developed provinces."[52] The Acehnese grievance that they are not enjoying their rightful benefits from the abundance of their natural resources is further compounded by the economic control enforced from Jakarta.

This economic control comes not only from the wealth going directly to Jakarta and then being redistributed in the form of subsidies, but also from central control of trade. Liddle writes that "Acehnese who wish to trade with Malaysia cannot do so directly; they must take their goods to Belawan for transshipment . . . it is a serious and continuing sore point in their relations with the center."[53] As in East Timor, it has also been a sore point that migrants from Java and other regions have taken the jobs created by the natural resources.

These economic grievances coincided with the emergence in Aceh during the 1970s of a secular-educated generation, which questioned the attitude among traditional Aceh elite that alliance with the center was in Aceh's best interest. They instead began to "argue that the centre's Javanese bias in resource distribution implied an 'internal colonial' relationship to Aceh which would only be corrected by Aceh moving towards a political autonomy in which it could retain control over its own resource revenue."[54] On December 4, 1976, Teungku Hasan di Tiro—a descendent of a famous hero who fought the Dutch, Teungku Chik di Tiro—announced his "Redeclaration of Independence" when he established GAM. His call for independence highlighted the grievances felt over Jakarta's internal colonialism. He asserted:

> During the last thirty years, the people of Aceh, Sumatra, have witnessed how our fatherland has been exploited and driven into ruinous conditions by the Javanese neo-colonialists . . . Aceh, Sumatra, has been producing a revenue of over 15 billion US dollar[s] yearly for the Javanese neo-colonialists, which they used totally for the benefit of Java and the Javanese.[55]

The response from the Indonesian military was to suppress this insurrection, and Hasan di Tiro fled in 1979 to establish a government in exile in Sweden. Despite the military's success, however, the Free Aceh Movement re-emerged in early 1989. The Indonesian response to GAM's attacks against the military was to double the number of troops stationed in Aceh (from 6,000 to 12,000) and designate the region as a Military Operations Area (Daerah Operasi Militer, DOM). The military were now able to operate in Aceh in much the same manner as they did in East Timor. There was a breakdown of the rule of law as the military sought to defeat GAM through whatever means were necessary. The result was widespread violations of human rights as the military embarked upon torturing and murdering suspected GAM supporters. Between 1989 and 1998, more than 1,000 people were killed, nearly 2,000 disappeared, and over 3,000 were tortured.[56] The result of designating Aceh a DOM was to create a climate of fear among the Acehnese, which led to resentment and ultimately support for GAM's goal of an independent state.

The fall of the Suharto regime in May 1998 paved the way for the DOM status to be removed in August. However, with GAM activists returning from exile and a sense of injustice prevailing because the new Habibie government was not prepared to prosecute those responsible for the human rights' violations, the level of violence escalated. On September 2, the chief of the armed forces, General Wiranto, ordered troops to remain in Aceh. Indeed, the number of troops deployed in Aceh increased in 1999, as the military carried out operations to capture suspected GAM leaders and sympathizers. Such operations by the end of 1999 had resulted in the deaths of 254 people and torture of 372.[57]

Resentment toward Jakarta—for economic exploitation and the military's human rights' abuses and the failure to prosecute once Suharto had fallen—led to an overwhelming call for an independent state. Although among the Aceh elite differences remained over whether to achieve this through violent struggle or nonviolent resistance, it is evident that independence had become the goal; Hasan di Tiro has even declared himself to be the head of state.[58] Since 1999, however, GAM and the Indonesian authorities have been engaged in a peace process under the auspices of the Henry Dunant Center, based in Geneva. Early signs of this process ending the conflict have not been encouraging. Indeed, 2001 was the worst year on record for conflict deaths; the Red Cross's conservative estimates are around fifteen hundred.[59] The violence was sufficient to cause a four-month shutdown of the ExxonMobil gas plant that services the giant Arun liquefied natural gas plant, causing an estimated loss of $350 million.[60] In April 2001, after peace talks had broken down, the Indonesian military embarked upon a series of operations designed to defeat GAM. With no effective civilian control over the military, the high incidence of human rights' abuses returned. In February 2002 a breakthrough appeared to have been achieved when GAM accepted autonomy as a basis for dialogue. This produced the December 2002 cease-fire agreement, which included details for a regional election to be held in 2004.

Although the December agreement was referred to as a "landmark" agreement, GAM's goal of independence has not been abrogated and within five months negotiations had broken down. On 19 May 2003, the Indonesian authorities launched a military offensive against GAM thus resuming their military approach to resolving the conflict.[61] Violence and bloodshed thus continue to characterize Indonesia's approach to nation building in Aceh.

Despite this gloomy assessment, a series of promising, albeit tentative developments have begun to address the demands for greater local political and economic control in Aceh—these have been the basis for the peace talks—but since these developments also apply to West Papua, I will examine them in the summary after the West Papua case study. In short, they amount to granting both provinces special autonomy status.

West Papua/Irian Jaya.   Located at the farthermost reach of Indonesia, West Papua is the country's largest province (twice the size of the UK) but has only two million inhabitants.[62] It is one of the world's least-explored areas, and the indigenous people scattered throughout the mountainous terrain retain many of their early customs. For example, the predominant religion is a mixture of animist beliefs and the worship of spirits, although Christian worship has increased. It is the most backward and underdeveloped of Indonesia's provinces.

Although West Papua was part of the Dutch East Indies when Indonesia gained independence, it remained under Dutch colonial rule. Dutch control did not end until 1962, when a UN Temporary Executive Authority (UNTEA) was established to govern the territory until a referendum could be held to determine whether the populace wanted to be part of Indonesia or have independence. In 1963, however, Jakarta effectively controlled UNTEA, and in 1969, West Papua officially became part of Indonesia with the signing of the "Act of Free Choice." Although the population was supposed to have a plebiscite, none was held. Instead, the Indonesian authorities selected pro-integrationalist tribal leaders who signed the Act of Free Choice on behalf of the people. The control Indonesian authorities held over UNTEA led to the creation of the Free Papua Movement (OPM) in 1963; its goal is for West Papua to secede from Indonesia. Given the diversity of the indigenous population, it is impossible to gauge the level of support for OPM; nevertheless, the local population exhibits strong anti-Indonesian sentiments. The desire for independence in West Papua was illustrated in June 2000, when a government-sponsored Papuan People's Congress proclaimed that West Papua had been independent since 1961.[63] Why then do the Irianese also want to leave Indonesia?

There are three broad reasons. The first is that unlike the majority of Indonesians, who are Malay, the Irianese are ethnically Melanesians. Indeed, one reason why West Papua was not incorporated into the Republic of Indonesia in 1949 was because some in Jakarta argued it would compromise Indonesia's cultural homogeneity. To what extent this ethnic difference is a source of tension is contentious. Dewi Fortuna Anwar argues that because Indonesia comprises over three hundred different ethnic groups, the ethnic differences between the Irianese and the rest of Indonesia "do not really constitute major stumbling blocks to . . . integration."[64] While the level of tension between West Papua and Jakarta is no doubt exacerbated by these ethnic differences, the fundamental source of grievance lies elsewhere: Indonesia's nation-building and state-making approach.

As with Aceh and East Timor, West Papua has suffered from Jakarta's internal colonial economic development program and the military's use of violence to suppress opposition. The second reason for anti-Indonesian sentiment is therefore that, like Aceh, the central government has exploited West Papua's natural resources and encouraged the migration of Javanese and other people to the province.

West Papua's primary natural resources are copper and gold; it has the world's third largest open-cut copper mine and the largest proven gold deposit. Since 1969, Freeport McMoran has been mining these resources and it dominates the local economy.[65] Its activities, though, have brought little benefit to the Irianese. Freeport has a terrible environmental record, its mining operation has necessitated the relocation of the local people (Amungme), less than 5 percent of the workforce are Irianese, and the wealth it does create goes to Jakarta. Coupled to these, West Papua has also been a major recipient of migrants via the government's transmigration program, and their arrival confirms Jakarta's control over West Papua's economy. Hence Catherine Caulfield's claim that the indigenous people "bitterly deprecate transmigration as a move to swamp them with people who share an ethnic and religious identity with Indonesia's military rulers."[66]

The final reason for the resentment toward Jakarta concerns the military's use of violence and abuse of human rights. West Papua has not gained the same amount of international press attention as either Aceh or East Timor, but the deployment of at least six battalions and operations conducted by ABRI Special Forces (Kopassus) and Strategic Reserve (Kostrad) indicate the instability of the province. Incidents that have been covered include the killing of eight OPM guerrillas in 1996 after they had taken fourteen environmentalists hostage.[67] This led to a reign of terror that lasted until October 1997, in which at least thirteen people were killed.[68] In the aftermath of Suharto's fall, coverage of the military's activities has increased. In July 1998, at least eleven people were killed on the island of Biak when they hoisted the West Papuan flag of independence,[69] while another thirty-one died when they did the same at Wamena in October 2000.[70] In 2001, violence continued in the province, and in November the president of the Papuan congress, Theys Hiyo Eluay, died in a car crash; the arrest of nine members of Kopassus suggests it was no accident. By 2002, there was evidence the Indonesian military were increasing their deployment of special forces in the province and also assisting the movement to West Papua of members of Laskar Jihad, one of the Islamic fundamentalist groups that have been heavily involved in communal fighting in both the Malukus and Sulawesi. The fear was that Laskar Jihad (now disbanded[71]) would be used, as prointegrationist gangs had been used in East Timor, to harass and intimidate opponents of continued Indonesian rule.[72]

Summary

Indonesia's state making and nation building failed because Jakarta's economic development approach mirrors the internal colonial model. The domination of bureaucracies and businesses by Javanese or other migrant groups inhibited the local people's ability to benefit from being part of Indonesia. Not only was the Indonesian state failing to meet their aspirations, but it was evident that the central region—Java—was exploiting their natural resources. To make matters worse, local resentment toward Jakarta's exploitation could not be voiced through political means since none existed, and if the people demonstrated, they became victims of ABRI's abuse of power. In such circumstances, fear and antipathy toward Jakarta is created, leading to calls for secession. Since the fall of Suharto, there have been some tentative steps toward resolving the underlying sources of Indonesia's internal ethnic problems.

One such step is the passing of Laws 22/1999 (local autonomy) and 25/1999 (revenue sharing with provinces and districts) in May 1999. These came into force in 2001 and, if they are fully implemented, will begin to address the economic and political grievances of Aceh and West Papua. For Aceh, autonomy would mean that the Acehnese authorities would keep 70 percent of the region's oil and gas revenues for the next eight years and, with a population 97 percent Muslim, would have the right to base Aceh's legal system on Islamic law. For West Papua, autonomy would mean 80 percent of the revenue from the region's natural resources would remain in the province, plus its name would change to Papua and it would be allowed to have its own flag and national anthem.[73] These laws, however, are problematic. They were quickly set up under the Habibie administration to forestall more radical demands for autonomy or even independence, and consequently they are poorly worded and contradictory. Neither the Habibie nor Wahid administrations took measures necessary to implement the laws, and because of this, implementation was inconsistent, with widespread confusion. Michael Malley even asserts that "local officials have accused the national government of acting inconsistently and trying to regain ceded authority."[74] In the case of Aceh, for instance, the 70 percent revenue is on net, not gross income, and the oil fields beyond Sumatra's territorial waters have not been given to Aceh.

The autonomy laws—now known as the Special Autonomy Act—are a crucial element in restoring stability to Indonesia and, despite their flaws, are steps in the right direction. However, problems remain. In the case of Aceh, twenty-one separate pieces of legislation that are needed to fully implement local autonomy had still not been passed by July 2002. In addition, it remains questionable whether in Aceh or West Papua autonomy is acceptable, with the desire for independence, undiminished, especially in the face of continued state violence. Adopting the language of human security, introduced in Chapter 1, this legislation does address the human security need for freedom from want. However, as witnessed in the continuing violence in Aceh and West Papua, the freedom from fear element of human security is sorely lacking. So long as human rights continue to be abused by state authorities, there can be little expectation of Indonesia emerging as a strong nation-state.

Overseas Chinese and National Identity

The ethnic security problems in Southeast Asia concern not only center-periphery relations; they also include threats to the nature of the national character. The ethnic violence that has threatened the stability of the region's new nation-states has occurred because of the perceived privileged economic status of ethnic Chinese migrants. Two Southeast Asian countries in particular have witnessed riots and violent attacks against their Chinese minority. In the case of Malaysia, the worst outbreak of violence was the May 1969 Kuala Lumpur race riots, but since then the government has initiated a series of policies that have helped lessen ethnic tension. Malaysia is one of the case studies; the other is Indonesia, where despite improving relations between its indigenous populace and the Chinese minority in the 1990s, the fall of the Suharto regime brought a wave of violence directed against the Chinese community.

Assimilation: Indonesia

If there is contention over whether Indonesia sought to assimilate its indigenous minorities in the Outer Islands, there is little doubt that Jakarta did seek to assimilate its Chinese population during the New Order regime.[75] The policy of assimilation (*pembauran*) was part of a two-pronged defense to safeguard Indonesian security from Communist China. The first measure was to assimilate the Chinese population and the other was to naturalize the Sino-Indonesians; this was largely successful, with Indonesian authorities estimating that by 1989 only five hundred thousand ethnic-Chinese out of five million had not opted for Indonesian citizenship.[76] The fear was that Sino-Indonesians might act as a fifth column in Indonesia through which Beijing could direct its subversive activities, hence the naturalization process to eradicate any confusion over the legal status of the Chinese population, and the assimilation program to adjust their identity and create loyalty to Indonesia. Since the demise of the PKI, the New Order regime also deprived the ethnic Chinese from having any direct political role. Internal security problems still remained with the Chinese minority, but the issues were over their economic position, not suspected ideological links to Communist China.

The assimilation of the Chinese population was, however, flawed. Although the goal was clear enough—the dissolution of "Chineseness" and adoption of local ethnic cultures—implementation of the program suffered from contradictions. This created the paradox of a Sino-Indonesian community whose linguistic and cultural world was Indonesian, yet was still regarded by indigenous people as different.

The eradication of Chineseness can be seen in the ways being Chinese was stigmatized and in the policies introduced to hinder the transfer of Chinese identity to the younger generation. The terms *pribumi* and non-*pribumi* were introduced to distinguish between the indigenous peoples (pribumi) and the migrants. Chinese culture is not equivalent to indigenous culture. There are no Chinese models in the theme park, "Beautiful Indonesia in Miniature"; events such as Chinese New Year could be celebrated only in private; and at the beginning of the

New Order regime Chinese language schools were closed. A quota system was introduced limiting the number of Sino-Indonesian students that could attend university. Citizens of Chinese descent had to carry identification cards, visitors entering Indonesia were informed that printed materials in Chinese were illegal, and during Suharto's presidency there was no Chinese cabinet minister, although there had been in the preceding regime, and no general or senior civil servant was of obvious Chinese ancestry.

Yet although transference to Indonesian was praised—such as intermarriage, adoption of an Indonesian name, and/or converting to Islam—the stigma attached to Chineseness remained. Thus marriage did not mean Chinese males could dispense with the identity card. Their children, regardless of how purely native their mothers, were still classified as nonpribumi, and access to public service still required declaring their former name. Not surprisingly, the Sino-Indonesian community perceived they were not accepted as full-fledged fellow citizens. This perception was not due simply to contradictions in the assimilation program but also because the pribumi resented the economic achievements of the Sino-Indonesians and the perceived favoritism they received during the New Order regime.

During that regime almost all the large conglomerates that dominated the Indonesian economy, apart from those owned by Suharto's children, were owned by Sino-Indonesians. It is estimated that although they constituted only 3 percent of the population, the Sino-Indonesians accounted for over 70 percent of Indonesia's corporate wealth. The frustration for the pribumi, especially indigenous entrepreneurs, is that this domination occurred because of political favoritism.[77] When Sukarno was ousted from power, there was a terrible massacre of communists in Indonesia, many of whom were Chinese.[78] The fear that they could be targeted again, coupled to the demise of the PKI, led Chinese businessmen to covertly fund generals and high officials in the New Order regime because they believed this would provide them with security against the indigenous communities. This created a close linkage between these businessmen and government officials, the best-known example being the billionaire Liem Sioe Liong's forty-year relationship with President Suharto. These close ties led to the accusation of political favoritism that in turn generated resentment toward Sino-Indonesian businessmen, hence Adam Schwarz's assertion that "*pribumi* businessmen believe Soeharto's patrimonial style of rule is the principal cause of the Chinese domination of Indonesia's private economy."[79] Schwarz concludes that the reason for Suharto's preference was not ethnicity per se but because no matter how economically strong it became, a Sino-Indonesian business elite was unlikely to be a political threat because the Sino-Indonesian community was so small.

The resentment of the pribumi toward the Sino-Indonesians and the failure of the New Order regime to assimilate the Chinese community into an Indonesian nation were vividly demonstrated in the riots that coincided with Suharto's downfall on May 13–14, 1998.[80] The riots were characterized by the systematic and brutal rapes of Chinese women and young girls, as well as the looting and burning of Chinese properties. Many Chinese fled Indonesia in the aftermath of the riots, although others stayed, hoping to create a more tolerant Indonesian society in the reformasi age.[81] It is estimated that over forty thousand left, and there was another emigration surge when Wahid's political demise became apparent.[82] The ambivalence shown by B. J. Habibie, Suharto's successor, immediately after the May riots in Jakarta and Solo was a poignant reminder of just how difficult resolving this "perennial source of ethnic conflict in Indonesia" might be.[83] Although he visited Chinatown in Jakarta, he did not condemn the riots or the rape of Indonesian-Chinese women and only did so belatedly on July 15.

In the aftermath of the New Order regime, the approach toward the Sino-Indonesians has markedly changed, especially under the Wahid administration. The failure of the assimilation approach can be seen in the Sino-Indonesians' resurgent interest in their Chinese ethnicity. A number of Chinese societies, including nongovernmental organizations and youth groups, have emerged to promote Chinese interests and to seek removal of discriminatory laws. In 2000, the Chinese were allowed to celebrate Chinese New Year openly, and since then, Chinese newspapers, magazines, books, and music have become widely available. The years of Suharto's rule and memories of the PKI demise, however, have limited the development of a political manifestation of Chinese ethnicity. In the 1999 elections the majority of Sino-Indonesians supported Megawati's nonracial party.

Whether this resurgence in Chinese ethnicity will improve relations with the pribumi remains questionable.[84] The May 1998 riots have certainly increased ethnic consciousness among the Chinese, but the goal is to assert this within an Indonesian identity—to acculturate rather than assimilate. Suryadinata concludes that while "more Indonesians have been able to accept the ethnic Chinese as part of the Indonesian nation, anti-Chinese feelings are still deeply rooted. Thus in the short-term Indonesia is still likely to see ethnic conflict between its citizens of Chinese and non-Chinese backgrounds."[85] This example of ethnic tension and the difficulties of nation building thus remains.

Acculturation: Malaysia

The Malaysian response to ethnic tension between the indigenous Malay (*bumiputera*—sons of the soil) and the migrants (Chinese and Indian) has been to pursue a policy of positive discrimination in favor of the Malay. Although a degree of ethnic tension remains in Malaysia, the policies directed at resolving this tension have been largely successful. Thus, unlike Indonesia, the riots in Kuala Lumpur after the 1997 financial crisis, as the people demonstrated against the corruption of officials, were not directed against the Chinese community as well. The Malaysian approach toward its ethnic Chinese has been one of acculturation rather than assimilation.

Since independence in 1957, Malaya and subsequently Malaysia, which was formed in 1963 with the amalgamation of Malaya and the territories of Sabah, Sarawak, and Singapore (the latter was removed in 1965), has witnessed ethnic tension between the indigenous Malay and the descendants of Chinese and Indian immigrants who settled in Malaya during the period of British colonial rule. This tension becomes particularly acute when the Malays perceive that the predominance of their culture and their political position is threatened. One such occasion was the national election in May 1969, when race riots between the Chinese and Malay communities lasted for five days and, according to official figures, resulted in 196 fatalities.

The violence erupted because during the 1960s there was growing disillusionment among the Malay population that they were not sharing in Malaysia's modest economic growth and that their government was not doing enough to improve their position. The Chinese too felt aggrieved. In their case it was because of the "special" position the Malaysian constitution granted the Malay, which made the Chinese feel like second-class citizens. This special status provides Malay citizens with positive discrimination in higher education, government employment, and other economic opportunities. It is designed to redress the economic imbalance between the bumiputeras and migrants that occurred during colonial rule. A consequence of Britain's management of Malaya was that the Malay population lagged behind the economic and educational advancement of the Chinese and Indian communities.

Since independence, a coalition government has ruled Malaya/Malaysia. This government, known until 1974 as the Alliance, is comprised of political parties representing the different ethnic communities in Malaysia. The main parties are the United Malays National Organisation (UMNO), which is the dominant party and represents the

Malay; the Malaysian Chinese Association (MCA) and the Gerakan, representing the Chinese; and the Malaysian Indian Congress (MIC). The general level of Malay disillusionment with UMNO during the 1960s was further compounded when in 1967, UMNO's leader, Tunku Abdul Rahman, appeared to appease the Chinese community by compromising on the National Language Act. As the 1969 election neared, so support moved away from the government coalition to the opposition.

Although the Alliance won the 1969 election, its majority had been severely reduced. The Chinese opposition party did well in the election, and it was thought that another state election might have to be called, resulting in greater Chinese gains. For the Malay it seemed the Chinese might gain control of the government and their special status would be endangered. With little faith left in the Alliance to protect their position in "their" country, the Malay turned on the Chinese community. John Funston captures the Malay fear when he writes, "Characteristically, such outbursts occur when the very identity if not existence of the community is felt to be threatened . . . [The] Malays perceived a direct threat to their identity and retaliated with the fanaticism of the religiously possessed in a holy war."[86]

In 1974, the Alliance was renamed the National Front (Barisan Nasional, BN) and has since pursued more vigorously the promotion of Malays via the New Economic Policy (NEP). This favoritism has not led to an increase in ethnic tension because the BN coalition has promoted the Malay while protecting the minorities' cultures and livelihoods. Thus while the national language is Malay, the symbols of the state are Malay, and the state religion is Islam, the Malaysian prime minister, Mahathir Mohamad, has nevertheless proclaimed that Malaysia is committed to multiculturalism: Chinese and Tamil language primary schools are government funded, a private Chinese college was approved in 1997, and Chinese and Indians can practice their customs and religion.[87] This is not to suggest that no ethnic tensions exist in Malaysia—for instance, there is a concern among the Chinese that having enjoyed the benefits of their special status, the Malay are unlikely to give it up—but there is an acknowledgement from the minorities that they can trust the BN coalition to look after their interests. Hence William Case notes, "[E]ven as UMNO proclaim[s] before [the] Malay . . . its defence of their birthright, it trie[s] to persuade the Chinese and Indians that it responsibly check[s] Malay chauvinism."[88]

Protection of Malaysia's different cultures is complemented by a goal of creating an overarching identity for all Malaysians to adopt. In

1991, Mahathir announced his Vision 2020, an ambitious goal of creating by 2020 a fully industrialized and true Malaysian nation (Bangsa Malaysia).[89] Bangsa Malaysia is "an inclusive concept, based upon loyalty to the country, its constitution and its language."[90] The idea expounds the goal of a nation-state in which people have different cultures, values, and religions, and while maintaining their separate identities, they also share an overarching identity of being Malaysian. What is interesting is that rather than being a clear case of regime-inspired acculturation, Vision 2020 also appears to be a reaction to Malaysian societal changes. A number of commentators have noted that because of the NEP, class divisions have increased within the ethnic communities. Consequently, poor Chinese and poor Malays have more in common with one another than they do with their wealthy compatriots and vice versa. In the business community, James Jesudason argues that "with the expansion of Malay capitalism, internal competition within the Malay business class has increased, making it difficult for Malays to have a unified conception of their economic interests against the other groups. This development in turn has eroded an important social basis of ethnic conflict."[91] Consequently, he argues that while conflict along ethnic lines cannot be ruled out, if conflict does occur it is equally likely to be Malay "lower-class resentment . . . directed towards corporate and capitalist co-ethnics as towards the Chinese businessmen."[92]

While it is too soon to argue that these changes will end Malaysia's ethnic tension, they could in the long term—by the year 2020 perhaps—create an overarching Malaysian identity containing values with which Malay, Chinese, and Indians will have an affinity. The financial crisis of 1997 and the subsequent political drama over the sacking and arrest of Anwar Ibrahim raised a not inconsiderable challenge to the BN coalition. K. S. Nathan warned that the economic crisis "could undermine the effort of the incumbent political leadership to forge a national community that transcends ethnic divides."[93] Yet it is notable that the issue the crisis raised for the Malaysian population was the process of democracy in Malaysia, not ethnicity. Ooi Kee Beng has even gone as far as to claim:

> Internal security, despite the rioting in Kuala Lumpur in 1999, is not as serious an issue as it used to be. In fact, the rioting shows that security is no longer the issue. The demonstrations, though carried out without permission, were often peaceful. The society had become stable enough for youths to take to the streets without fear of the demonstrations turning into racial riots. Hopefully, such a fear is now passing into history of a bygone stage in Malaysian nation-building.[94]

The riots and the Anwar Ibrahim case are examined in Chapter 3, but at present it appears that Malaysia has gone a long way toward managing, if not entirely resolving its ethnic security problem.

Conclusion

This chapter has examined one of the domestic or internal security problems that plagues Southeast Asia: ethnic conflict. At the time of writing, the Burmese authorities continue their resort to violence against the ethnic minorities that reside along the Burma/Thailand border. Likewise, in Indonesia the use of force by the TNI against GAM and Papuan guerrillas continues. In order to understand why these incidents occur, it is necessary to appreciate that these states are engaged in a policy of nation and state building. The continuing violence indicates that the policies are failing, and this can be explained by making identity the referent object of security—that is, seeing the different groups' ethnic identity as the "thing" that is threatened and thus needs defending. The threat comes from the nation-building policies of either assimilation or acculturation by the majority ethnic group that forms the elite.

This is not to argue that identities are fixed; indeed, they change over time as new (foreign) influences come to bear. This has certainly been true of Southeast Asia where aspects of Chinese and especially Indian culture have been adopted. Yet it is possible to see identities challenged at particular moments in time, and at these moments identity can be thought of as a referent object.[95] This challenge to an ethnic group's identity lies at the heart of the Copenhagen School's societal security. The threat can either be direct through repressive measures against the expression of the identity, or it can arise from more insidious methods, such as an economic model that favors certain ethnic groups, thus penalizing segments of the population on ethnic grounds.

A direct threat by a majority group to the identities of the state's minorities was the Burmanization (or Myanmafication) approach of the Burmans in Burma. This attempt to impose a monoethnic identity on the state's minority groups, coupled to an exploitative development program, created a backlash to the elite's nation- and state-building policies. Burma consequently remains a weak state, with minorities such as the Shan and Karen continuing to resist Rangoon's control. In Indonesia it is argued that the authorities sought to acculturate rather than assimilate their peripheral groups. However, implementation of a neocolonial economic model brought a backlash along ethnic lines, which occurred because the peripheral communities were prevented from occupying positions of power within the state bureaucracy. Javanese migrants took these positions, referred to in East Timor as Battalion 702. Thus, while Jakarta has professed a nation-building policy of multiculturalism, the reality is that non-Javanese have found that opportunities to enhance their economic and social well-being in Indonesia are stymied by their ethnicity. The failure of Indonesia's nation- and state-building policies was manifest from the 1970s onward, with separatist forces emerging in Aceh, Irian Jaya (West Papua), and East Timor. The latter's successful bid for secession in August 1999 indicates the failure of Jakarta's approach, as does the continuing need to resort to violence in Aceh and West Papua.

The issue of sizable Chinese minorities has been a source of internal conflict and violence in Malaysia and Indonesia. In Malaysia the pursuit of acculturation can be seen in the call for a Malaysian identity to complement the indigenous identities of the bumiputeras and nonbumiputeras. Through a power-sharing arrangement in government, albeit an unequal one, coupled to a policy of positive discrimination for the Malay, Malaysia has made significant progress in lessening if not eliminating this source of ethnic conflict. Not so in Indonesia, where the violence directed against the Sino-Indonesians in 1998 was clear evidence of Indonesia's failure to assimilate its Chinese population. Whether the acculturation approach adopted by the Sino-Indonesians since 1998 will achieve racial harmony remains to be seen.

Notes

1. Benedict Anderson, *Imagined Communities*, 2nd ed. (London: Verso, 1991), pp. 6–7.
2. For societal security see Barry Buzan, Ole Wæver, and Jaap de Wilde, *Security: A New Framework for Analysis* (Boulder: Lynne Rienner, 1998), Ch. 6.
3. Barry Buzan, "Societal Security, State Security and Internationalisation," in Ole Wæver, Barry Buzan, Morten Kelstrup, and Pierre Lemaitre, *Identity, Migration and the New Security Agenda in Europe* (London: Pinter, 1993), p. 43.
4. The negative aspects of "Batakness" included pig eating and cannibalism. The missionaries who spread Christianity did so by respecting those elements of Batak culture that did not directly confront Christian tenets. Thus, Dahm notes, "the Bataks, at least in the beginning, did not have the feeling of sacrificing their cultural identity." Bernhard Dahm, "Ethnic Groups, Colonial Conquest and Nationalism in Sumatra," in Thomas Engelbert and Andreas

Schneider (eds.), *Ethnic Minorities and Nationalism in Southeast Asia* (Frankfurt am Main: Peter Lang, 2000), pp. 18–19.

5. Charles F. Keyes, *Isan: Regionalism in Northeastern Thailand,* Data Paper 65 (Ithaca, NY: Cornell University Southeast Asia Program, 1967).

6. For an excellent coverage of the Isan, see David Brown, *The State and Ethnic Politics in South-East Asia* (London: Routledge, 1994), pp. 170–205.

7. Michael Hechter, *Internal Colonialism: The Celtic Fringe in British National Development 1536-1966* (London: Routledge & Kegan Paul, 1975), p. 10.

8. D. R. SarDesai, *Southeast Asia: Past & Present,* 4th ed. (Boulder: Westview Press, 1997), p. 17.

9. Myanmar is the Burman name for the country; as a significant component in the current regime's Burmanization of the country it is not accepted by the minority groups. I have used the name Burma throughout the book.

10. There is some controversy over the name given to the majority ethnic group. In this text Burman refers to the majority ethnic group that inhabits Burma's heartland of the Irrawaddy River Valley and the delta area, while Burmese denotes all the peoples of Burma.

11. Brown, *The State and Ethnic Politics in South-East Asia*, p. 50.

12. David I. Steinberg, *The Future of Burma: Crisis and Choice in Myanmar* (Lanham, MD: University Press of America, 1990), p. 75.

13. Brown, *The State and Ethnic Politics in South-East Asia*, p. 45.

14. Ibid., p. 46.

15. Josef Silverstein, *Burmese Politics: The Dilemma of National Unity* (New Brunswick, NJ: Rutgers University Press, 1980), p. 239.

16. Brown, *The State and Ethnic Politics in South-East Asia*, p. 50.

17. For details of the Karen, how they have been threatened, and their reaction to the threat, see Yoko Hayami and Susan M. Darlington, "The Karen of Burma and Thailand," in Leslie E. Sponsel (ed.), *Endangered Peoples of Southeast and East Asia: Struggles to Survive and Thrive* (Westport, CT: Greenwood, 2000), pp. 137–155.

18. Rodney Tasker, "Brass Taxed," *Far Eastern Economic Review*, 27 June 2002, p. 19; hereafter the *Far Eastern Economic Review* is referred to as *FEER*.

19. Gustaaf Houtman, *Mental Culture in Burmese Crisis Politics* (Tokyo: Institute for the Study of Languages and Cultures of Asia and Africa, Tokyo University of Foreign Studies, 1999), p. 53.

20. Ibid.

21. Mikael Gravers, *Nationalism as Political Paranoia in Burma* (Richmond, UK: Curzon, 1999), p. 109.

22. Nick Cheesman, "Seeing 'Karen' in the Union of Myanmar," *Asian Ethnicity* 3/2 (September 2002), p. 219.

23. Josef Silverstein, "The Civil War, the Minorities and Burma's New Politics," in Peter Carey (ed.), *Burma: The Challenge of Change in a Divided Society* (Basingstoke, UK: Macmillan, 1997), pp. 145–146.

24. Ibid., p. 140.

25. For details see Robert H. Taylor, "The Constitutional Future of Myanmar in Comparative Perspective," in Peter Carey (ed.), *Burma: The*

Challenge of Change in a Divided Society (Basingstoke, UK: Macmillan, 1997), pp. 57–62.

26. Tin Maung Maung Than, "Myanmar: The Dilemma of Stalled Reforms," *Trends in Southeast Asia*, No. 10 (Singapore: Institute of Southeast Asian Studies, 2000), p. 10.

27. Silverstein, "The Civil War, the Minorities and Burma's New Politics," p. 144. On the day before the Panglong Agreement, U Aung San addressed the delegates and warned, "If we want the nation to prosper, we must pool our resources, manpower, wealth, skills, and work together. If we are divided, the Karens, the Shans, the Kachins, the Chins, the Burmese, the Mons and the Arakanese, each pulling in a different direction, the Union will be torn, and we will come to grief." Quoted in Annemarie Esche, "Nation, Nation-State and Ethnicity (with reference to the Union of Myanmar)," in Thomas Engelbert and Andreas Schneider (eds.), *Ethnic Minorities and Nationalism in Southeast Asia* (Frankfurt am Main: Peter Lang, 2000), p. 86.

28. Silverstein, "The Civil War, the Minorities and Burma's New Politics," p. 148.

29. Ibid., p. 147.

30. Bertil Lintner, "The Proof of the Pudding," *FEER*, 16 May 2002, pp. 12–14; Barry Wain, "Rangoon Rebirth," *FEER*, 27 June 2002, p. 61.

31. Support for the current process is manifest in the New Panglong Initiative in 2001 and the September 2002 Copenhagen Declaration.

32. Quoted in John McBeth, "Why Did We Fail?" *FEER*, 1 August 2002, p. 48.

33. For details of the violence in Kalimantan, see Catherine Philp, "Refugees flee head-hunters in race to the coast," *The Times*, 26 February 2001; John Aglionby, "Below this mud lie 118 victims of new bloodshed in Indonesia," *The Guardian*, 28 February 2001; and Anne Schiller and Bambang Garang, "Religion and Inter-ethnic Violence in Indonesia," *Journal of Contemporary Asia* 32/2 (2002), pp. 244–254.

34. For an account of Laskar Jihad, including its antisecessionist stance, see Michael Davis, "Laskar Jihad and the Political Position of Conservative Islam in Indonesia," *Contemporary Southeast Asia* 24/1 (April 2002), pp. 12–32.

35. R. William Liddle, "Coercion, Co-option, and the Management of Ethnic Relations in Indonesia," in Michael E. Brown and Šumit Ganguly (eds.), *Government Policies and Ethnic Relations in Asia and the Pacific* (Cambridge, MA: MIT Press, 1997), p. 307.

36. Marcus Colchester, "Banking on Disaster: International Support for Transmigration," *The Ecologist* 16 2/3 (1986), p. 62.

37. Peter Carey and Steve Cox, *Generations of Resistance: East Timor* (London: Cassell, 1995), p. 9. For an additional view of cultural genocide, see A. Barbedo de Magalhães, *East Timor: Indonesian Occupation and Genocide* (Porto Codex: Oporto University, 1992), Ch. 7.

38. John Pilger, "Spoils of a massacre," *The Guardian: Weekend*, 14 July 2001, pp. 18–29.

39. Figures from Stephen Sherlock, "Political Economy of the East Timor Conflict," *Asian Survey* 36/9 (September 1996), p. 836.

40. Carey and Cox, *Generations of Resistance*, p. 9.

41. For details of the atrocities committed by the Indonesian armed forces in the initial period of their occupation of East Timor, see John G. Taylor, *Indonesia's Forgotten War: The Hidden History of East Timor* (London: Zed Books, 1991).

42. Sherlock, "Political Economy of the East Timor Conflict," pp. 845–846.

43. Chisako M. Fukuda, "Peace Through Nonviolent Action: The East Timorese Resistance Movement's Strategy for Engagement," *Pacifica Review*, 12/1 (February 2000), p. 19.

44. John Aglionby, "Timor refugees choose at last," *The Guardian*, 7 June 2001.

45. For an account of UNTAET's initial performance, see Jarat Chopra, "The UN's Kingdom of East Timor," *Survival* 42/3 (Autumn 2000), pp. 27–39.

46. John Aglionby, "Historic presidential vote for East Timor," *The Guardian*, 5 April 2002; Mark Dodd, "Poor, but Free," *FEER*, 30 May 2002, p. 20.

47. Dini Djalal, "Silencing the Voices of Aceh," *FEER*, 5 July 2001, p. 25.

48. John Gittings, "Aceh rebels agree to truce with Jakarta," *The Guardian*, 10 December 2002.

49. The five principles of Pancasila are: Belief in the one and only God; just and civilized humanity; the unity of Indonesia; democracy guided by the inner wisdom in the unanimity arising out of deliberations amongst representatives; and social justice for the whole of the people of Indonesia. For more on these principles, see the Internet site: http://www.ri.go.id/pancasila.htm.

50. Brown, *The State and Ethnic Politics in South-East Asia*, p. 156.

51. For details on Indonesia's redistribution of its wealth to the regions, see I Ketut Putra Erawan, "Political Reform and Regional Politics in Indonesia," *Asian Survey* 39/4 (July/August 1999), pp. 588–612.

52. Priyambudi Sulistiyanto, "Whither Aceh?" *Third World Quarterly* 22/3 (June 2001), p. 439.

53. Liddle, "Coercion, Co-option, and the Management of Ethnic Relations in Indonesia," p. 307.

54. Brown, *The State and Ethnic Politics in South-East Asia*, p. 151.

55. Ibid., p. 155.

56. Figures from Sulistiyanto, "Whither Aceh?" p. 442.

57. Ibid., p. 446.

58. Hasan di Tiro detests the Javanese even more than the Dutch; see Donald K. Emerson, "Will Indonesia Survive?" *Foreign Affairs* 79/3 (May/June 2000), pp. 99–100.

59. Michael S. Malley, "Indonesia in 2001: Restoring Stability in Jakarta," *Asian Survey* 42/1 (January/February 2002), p. 128.

60. John McBeth, "ExxonMobil Under Siege," *FEER*, 8 August 2002, pp. 36–38.

61. Initial details for the cease-fire agreement's collapse and the resumption of a military solution can be found in John Aglionby, "Jakarta Orders Attack on Aceh," *The Guardian*, 19 May 2003; John Aglionby, "Indonesia Uses UK Hawks in Aceh Offensive," *The Guardian*, 20 May 2003; and John McBeth, "Return to War," *FEER*, 22 May 2003, p. 20.

62. This region has several names. West Papua is the name preferred by nationalists, and they used the name on December 1, 1961, when the people proclaimed independence from the Dutch. In March 1973, under Indonesian rule the region was named Irian Jaya; previously it had been called West Irian. In 2000, to show that Indonesia was sensitive to Irianese demands for greater autonomy although not independence, it was renamed Papua, and the Morning Star flag was legalized. By the end of 2000, however, the flag had been banned.

63. John Aglionby, "Papuans renew their drive for freedom," *The Guardian*, 3 July 2000.

64. Dewi Fortuna Anwar, "Indonesia: Domestic Priorities Define National Security," in Muthiah Alagappa (ed.), *Asian Security Practice: Material and Ideational Influences* (Stanford: Stanford University Press, 1998), p. 494.

65. John McBeth, "Company Under Siege," *FEER*, 25 January 1996, pp. 26–28.

66. Catherine Caulfield, *In the Rainforest* (London: Heinemann, 1984), p. 198.

67. For details see Nick Rufford, "British hostages plead for army to hold back as deadline nears," *The Sunday Times*, 21 January 1996.

68. Dan Murphy, "Hearts and Minds," *FEER*, 29 April 1999, p. 21.

69. Dan Murphy, "The Next Headache," *FEER*, 29 April 1999, pp. 20–21.

70. Ben Dolven, "A Rising Drumbeat," *FEER*, 16 November 2000, pp. 72–75.

71. Robert Go, "Laskar Jihad disbands in face of blast outrage," *The Straits Times*, 16 October 2002.

72. John Roberts, "Indonesian military steps up repression in West Papua," 8 June 2002. See the Internet site http://www.wsws.org/articles/2002/jun2002/papu-j08.shtml. For collusion between the military and Laskar Jihad see Davis, "Laskar Jihad, and the Political Position of Conservative Islam in Indonesia," pp. 19–20.

73. Peter Searle, "Ethno-Religious Conflicts: Rise or Decline? Recent Developments in Southeast Asia," *Contemporary Southeast Asia* 24/1 (April 2002), pp. 2-4.

74. Malley, "Indonesia in 2001: Restoring Stability in Jakarta," p. 129.

75. Although even in this case it has been argued that under the New Order regime there was a conscious attempt to maintain the Sino-Indonesian identity in order to help foster an Indonesian identity among the diverse indigenous ethnic groups. See Ariel Heryanto, "Ethnic Identities and Erasure: Chinese Indonesians in Public Culture," in Joel S. Kahn (ed.), *Southeast Asian Identities: Culture and the Politics of Representation in Indonesia, Malaysia, Singapore, and Thailand* (Singapore: Institute of Southeast Asian Studies, 1998), pp. 95–114.

76. Since there was not an official census of the ethnic Chinese, these figures are only estimates. For Indonesian concerns over the security problem vis-à-vis China that the Chinese community created, see Rizal Sukma, *Indonesia and China: The Politics of a Troubled Relationship* (London: Routledge, 1999), pp. 140–143.

77. For details of these frustrations, see Adam Schwarz, *A Nation in Waiting: Indonesia in the 1990s* (Boulder: Westview, 1994), pp. 120–132.

78. The CIA reported the massacre as one of the worst in the twentieth century; see Pilger, "Spoils of a massacre," pp. 24–25.

79. Schwarz, *A Nation in Waiting*, p. 131.

80. For three possible explanations for the attacks, see Leo Suryadinata, "Chinese Politics in Post-Suharto's Indonesia," *Asian Survey* 41/3 (May/June 2001), pp. 506–509.

81. For more on the riots and the Indonesian-Chinese response, see Margot Cohen, "Turning Point," *FEER*, 30 July 1998, pp. 12–18.

82. John McBeth, "Voting with Their Feet," *FEER*, 12 July 2001, pp. 22–24.

83. Searle, "Ethno-Religious Conflicts: Rise or Decline?" p. 6.

84. For a succinct coverage of post-Suharto pribumi/non-pribumi relations, see Margot Cohen, "Exploring a Painful Past," *FEER*, 19 September 2002, pp. 62–65.

85. Suryadinata, "Chinese Politics in Post-Suharto's Indonesia," p. 524.

86. N. J. Funston, *Malay Politics in Malaysia: A Study of the United Malays National Organisation and Party Islam* (Kuala Lumpur: Heineman, 1980), p. 211.

87. For details see Harold Crouch, "Malaysia: Do Elections Make a Difference?" in R. H. Taylor (ed.), *The Politics of Elections in Southeast Asia* (New York: Woodrow Wilson Center, 1996), pp. 131–133; and "MCA to help raise funds for new Chinese college," *The Straits Times*, 7 July 1997.

88. William Case, "Malaysia: Aspects and Audiences of Legitimacy," in Muthiah Alagappa (ed.), *Political Legitimacy in Southeast Asia: The Quest for Moral Authority* (Stanford: Stanford University Press, 1995), p. 104.

89. Malaysian foreign minister Abdullah Ahmad Badawi contended that Malaysia "cannot go into the 21st Century with people living a separate identity except that they hold the same passport, hold the same identity card." For Badawi the creation of a Malaysian identity is a clear objective. See Frank Ching, "Forging Malaysia's Identity," *FEER*, 29 August 1996, p. 36.

90. T. N. Harper, "New Malays, New Malaysians: Nationalism, Society and History," in *Southeast Asian Affairs 1996* (Singapore: Institute of Southeast Asian Studies, 1996), p. 242.

91. James V. Jesudason, "Chinese Business and Ethnic Equilibrium in Malaysia," *Development and Change* 28/1 (1997), p. 131.

92. Ibid., p. 139.

93. K. S. Nathan, "Malaysia: Reinventing the Nation," in Muthiah Alagappa (ed.), *Asian Security Practice: Material and Ideational Influences* (Stanford: Stanford University Press, 1998), p. 548.

94. Ooi Kee Beng, "New Crisis and Old Problems in Malaysia," in Ho Khai Leong and James Chin, (eds.), *Mahathir's Administration: Performance and Crisis in Governance* (Singapore: Times Books International, 2001), pp. 117–118.

95. For a defense of their position, see Barry Buzan and Ole Wæver, "Slippery? Contradictory? Sociologically Untenable? The Copenhagen School Replies," *Review of International Studies* 23/2 (April 1997), pp. 241–250.

3

Political Security
and Regime Legitimacy

I n the previous chapter the nation- and state-building approaches of
Southeast Asian states were examined to highlight the ethnic dimension of the region's internal security problems. The link between legitimacy and security issues does not, though, come only from ethnic challenges. Another internal security problem, because it raises the question
of regime legitimacy, is the challenge of political ideologies. This challenge was manifest during the Cold War with the internal security threat
posed by various communist movements that were active in Southeast
Asia. Since the end of the Cold War, this security threat has taken the
form of calls for greater democracy, encapsulated in the cries of *reformasi* that brought down the Suharto government in Indonesia and posed
a serious challenge to the government of Malaysia.

This chapter highlights the criteria for ascertaining regime legitimacy and then examines these criteria with respect to Indonesia, Malaysia,
and Thailand.

Security and Regime Legitimacy

The term *regime* refers to the institutions, principles, and procedures
that constitute the political system. Thus Western liberal democratic
regimes include the principles of participation and competition among
institutions such as political parties, and an accountable executive and
legislative plus an independent judiciary. Institutions also include the
constitution, legal system, and elections that provide procedures for the
acquisition of power and the exercise of that power when in office.
Regime type refers to the categories of democracy, authoritarianism,

and totalitarianism; it is possible, therefore, for a regime to witness several changes of government. While this means specific individuals should not be regarded as regimes, in some cases the regime does become personified by a particular person. For example, the New Order regime in Indonesia was personified with President Suharto. Once Suharto was forced out of office in 1998, the regime was replaced.[1]

In order to address the question of regime security, it is necessary to utilize the securitization work of the Copenhagen School and in particular the notion of political security, since this refers to the legitimacy of the regime. If the regime is not regarded as legitimate by the population, then it and the elite in power are likely to face a challenge. Since the regime encompasses the political and legal system, such a challenge is likely to require activity outside normal politics. It was noted in Chapter 1 that according to the Copenhagen School, the use of extraordinary measures—that is, activity outside normal politics—is a criterion for determining if an issue has become a security issue. Thus the use of extraordinary measures by the populace, such as storming government buildings in order to overthrow the elite and/or regime, signifies that the challenge has moved from being a political issue to a security issue. Whether such activity is successful in removing the regime will depend upon the level of collaboration the anti and proregime supporters muster from the populace. During the Cold War the activities of the numerous communist parties in Southeast Asia, such as the Communist Party of Malaya (CPM) and Communist Party of Thailand (CPT), were a security issue because they threatened the regimes' legitimacy. They failed to remove the incumbent regimes because they were not able to gain the support of the general population in those countries. Elsewhere in Southeast Asia, such as Vietnam, Laos, and Cambodia, the communists were successful.

The key in this chapter is determining whether heated public debate, such as evidenced by the calls for reformasi, indicates a desire for political reform that endangers the regime or whether it is a desire to replace the government. The former is a security threat because the regime's survival is at stake, whereas the latter will become a security issue only if the regime does not have adequate procedures for the government to be replaced. If adequate procedures exist for the population to express their dissatisfaction, then demands for change, because they can be satisfied within the existing political framework and do not require extraordinary measures, can be regarded as political not security issues.

A difficulty arises when even though the regime does have adequate procedures for the government to be replaced—the regime has effective self-renewal—the incumbent elite regards demonstrations as a threat to its survival and expresses this challenge as a threat to national security. Such an expression could be manifest by declaring martial law and deploying armed forces on the streets. In this case the demonstration is not a security threat either to the regime or the state, but the elite is making a securitizing move by claiming the need to take extraordinary measures to suppress the demonstrators. If the demonstrators are representative of the population, the populace are likely to regard these extraordinary measures as illegitimate and the government as acting outside the rule of law. The government's attempt to securitize the issue has failed. However, if the regime's institutions and procedures are incapable of checking this abuse of power—the measures could include arresting antigovernment leaders on charges widely regarded as trumped up and/or shooting demonstrators by the armed forces—the regime's legitimacy will be eroded. In essence, the regime has failed to protect the people's right to replace the government and thus no longer has effective self-renewal. In such circumstances, incidents of violence initiated by antigovernment demonstrators against government forces are likely to be acceptable to the wider population, because they realize that extraordinary measures are needed. The demonstrators make the securitizing move, which is accepted by the population because they see no means of removing the current elite within the current regime. It has then become a security issue because the regime's survival is threatened. Although not reaching the level of a security threat, the general unease that Malays felt toward their government's persecution of Anwar Ibrahim is a case in point; the regime's credibility was damaged by it. This is discussed further in the Malaysian case study below.

The referent for security in this chapter therefore is the regime; and whether it is faced by an existential threat is determined by the degree of legitimacy it commands. The previous chapter highlighted that a shared identity was important in establishing a sense of loyalty to the state among the populace. The notion of sharing an identity or values has also been used to enhance regime legitimacy. For example, in the late 1980s the Singaporean government introduced the notion of "Shared Values" as an important nation-building tool. These five values are designed partly to establish principles with which Singapore's multiethnic society have an affinity.[2] The degree to which individuals identify with these values varies, but what is important is that whether Chinese, Indian, or Malay, they have as Singaporeans at least some affinity with them. How far these values have helped create a

Singaporean national identity is questionable. In the wake of the foiled terrorist attacks in Singapore after the September 11, 2001, attacks in the United States, the Singaporean government and Muslim associations there were quick to emphasize that although the terrorists detained were all Muslims, the predominately Chinese population should not direct their anger at Singaporean Muslims.[3] The implication is that despite attempting to highlight values shared by the different ethnic communities and using this to develop a national identity, the fear remains that ethnicity is a divisive issue in Singapore. The issue of terrorism is examined in Chapter 7; of relevance here is that Shared Values are not just about nation building but were introduced also to enhance the regime's legitimacy.

Singapore's style of government is a paternal one, sometimes referred to as "soft authoritarianism," where the elite determines what is in the best interests of the population. This paternalistic approach was the result of the government's unhappy experience with democracy between 1959 and 1965. The People's Action Party (PAP), which has held power since 1959, consisted of a coalition of Western-educated professionals under the leadership of Lee Kuan Yew. In 1961, when Singapore joined the Malaysian Federation, the left wing of PAP split to form the Barisan Socialis, which jeopardized the PAP's working majority. The difficulties this created, in conjunction with the problems that arose from the merger with Malaysia, left the PAP opposed to participatory politics. Leonard Sebastian writes:

> In principle, it was felt that representative politics was unsuitable for the Singapore masses, who lacked the political culture to participate and were deeply divided along ethnic and religious lines. The perception in the minds of the PAP elite was that democracy played into the hands of dangerous ideologues, such as communists and communalists, who were adept at exploiting the racial cleavages and religious prejudices of the masses. Hence when merger with Malaysia failed in 1965, Lee Kuan Yew turned his back on democratic socialism and opted instead for a strict uncompromising style of government.[4]

There are small and tentative signs that this is beginning to change, which will be examined later, but the following comment from a second-generation member of the elite remains relevant to the paternal style of Singapore's regime: "I don't believe that consultation with the people is a very productive exercise. People, even with education, tend to be irrational."[5]

By the 1980s, there was concern that the PAP was out of touch with the people. In 1981, its monopoly of parliament was broken when an opposition candidate won a by-election, and in the 1984 general election the PAP's vote fell to 62.9 percent and two opposition candidates were elected. Shared Values were therefore introduced as a means of arresting this decline of support by bridging the gap between the elite and the common people. By identifying its policies with these values, the PAP portrays itself as a defender of Singaporean interests, which in turn enhances the regime's legitimacy.

There are two criteria for determining the legitimacy of a regime: the manner in which governments acquire power and even more important, how they exercise that power.

Attainment of Power

If a government acquires power outside the legal framework, such as through a coup d'état, then it could be expected that not only would the government lack legitimacy in the eyes of the population, but the regime's legitimacy would also be damaged—indeed, the new government might establish a new regime. However, acquiring power outside the legal framework may have very little effect on the regime's legitimacy. For instance, formal provisions for the accession of a new government may not be well established, and traditional forms of power acquisition may carry more weight in conferring legitimacy. Such traditional forms may include the patron-client relationship that exists within the "Asian Way" of governance. According to both Malay and Confucian values, the ruled show deference to the ruler, and in return the ruler reigns in a just and fair manner. In other words, the manner in which the elite rules, rather than how power was conferred, determines the regime's legitimacy. The acceptance of a new government that installs a new regime, regardless of how it gained power, could also be explained by the circumstances in which it came to power. For example, it may have brought about the removal of a despotic regime or of an authority installed by an external agency such as a colonial power.

The question of dubious legality in the accession to power, and its relative unimportance to regime legitimacy, can be witnessed in the Philippines in early 2001, when the Estrada administration was replaced by the Arroyo administration. Joseph "Erap" Estrada had won the 1998 presidential election by a large majority and so enjoyed a popular mandate; however, his support waned as it became increasingly evident that the administration was corrupt. By the end of 2000, impeachment proceedings had begun on four counts: bribery, corruption, violating the constitution, and betraying the public trust.[6] In January 2001, the Philippine senate narrowly voted to suppress key documents necessary in the impeachment trial—widely regarded as a result of Estrada calling in personal favors from senators—which triggered a four-day protest in the streets of Manila. Hailed as People Power II, the sequel to the demonstrations that brought down the Marcos government and led to the installation of the current regime, the protests paved the way for Gloria Macapagal Arroyo to be sworn in as the next president.[7]

Arroyo's accession relied on a controversial interpretation of the constitution and the assistance of the military. The Philippines' supreme court ruled that Estrada had vacated his position and therefore Arroyo, as vice-president, should assume office. Estrada, however, had not provided a written letter of resignation and indeed publicly refuted her right to be president.[8] It is also evident that the Philippines' military played an important role. Claiming that the situation was volatile, as evidenced by a bomb explosion in Manila in December 2000; that the communists were seeking to take advantage; and that the armed forces were becoming divided over the president's impeachment, the chief of staff, General Angelo Reyes, withdrew the military's support for the Estrada administration.[9] It was a bloodless coup. The fact it was a coup—and referred to as such by those who supported the street protests—is an indication that the dubious legality of Arroyo's accession did not lessen her administration's or the regime's legitimacy.[10] What mattered was that the corrupt Estrada administration had not been able to survive, and on these grounds Arroyo's administration will also be judged. In other words, it is the manner in which the elite rule that matters, more than how they came to power.

Performance When in Power

Muthiah Alagappa divides how governments use power as a means of achieving legitimacy into two parts.[11] The first is whether they operate, or at least are seen to operate, within the rule of law, and the second is whether they enhance the well-being of the community. The first is essentially concerned with the abuse of power by the ruling elite and the issue of corruption, while the second concerns the government's performance. A government that uses coercion or force against the population and is riddled with corruption would be expected to lack legitimacy. This, though, needs some clarification. With regard to coercion or force, it depends upon whether the majority sees this action as a means to restore stability. For instance, the failure of the Wahid administration in Indonesia to quell the rioting and stop the bloodshed in the "Spice Islands" and elsewhere on the archipelago appeared to confirm the view that he was a weak president.[12] If, of course, the coercion is directed against the population as a whole, the government and regime will be illegitimate. The barbaric Cambodian regime installed by Pol Pot's Khmer Rouge, which reigned between 1975 and 1979, and the military regime that rules Burma clearly lack legitimacy.[13]

In the aftermath of the 1997 financial crisis in Southeast Asia, the issue of corruption has become a more prominent criterion for legitimacy. Prior to this, practices that could be regarded as corrupt, but were of course not referred to as such, were seen as intrinsic to the Asian Way of governance and business. For example, Lee Kuan Yew has admitted that nepotism is a Confucian weakness, and Amitav Acharya writes that "*guanxi*—roughly, the use of personal connections to one's advantage outside the legal framework—is now said not to be a good Asian value."[14] The prominence of corruption as a criterion for challenging the legitimacy of governments and regimes was captured in the popular acronym, *KKN*–Korupsi (corruption); Kolusi (collusion); Nepotisme (nepotism). Public concern over corruption, as noted above, resulted in the fall of the Estrada administration in the Philippines and was the basis of impeachment proceedings against Wahid's government in Indonesia, although in the latter case the impeachment process increasingly focused on Wahid's performance as president. Concern with corruption, especially over the damage it does to legitimacy, has also been evident since the late 1990s in China. Jiang Zemin, the former Chinese president, said that it represents a "life and death" struggle for the party.[15]

The manner in which a government reigns confers legitimacy not just on whether it abides by the rule of law but also on how well it performs. Legitimacy gained from performance reflects the elite's responsibility to use the concentration of power in their hands to improve the people's well-being. Failure to do this not only reduces the legitimacy of the government but, if successive administrations also fail, also brings the regime's legitimacy into question, depending upon the regime's capacity for self-renewal. In this respect a democratic regime, where the electorate can replace an ineffective government, is more likely to survive an economic downturn than an authoritarian one. For example, when the economic crisis of the late 1990s hit Indonesia, the subsequent overthrow of the Suharto government ended Indonesia's authoritarian New Order regime. Democratic regimes are not immune to such legitimacy crises; where democracy is relatively new and a commitment to democratic values is absent, it could be replaced by an authoritarian regime. This was the case with the Weimar Republic in Germany and has occurred in Burma, Thailand, the Philippines, and Indonesia. However, it was noticeable that the democracies of the region, such as the Philippines and Thailand, were able to ride out the 1997 financial storm without a security threat to their regimes emerging.

Whether the government's poor performance can create a security threat to the regime is therefore dependent upon the regime's self-renewal capabilities. If the regime does not have established procedures for the people to replace an ineffective government, then it is not creating conditions for stability and security during difficult times. Thus when the government's performance is poor, the pressure to replace it also brings pressure to replace the regime. Where conditions for effective self-renewal are in place, however, then performance, while remaining important to the incumbent government, is less important for the continued survival of the regime. In essence, regime legitimacy is achieved where the government is accountable to the people, because the people have a stake in the decisionmaking process. Indeed, the population's ability to replace an ineffective government within the regime's established procedures ultimately prevents domestic political problems from becoming security problems.

It is therefore important to consider the two types of regimes and their capacity for self-renewal that exist in Southeast Asia: authoritarian regimes that include communist and military regimes; and democratic regimes that, although not liberal democracies, nevertheless have the trappings of democracy. These democracies are often referred to as "Asian-style democracies" because of the paternal style of rule. It is useful to distinguish between these regimes and authoritarian regimes not because of democracy per se, but because the former have elections that allow for self-renewal.

Authoritarian regimes may enjoy legitimacy when they acquire power because they have either removed a regime established by a former colonial state or removed an ineffective government. The problem faced by these types of regimes is maintaining their legitimacy. To do this, they tend to rely upon performance, and regardless of how long the regime has been in place or how successful governments have been, if the performance drops, then so does the regime's legitimacy. Hence the collapse of the communist regimes in Eastern Europe and the USSR, and the New Order regime in Indonesia.

Even if authoritarian regimes are successful, however, they suffer from a paradox. On what grounds does a military regime that comes to power in order to restore law and order, maintain its legitimacy once law and order are restored? In Burma the military regime changed its name from the State, Law and Order Restoration Council (SLORC) to the State, Peace and Development Council (SPDC) because the former implied a temporary mandate. Needless to say, the name change has not solved its legitimacy crisis.

The authoritarian regime could argue that it creates the stability necessary for economic development, but the paradox remains. If the regime increases the economic and social well-being of the population, this could create new groups (entrepreneurs, middle classes) that demand political participation. Such political participation might initially manifest in the rise of a civil society and, in time, in the desire to have a direct impact on the state's decisionmaking through elections. Alagappa writes that sustained "capitalist development contains the seeds that can destroy authoritarian rule. Combined with a capacity for *limited* self-renewal, these considerations contribute to the erosion of legitimacy and, eventually, to a crisis" (emphasis added).[16]

Singapore is a useful case study to examine in this regard, not least because the regime falls between being authoritarian and democratic— hence the phrase "soft authoritarianism"—but is coping with the problems that affect authoritarian regimes. Singapore became an independent sovereign state in 1965, when it was expelled from the Malaysian Federation. For Lee Kuan Yew, Singapore's leader until November 1991 and now senior minister, it was not at all evident the small island-state would survive; he reasoned it could do so only through economic development. Thus from the outset, and this remains true today, the regime has based its legitimacy on performance, with the added incentive for Singaporeans to support the regime because, the PAP argues, Singapore's survival depends upon it. In simplistic terms, if Singapore's economy fails, so does Singapore. In 1996, Goh Chok Tong, the prime minister, warned the population ahead of the 1997 election that if "Singapore falters we will have no option but to ask Malaysia to take us back. Such a merger will be on Malaysia's terms."[17]

The PAP government establishes the goals to be achieved and the means used to achieve them. The bureaucracy has been co-opted into the PAP so that no effective distinction exists between the civil service and political elite. Indeed, Goh Chok Tong and much of the second-generation cabinet are former civil servants. As Sinnathamby Rajaratnam, one of the PAP's founding members has remarked: "It did not take long before we established a close link between us and the civil service. In fact, after the first two elections, the PAP became an administration. It was no longer a party. And the civil service became part of that."[18] This close identification between the institutions of the state and the government blur the distinction between the regime and government. In Singapore a challenge to the government's legitimacy inevitably entails a challenge to the legitimacy of the regime. Indeed, given the circumstances in which Singapore acquired sovereign statehood, this legitimacy could even affect the state, which might explain Goh Chok Tong's 1996 warning noted above. Cho-Oon Khong concurs that the survival of the state could be endangered when he writes: "[I]nsofar as the state was the creation of a particular leadership, questions of legitimacy directed at the government and impinging on the political regime may possibly extend even further to the nation-state itself."[19]

Since the 1980s, political opposition to the PAP has emerged and there is some semblance of choice for the Singaporean electorate; however, this does not mean there is effective self-renewal in the Singaporean regime. In the 1997 election only 36 seats out of 83, less than half, were contested. The PAP hounded an opposition candidate, Tang Liang Hong, whom they accused of endangering the stability of the state by "threatening the delicate harmony between the island's Chinese, Malay and Indian communities."[20] The PAP elite filed thirteen lawsuits against Tang, claiming that "by denying their accusations he damaged their credibility with voters."[21] The PAP elite also filed ten defamation lawsuits against the leader of the opposition Workers' Party, J. B. Jeyaretnam, because he read aloud a statement from Tang at an election rally. Jeyaretnam was found guilty of defamation and ordered to pay damages.[22] In August 2001, after losing a bankruptcy petition in a separate case, he lost his seat in parliament after being declared bankrupt.[23] The November 2001 election saw a repetition of the 1997 election, with only 29 out of the 84 seats contested and opposition candidate Chee Soon Juan facing legal action after accusing the prime minister of misusing public funds. In August 2002 he was found guilty of defamation and ordered to pay damages.[24]

There are tentative signs the regime is recognizing the need to ensure that disaffection with the government can be expressed through political channels, including parliament.[25] This is crucial in establishing self-renewal. One such channel is the Nominated Member of Parliament (NMP) scheme, where prominent members of Singaporean society sit in parliament for two years and provide an independent voice. There are currently provisions for nine NMPs, although the extent to which they represent a critical voice toward PAP policy is questionable. The importance of establishing constructive criticism of government policies was recognized by Goh Chok Tong after the PAP's landslide victory in the 2001 general election, a victory that was the PAP's third best result since independence. After the election the prime minister considered partially lifting the party whip so that twenty PAP MPs could act as an alternative policies group to be called the People's Action Forum.[26] PAP MPs, however, have rejected the forum and while there has been an attempt to encourage more debate in Parliament, the whip remains on matters affecting the budget, the constitution, no-confidence motions, and issues of critical national importance, such as security.[27]

Notwithstanding these recent developments, including a surprisingly good victory in the 2001 general election that far surpassed PAP's own expectations, the Singapore regime suffers from its legitimacy being too dependent upon performance.[28] If Singapore is to avoid internal security problems during difficult times, it will need to ensure that popular disaffection with the PAP can be expressed through political channels. A viable alternative to the PAP government is essential to the regime's self-renewal and, in Singapore's case, possibly the state itself. Hence Cho-Oon Khong's warning that while "the legitimacy of the leadership, regime, and state currently appears secure, Singapore's leadership must discover a more durable basis of legitimacy if the regime's viability is to be maintained over the long-term. Indeed, it is certain to need those new means of ensuring its legitimacy as social and economic change in the future is likely to create new—and possibly more serious—challenges to its authority."[29]

In addition to Singapore's soft authoritarianism and the region's military regimes, another form of authoritarian rule in Southeast Asia is communism. However, although the communist regimes in the region have survived the end of the Cold War, their interest in developing market economies reveals the failure of their regimes to provide an alternative path of development. Vietnam began its economic renovation in 1986 with *doi moi* and is currently seeking to follow the Chinese experiment of a market economy while retaining a communist political system.[30] Whatever success this achieves, it indicates that communism as an alternative model for development has failed. Of course, even if Vietnam, China, and Laos can produce the economic growth their neighbors have enjoyed, can they maintain their political systems while liberalizing their economies? It seems likely they will face the same problems as the region's other authoritarian regimes.

This is not to suggest that democratic regimes do not have legitimacy crises. It was noted earlier that where democracy is new, the commitment to democratic values and associated institutions and procedures

may be absent. In a new state that is home to a diverse ethnic population, it is possible the elite will rely upon primordial loyalties to assume
power and then exercise that power to benefit their own people instead
of the population as a whole. In the previous chapter this was labeled a
monoethnic regime. In such circumstances the components of a democratic system, such as universal suffrage and freedom of association and
expression, become tools for a bitter conflict, with elections becoming
battlegrounds marred by violence as campaigns arouse hatred. The
fledgling democracy is seen as part of the cause for the violence and
breakdown of law and order, and hence the willingness to accept an
authoritarian regime that will restore peace and stability. Samuel
Huntingdon captures this logic perfectly when he writes: "Under a democratic regime, radicalism, corruption and disorder reach unacceptable
levels and the military overthrow it to considerable popular relief and
acclaim."[31] Such popular relief was evident in Thailand when the democratic regime was replaced by the military in 1976. The elections in
April that year had been the most violent in Thai history, and when the
coup occurred in October, the Thai middle class "was quite willing to
trade chaotic parliamentary democracy for stable military dictatorship,
to exchange individual freedom for national security and domestic tran-
quillity, and to adopt short-term pragmatic solutions to problems rather
than the troublesome pursuit of long-term reforms."[32]

The criteria for judging whether the regime's survival is under
threat, therefore, hinges on its legitimacy, and that is dependent not so
much on how it came into force but the performance of successive governments and whether the regime provides for effective self-renewal. In
the former case, a series of ineffective governments will raise doubts
regarding the effectiveness of the political system, that is, the regime;
this is as true for democratic regimes as for authoritarian ones. In the
latter case, if the people cannot replace ineffective governments within
the rule of law, because the regime does not provide such procedures,
then they have little choice but to replace the regime when they want to
change the government—that is, to challenge the regime's survival.

Case Studies: Indonesia, Malaysia, and Thailand

We now turn to three case studies that highlight the issue of regime
legitimacy and security. These three countries all experienced political
challenges as a consequence of the financial crisis that swept across
Southeast Asia in the late 1990s. However, the security problems they

faced varied in intensity. In Indonesia the security threat was so severe that the regime collapsed; in Malaysia the regime survived but dissatisfaction was evident; while in Thailand, the final case study, the problems did not result in a security challenge to the regime. The case studies thus constitute a spectrum with lessening intensity of the security threat.

Indonesia

On May 21, 1998, after over thirty years as Indonesia's president, Suharto resigned from office. A series of demonstrations that began in earnest in February had by May worsened into riots and violence spreading from Jakarta to engulf Yogyakarta, Bandung, and Surabaya. With newspaper headlines such as "A nation descends into anarchy" and "Suharto returns to war zone" echoing the chaos, Indonesia's New Order regime was facing a security threat—a threat to its survival.[33] Throughout 1998, students had been demonstrating about ending the regime's corruption, collusion, and cronyism, overhauling the political system, and lowering prices on basic necessities. The threat was captured in the cries of reformasi, which essentially meant reform of the political system by removing the incumbent regime and its personification, Suharto.[34]

The catalyst for the regime's fall was the financial crisis sweeping through Southeast Asia, although disaffection with the regime predated this event. The Indonesian rupiah devalued by 10 percent on October 3, 1997, the biggest one-day fall for any currency during the crisis; by January 21, 1998, the rupiah was worth one-sixth of its July value. With considerable foreign debts, the economy faced an intolerable burden with the devaluation of the rupiah. Companies were closing, unemployment rose by four million in a few months, and labor leaders were predicting that another two million would lose their jobs by the end of the year; another estimate put this as high as eight million.[35] The cost of basic necessities was rising—cooking oil and gasoline had tripled in price—and the banking system was collapsing. The financial crisis was impacting all Indonesians, and workers joined students in their demonstrations.[36]

The rioting began with the fatal shooting of four students from Trisakti University on May 12. In the violence that ensued, more than five thousand buildings were torched and over one thousand people killed; the Chinese community was the main target of the violence. Seven days later, after it was evident that Suharto had lost the support

of the military and the chairman of his own party had called for his resignation, Vice-President B. J. Habibie became the new president.[37] In
June the following year, Indonesia witnessed its first free and peaceful
general election since 1955, and in October 1999, the People's Consultative Assembly (Majelis Permusyawaratan Rakyat, MPR) elected
Abdurrahman Wahid as the new Indonesian president. The current president, Megawati Sukarnoputri, subsequently replaced Wahid in July
2001.

The question here is why did the demand for political change
become a threat to the survival of the regime and hence a security
issue? The fall of Suharto's New Order regime seemed especially
unlikely given the commonly held view that it was secure. In a piece
published in 1998, Dewi Fortuna Anwar expressed this position, noting
that since "the government has succeeded in developing the economy
and improving the general standard of living, it has been able to forestall serious challenges to its authority."[38] Herein, though, lies the
answer to why the regime fell. The Suharto government and the New
Order regime based its legitimacy on performance.

The New Order regime was the third regime to rule Indonesia since
it gained independence from the Dutch. Prior to this, Indonesia had
experienced a parliamentary democracy (1949–1957) and the authoritarian rule of Sukarno known as Guided Democracy (1958–1965).
Suharto's legitimacy was based on economic development producing a
rising living standard for the Indonesian population. In order to achieve
this, Suharto argued that political stability was necessary, which meant
the continuation of authoritarian rule. Indeed, the New Order regime
was arguably totalitarian. Suharto not only controlled parliament
through the appointment of well over half its members, but he also
politicized the civil service and codified the armed forces' political role
by enabling ABRI (Indonesian Armed Forces) to be represented in the
legislature. The civil servants became members of Golkar, Suharto's
party, and in 1973, under pressure from the government and armed
forces, the opposition merged into two parties—the United Democratic
Party (PPP) and the Indonesian Democratic Party (PDI). The degree of
control the regime was able exert in these parties was manifest in 1996,
when the government ousted Megawati Sukarnoputri (Sukarno's daughter) from the PDI leadership; she was subsequently excluded from the
list of candidates that could compete in the May 1997 general election.
In addition to the legislature and government bureaucracy being sub-
servient to the executive, the press were state controlled and the only

trade union recognized by the government was the government-sponsored All-Indonesian Workers Union (SPSI).

This concentration of power in the executive coincided with some impressive economic successes for Indonesia. Under Suharto, per capita GDP rose by an average of 4.3 percent annually from 1965 to 1988, one of the highest sustained growth rates of any country in the world. From 1988, the economy grew by almost 7 percent a year. A successful family-planning program and measures to increase rice production dramatically reduced malnutrition and infant mortality. Illiteracy also declined significantly. But perhaps Suharto's greatest achievement was poverty alleviation. Some economists estimate that more than 70 percent of Indonesians lived in poverty in 1970. By 1990, this figure had dropped to about 15 percent. In the mid-1980s, Suharto was dubbed the "Father of Development."

These figures, however, mask the uneven economic prosperity of Indonesia. Economic development and prosperity was concentrated in the central islands such as Java and in the hands of the Indonesian Chinese community. In 1993, it was estimated that 1 percent of the population secured 80 percent of the country's wealth, and the concentration of that wealth was in the hands of nonpribumi.[39] This concentration of wealth in the hands of the few fueled speculation that the government was corrupt, with lucrative projects and business licenses being awarded to Suharto's close associates and family. Indeed, by the time the New Order regime fell, the acronym KKN had come to personify Suharto and his regime. With the majority of Indonesia's wealth in the hands of a nonindigenous minority, the impression was created that under the New Order regime the economic disparity that had existed under Dutch colonial rule had been repeated.

With political power concentrated in the hands of a dictator, few political avenues were available for the population to express dissatisfaction. When they did so, they were met with violence, as in the Tanjung Priok shootings in 1984. After authorities removed posters detailing political issues from a prayer house in the Tanjung Priok district of Jakarta, fifteen hundred marched in protest. The army responded by shooting the demonstrators, killing hundreds. Student demonstrations in Jakarta in 1974 and in Bandung in 1978 also signified a lack of political avenues to express dissatisfaction with the government. This situation, coupled with Indonesia's uneven economic performance, contributed to the labor unrest of the 1990s.

Resentment over Indonesia's uneven economic development was

seen in Medan in April 1994, when what began as a protest by factory
workers over pay and the right to organize a union outside the SPSI,
flared into a riot and attacks against the ethnic Chinese community.[40]
The frustration created by the disparity in economic prosperity was not
confined to urban factory workers; the countryside also experienced
riots.[41] The economic disparity between central Java and the outer
islands and peripheral communities also helps explain the disturbances
in Aceh and Irian Jaya (West Papua) noted in the previous chapter.

In the summer of 1996, Megawati's position in the PDI was challenged, and ten thousand demonstrators took to the streets of Jakarta in
her support. The demonstrators were a mixture of workers, students,
journalists, and others; crucially, they were representative of the entire
Indonesian population. The demonstrations erupted into riots in
December and again in April 1997. The financial crisis of 1997 was the
final straw for a population increasingly frustrated over the disparity in
economic development, with little opportunity within the regime to
replace Suharto's government. The demonstrators in 1998 were therefore taking extraordinary measures, and with the support of the people,
they securitized the issue. It became evident to the elite, including the
military, that the regime's survival was not possible and that Suharto
would have to resign. While the machinations of the elite in 1998 might
very well explain why Suharto fell as quickly as he did, the underlying
reason why the regime collapsed was because its legitimacy was based
on performance and there was no provision for effective self-renewal.[42]
The regime's failure to establish procedures for self-renewal and to air
grievances meant that when the government's performance was poor,
securitising rather than politicizing was the only means available to the
people.

The extent to which the end of the New Order regime will keep
political issues from becoming securitized will depend upon the population's ability to renew the government. If the current regime establishes
effective self-renewal, then it will likely achieve enduring legitimacy.
The initial signs, however, were not encouraging.[43] The armed forces
retained a political role with 7.6 percent of the seats in parliament,
which gave it four seats more than reformasi leader Amin Rais's party
won in the 1999 election. In addition, 34 percent of the MPR delegates
who voted for the new president in October were not elected but
appointed by the military and political elite.

By mid-2002, the signs were mixed. There were some positive
developments toward achieving legitimate governmental self-renewal.
In November 2001, the MPR's role in electing the president was ended

and its role in impeaching him or her was greatly diminished. Instead, the people would directly elect their president. Despite current president Megawati arguing that Indonesia was not yet ready for direct presidential elections in 2004, and that the MPR should retain a role, in August 2002, the MPR not only introduced direct presidential elections, it also removed the military from parliament. Both of these milestones come into effect in 2004.[44] However, in other respects the signs are not so promising. Megawati is not a reformist and maintains close ties with the military.[45] Intolerance toward protestors has increased, not just those in Aceh and West Papua but also in Jakarta. This paints a picture not of a government establishing a regime with effective self-renewal, but one seeking to safeguard its own position in power. For Sidney Jones of the Brussels-based International Crisis Group, this is not a surprise: "The picture that has emerged is of an extremely conservative, if not anti-reformist president. The [reform] spirit of 1998 is dead in the administration, if not in the populace at large."[46]

In late 2002, the regime was faced with responding to the Bali bombings on the night of October 12. Prior to this terrorist attack, the authorities in Jakarta had rejected the claim that Indonesia had a terrorist problem and had thus refused to act against suspected terrorists, most notably the Jemaah Islamiah (JI) and its leader, Abu Bakar Bashir. While it is too soon to know what effect the Bali bombing will have on the regime and the progress of democratization, it did force authorities to recognize the existence of a terrorist network in Indonesia, and Bashir was detained. The immediate impact of the bombing was to reveal a degree of frustration with the regime—most notably from the two organizations that represent one-fourth of the population (the Muhammadiyah and Nahdlatul Ulama)—because of the perception that the political system and the leadership are weak.[47] The development of a democratic regime in Indonesia thus faces a critical and testing time.

Malaysia

The cries for reformasi to remove a corrupt and unrepresentative government were not restricted to Indonesia. In September 1998, following the arrest of the recently sacked deputy prime minister, Anwar Ibrahim, calls for reformasi were heard among the protestors who took to the streets in Kuala Lumpur. Thousands demonstrated, often in defiance of police firing tear gas and chemically laced water, and in October 1998, for the first time in the crisis, protestors threw stones, bricks, and gasoline bombs at the police.[48] Two years later, in his annual independence eve address on August 30, 2000, Malaysia's prime minister, Mahathir Mohamad, spoke of Malaysia being under siege from foreigners and extremists seeking to overthrow the government by armed force.[49] The government, he assured his audience, would not be deterred if it felt national security was threatened. Mahathir's securitizing move has precedents in Malaysian politics. In 1984, the government tabled a white paper entitled the "Threat to Muslim Unity and National Security," in which the opposition Muslim-based party PAS (Parti Islam Se-Malaysia) and extremists were labeled as possible threats to national security. It is in this context that the violence that erupted in Memali in November 1985, when police attempted to arrest PAS member Ibrahim Mahmood, can be understood.[50] Has Malaysia's regime faced a security threat?

The political events in Malaysia since the arrest of Anwar Ibrahim have raised the question of regime legitimacy for the first time since the May riots of 1969. The legitimacy of the regime has been largely untroubled because the coalition government (Barisan Nasional, BN), which is comprised of eleven parties, draws its support from the different ethnic communities that constitute the population of Malaysia. Even though the November 1999 election was not a success for the BN, it still gained 56 percent of the vote (down from 65 percent). Thus, although dominated by the United Malays National Organisation (UMNO)—and the BN is committed to the principle of Malay dominance—the government has nevertheless been able to represent minority ethnic groups via the BN membership of, among others, the Malaysian Chinese Association (MCA); Gerakan; the Malaysian Indian Congress (MIC); and other parties representing the indigenous groups in East Malaysia. Of equal importance is that those segments that do not feel represented by the coalition government are able to express their dissatisfaction via opposition parties: the Parti Islam Se-Malaysia (PAS); the Democratic Action Party (DAP); and more recently, the multiethnic Keadilan (National Justice Party) party led by Anwar's wife, Wan Azizah. The regime has thus enabled the population to have an impact on the state's decisionmaking apparatus. Consequently, William Case notes that "strongly Islamic Malays and working-class Chinese may doubt, even deny, the government's authority, but they seem at another level to accept the worth of the regime."[51]

Why then did the arrest of Anwar and subsequent events create a legitimacy crisis and to what extent have these events become securitized? The manner in which Anwar was ousted created disquiet among

Malays. In the eighteen days between his sacking and arrest, Anwar had toured the country giving talks on the rampant KKN afflicting the government and hence the need for change. His detention under the Internal Security Act (ISA) occurred after he led an enormous rally in Kuala Lumpur on September 20, 1998. Although the grounds for his subsequent arrest were a mixture of corruption charges and sexual misdemeanors, it was widely regarded by Malays as politically motivated. The court case itself was seen as unfair, with Mahathir declaring him guilty of sexual misdemeanors and homosexuality before the court case began. He was beaten while in police custody, and the prosecution's witnesses reversed their testimony of being sodomized by Anwar, saying their confessions were not voluntary and, in the case of Manawar Anees, were extracted after four days of interrogation.[52] Judge Augustine Paul ruled that these statements were irrelevant unless the defense submitted a motion alleging ill intent by the prosecution. If the defense could not substantiate the allegation, then they would face a charge of contempt of court.[53] This was not an idle threat; the judge had previously sentenced Anwar's defense lawyer, Zainur Zakaria, to three months in jail for submitting an affidavit claiming the prosecution had abused their position.[54] The Malaysian special branch chief, Mohamad Said Awang, "admitted that he might lie to the court if told to do so by government ministers" and a report by the special branch submitted to Mahathir in 1997 stated that the sexual allegations against Anwar were baseless.[55] In April 1999, Anwar was sentenced to six years in jail for corruption, which led to street protests, and when in September there were reports of high levels of arsenic in his blood, tens of thousands marched because they believed the government to be culpable. The September march degenerated into violence, with the police resorting to tear gas, chemical water, and bludgeons. When the sodomy trial was reconvened in 2000, Anwar's defense lawyer, Karpal Singh, was arrested for "uttering seditious words" while defending Anwar in court.[56] Anwar was found guilty and sentenced to fifteen years in jail—nine for sodomy plus the six for corruption.

The Malaysian judicial system was criticized internationally, and many within Malaysia did not believe the charges and Anwar's image was undamaged. Indeed, the trial raised disturbing insights into their government's use of the ISA and sedition laws to silence critics. Reports by the foreign press of the street demonstrations also were censured.[57] These events were not new, however; the ISA had been used previously to quell opposition, such as "Operation Lalang" in 1988, in which over a hundred people were arrested. The reason why the government's actions caused such unease reflects the emergence of a new middle class in Malaysia that is less willing to accept the autocratic style of the leadership. These people when they were younger were influenced by such organizations as the Malaysian Youth Movement (ABIM), which had been headed in its early years by Anwar. Mahathir's public shaming of Anwar also breached deeply held Malay beliefs against such behavior.

The November 1999 general election was one of the dirtiest ever, and the result—one of UMNO's greatest electoral setbacks—confirmed the damage the Anwar trial had done to the government. The decision by the opposition parties to form their own coalition—the Barisan Alternatif (BA)—also aided PAS, DAP, and Keadilan in the election. However, those who doubted if the BA could remain intact until the next elections in 2004 proved correct. Tensions existed between the PAS and DAP over PAS's ambiguous position on setting up an Islamic state, while PAS and Keadilan differed on who would lead Malaysia if BA won; PAS wanted its leader installed as the Malaysian prime minister, not Anwar. The BA eventually collapsed in September 2001, when DAP parted with PAS after the latter proposed turning Malaysia into an Islamic state upon forming a government.

While the Anwar trial revealed the extent of government control over the press and judiciary, and Kuala Lumpur witnessed riots and battles with the police, the regime itself was not threatened. The issues raised in Malaysia did not become security issues. The electorate participated in the 1999 elections and was able to express their dissatisfaction with UMNO by reducing its parliamentary representation by 22 seats. The BN coalition government was still able to win more than the two-thirds majority (148 out of 193 seats, or 77%) widely regarded as necessary for providing a strong mandate, because the system is so heavily loaded in favor of the government. That the election result did not lead to disturbances, despite not being free and fair, is an indication of just how secure the regime is.[58] The reason why the BN coalition won is also because of the strong Chinese support for the government. Calls for change in Indonesia, while acting as the catalyst for reformasi in Malaysia, also enabled the government to warn that the violence witnessed in Indonesia, especially against the Chinese, could arise if the opposition won the election. Hence the Chinese support for the status quo.

In the summer of 2000, Mahathir's annual independence eve address, with its emphasis on Malaysia being under siege, painted a bleak picture. The country appeared set for political instability, with the leadership of UMNO likely to be contested before the next general election and UMNO needing to regain much of the Malay vote it lost to PAS. At the height of the Anwar trial—with the accused a victim of police brutality, doubts concerning the validity of the prosecutor's case, and riots in Kuala Lumpur—it seemed that the regime was on the verge of a serious threat to its survival. This, though, did not occur, despite widespread cynicism about the government's explanation of events. This cynicism was seen in such events as the attempt to implicate PAS in the arms heist in July 2000 and the decision to abrogate an agreement to pay petroleum royalties to Terengganu (a state that voted in PAS), which was widely regarded as an act of political vengeance.

Malaysia, however, has recovered from the trauma of the Anwar trial. This is perhaps best seen in the June 2002 decision of Mahathir when, confident he had seen Malaysia and UMNO through the traumatic experience of the Anwar trials, he announced he would resign as prime minister by October 2003.[59] The events of 1998–2000 ultimately remained at the political end of the securitization spectrum, and this was manifest most strongly in the population's acceptance of the government's use of the sedition acts and ISA. However, the disturbances indicated the Malaysian regime had been tarnished.

Thailand

The financial crisis that swept through Southeast Asia and beyond in the late 1990s had its origins in Thailand.[60] It acted as the catalyst for the reformasi movement that brought down the New Order regime in Indonesia and challenged the BN coalition government in Malaysia. A challenge to the regime's survival might have been expected in Thailand, given that there have been fifteen constitutions and seventeen military coups (only seven successful) since its absolute monarchical system was overthrown in 1932. Indeed, public discontent with the corruption of the democratic government of Chatichai Choonhavan led to near universal support for the army coup of 1991. The incompetence of Chavalit Yongchaiyudh's government to manage the 1997 financial crisis led to his resignation in November 1997 and his replacement by Chuan Leekpai. Unlike Indonesia or Malaysia, the political fallout from the financial crisis did not coincide with demonstrations or riots on the streets of Bangkok, although there was political tension between the opponents and supporters of the new constitution when it was debated in September.[61] Although the military had established plans in case clashes occurred between the two sides, the likelihood of a military coup was marginal.[62]

That riots did not occur is indicative of the current regime's provisions that enable the new middle classes in Thai society to influence the state's decisionmaking and replace ineffective and corrupt governments. The damage done to the military's reputation by the violent unrest in May 1992, which brought the ruling military government to an end, has also dampened the military's enthusiasm for getting involved in domestic politics.[63] Indeed, since 1992 the ability of the military to rule Thailand again has been steadily reduced. Only an elected member of parliament can now become prime minister, thus preventing military leaders from assuming power, and the Internal Peace-Keeping Command Act, which gave excessive power to the military, has been repealed. Civilian control over the military was reinforced when Prime Minister Chuan assumed the defense portfolio (only the second civilian to hold the post) in 1998, and the army chief, Surayud Chulanont, resigned from the senate (the first general to do so) in support of the principle that the military should stay outside politics.[64]

The new constitution is designed to improve democratic governance and root out corruption by increasing openness, transparency, and accountability. It has met with some success with the National Counter Corruption Commission (NCCC) and the Constitutional Court—both creations of the 1997 constitution—forcing Deputy Prime Minister and Minister of the Interior Sanan Kachornprasat to resign both from the cabinet and as secretary-general of the Democrat Party when he was found guilty of misrepresenting assets as a loan. The elections to the new senate in 2000 also revealed the powers of the election commission. This body announced that improper proceedings had taken place and ordered the re-election of seventy-eight senators; in some provinces the elections were held four times before the commission was satisfied. While this made the elections messy, it nevertheless gave credibility to the political reform process. This is not to suggest that old-style Thai politics, based on patron-client relationships and money, has been removed, and indeed, with the election in 2001 of Thaksin Shinawatra as prime minister, it might return. The 1997 constitution does provide greater political accountability than in the past, however; Thaksin himself was investigated by the NCCC. While such independent bodies as the NCCC and Constitutional Court continue to operate, democratic governance will be strengthened, but whether such strengthening will continue under the Thaksin administration is questionable.[65]

What is evident in surveying the Thai political landscape since the financial crisis in 1997 is that, while there has been much activity, it has remained at the politicized end of the security spectrum. Thailand's democratic regime, which is evolving with the 1997 constitution, did not face a security threat. Its survival was not in question, because of the military's willingness to accept civilian political control and the electorate's acceptance of the political process of self-renewal, albeit one with a high incidence of vote buying and electoral fraud. While political participation remains, especially among the middle classes, the likelihood of domestic dissatisfaction rising high enough to become a security threat is remote.

Conclusion

When the regime's legitimacy is questioned, which tends to happen when the process of government self-renewal is either nonexistent or regarded as inadequate, then violent unrest may occur. This violence can take the form of guerrilla warfare, as was the case with the communist challenge, or street demonstrations and riots that lead to running battles with government forces. In either case, the regime faces a threat to its survival and will thus regard the challenge as a security issue. Although a democratic regime is not immune to such challenges, so long as it provides the population with an effective means of replacing an unpopular government (such as legitimate popular participation in politics), it will have in place the necessary procedures to enable heated debates to remain political issues and not deteriorate into security issues. This can be seen in Thailand, where, Duncan McCargo states: "No government can assert its legitimacy without reference to popular participation. Yet, without substantial decentralization of the bureaucratic order, and the creation of more effective local government structures, it seems unlikely that popular dissatisfaction with representative politics will decline."[66] In other words, while Thai citizens might be dissatisfied with elements of the regime, such disaffection can remain at the politicized end of the spectrum because the regime has effective self-renewal. Disaffection need not become securitized because replacing an unpopular government does not equate to replacing the regime.

The extent to which a democratic regime can prevent politicized issues from deteriorating into securitized issues is dependent upon the level of support for democratic governance among the population, and also the type of democracy practiced. Where the principles of democra-

cy are new, it is possible that open competition between opposing political factions will create endless crises that fail to provide the stability
necessary to improve living standards. In such circumstances, the stability provided by authoritarian regimes is likely to be welcomed, which
was the case in Southeast Asia during the early period of postcolonial
rule. The problem these regimes face is maintaining their legitimacy
when the population is incapable of replacing the elite because the
regime has no effective self-renewal procedures. The issue of regime
survival and thus an internal security problem re-emerges, as the population can only replace the incumbent government by overthrowing the
regime. In Southeast Asia this was the case in the Philippines when
Marcos was removed in 1986 and in Indonesia when Suharto resigned
in 1998.

Where democracy is practiced, the danger of political issues
becoming security issues is dependent on the effectiveness of self-
renewal procedures. In Singapore the PAP government is so closely
associated with the political institutions that any challenge to the government is seen as a challenge to the regime and even the state. In the
case of Singapore, therefore, because there is no effective self-renewal,
political issues can quickly become securitized. Indeed, the PAP elite is
not averse to using security language to curtail political debates on the
grounds of national security. Conversely, where the democratic process
enables the electorate to replace unpopular governments, the likelihood
of political issues degenerating into security issues is lessened. Hence
the lack of a security threat in Thailand and the Philippines in the aftermath of the 1997 financial crisis.

Notes

1. Not all institutions must be replaced for a regime change to occur; for
example, Indonesia retains the original constitution adopted in 1945. Yet while
this constitution has been in operation, Indonesia has undergone three regime
changes: Sukarno's Guided Democracy, Suharto's New Order, and the current
development of democracy under Megawati Sukarnoputri. The 1945 constitution was superseded by a federalist constitution drafted with the Dutch in
December 1949. On July 5, 1959, Sukarno restored the 1945 constitution by
presidential decree, and it has been in effect since.

2. The five values are: "nation before community and society above self;
the family as the basic unit of society; respect and community support for the
individual; consensus instead of conflict; and racial and religious harmony."
Shared Values continue to be used by the Singaporean government. In August
2002, Goh Chok Tong, Singapore's prime minister, referred to them when

addressing the importance of the people's attachment to the country. See "Singapore is the sum of our dreams, our fears, our sweat," *The Straits Times*, 19 August 2002. For more on Singapore's identity, see David Brown, *Contemporary Nationalism: Civic, Ethnocultural & Multicultural Politics* (London: Routledge, 2000), Ch. 5. The principles are quoted from N. Balakrishnan, "SINGAPORE 1: Values Offer Shares in Confucian Society: Esprit de Core," *Far Eastern Economic Review*, 7 February 1991, pp. 27–28; hereafter the *Far Eastern Economic Review* is referred to as *FEER*.

3. "Don't let actions of a few destroy the social fabric," *The Straits Times*, 22 September 2002.

4. Leonard C. Sebastian, "Values and Governance Issues in the Foreign Policy of Singapore," in Han Sung-Joo (ed.), *Changing Values in Asia: Their Impact on Governance and Development* (Tokyo: Japan Center for International Exchange, 1999), p. 226.

5. Cho-Oon Khong, "Singapore: Political Legitimacy Through Managing Conformity," in Muthiah Alagappa (ed.), *Political Legitimacy in Southeast Asia: The Quest for Moral Authority* (Stanford: Stanford University Press, 1995), p. 134.

6. The charges centered on but were not restricted to an accusation from Estrada's former political ally, Luis Singson, that the president had received around £7 million in kickbacks from a gambling syndicate. See John Gittings, "Foes say Manila leader got payoffs," *The Guardian*, 18 October 2000; and John Aglionby, "Philippines president tried for corruption," *The Guardian*, 8 December 2000.

7. For details see Deidre Sheehan, "More Power to the Powerful," *FEER*, 1 February 2001, pp. 16–20.

8. James Hookway, "I Only Said I Was Tired," *FEER*, 25 April 2002, pp. 44–46.

9. For details of an interview with Gen. Angelo Reyes, see Deidre Sheehan, "Duty-Bound," *FEER*, 15 February 2001, p. 23.

10. Former Philippine president Fidel Ramos, who led a protest from the airport to the city center, stated in an interview to the *Far Eastern Economic Review:* "Belabouring the issue of the coup is a secondary matter now. We have done two People Power turnovers in 15 years. I hope we will not have another one in the next 15 years. We have to strengthen our democratic institutions." This is a strong indication that regardless of earlier denials in the interview that it was an unconstitutional coup, it was exactly that. See Nayan Chanda, "Mr. Citizen Speaks," *FEER*, 22 February 2001, p. 24.

11. Muthiah Alagappa, "The Anatomy of Legitimacy," in Muthiah Alagappa (ed.), *Political Legitimacy in Southeast Asia: The Quest for Moral Authority* (Stanford: Stanford University Press, 1995), p. 21.

12. John Aglionby, "Wahid's whirlwind visit to Borneo fails to mollify his critics," *The Guardian*, 9 March 2001.

13. In 1990, although the Burmese opposition party, the National League for Democracy, won an overwhelming victory in the national election, it was not allowed to assume office, and thus the current military government does not have a popular mandate to legitimize its rule.

14. Amitav Acharya, "Southeast Asia's Democratic Moment," *Asian Survey* 39/3 (May/June 1999), p. 422.

15. Quoted from Danny Gittings, "Empty docks in China's graft trials," *The Guardian*, 14 September 2000.

16. Muthiah Alagappa, "Contestation and Crisis," in Muthiah Alagappa (ed.), *Political Legitimacy in Southeast Asia: The Quest for Moral Authority* (Stanford: Stanford University Press, 1995), p. 63.

17. "Singapore's Sheepdog Trials," *The Economist*, 14 September 1996, p. 71.

18. Quoted from Cho-Oon Khong, "Singapore: Political Legitimacy Through Managing Conformity," p. 118.

19. Ibid., p. 116.

20. Nick Cumming-Bruce, "Singapore to bankrupt dissident by legal action," *The Guardian*, 29 January 1997.

21. "Denial libels accusers," *The Guardian*, 30 May 1997.

22. This case caught international attention with Jeyaretnam's hiring of British QC, George Carmen, and although Jeyaretnam achieved a qualified success, an appeals court found in favor of the PAP and quintupled the damages Jeyaretnam would have to pay. Unable to pay these damages, Jeyaretnam would have to vacate his seat in parliament. This did not occur, however, as it was agreed that Jeyaretnam could pay in five installments and thus avoid bankruptcy proceedings and keep his seat in parliament. See Nick Cumming-Bruce, "British QCs in Singapore legal battle," *The Guardian*, 19 August 1997; John Gittings, "Singapore court bankrupts MP," *The Guardian*, 24 July 1998; and *FEER*, 15 October 1998, p. 16.

23. Tim Huxley, "Singapore in 2001: Political Continuity Despite Deepening Recession," *Asian Survey* 42/1 (January/February 2002), p. 160. Also see Diane K. Mauzy and R. S. Milne, *Singapore Politics Under the People's Action Party* (London: Routledge, 2002), pp. 134–136.

24. "SDP chief to appeal against court ruling," *The Straits Times*, 23 August 2002.

25. For a brief and current account of political debate in Singapore, see Zuraidah Ibrahim, "Is politics coming back to Singapore?" *The Straits Times*, 12 October 2002.

26. Huxley, "Singapore in 2001," p. 162. One idea for increasing the opportunity to express dissatisfaction outside parliament that has been unsuccessful is Speakers' Corner. In September 2000, Singapore established its own version of London's Hyde Park Speakers' Corner. Located in Hong Lim Park, it provides Singaporeans with a public platform to speak on issues of interest and concern. The speakers are not immune from the state's defamation laws, however; it has proven a flop because speakers must register with the police and the authorities were taping some of the speeches. See John Aglionby, "One small step for Singapore," *The Guardian*, 28 April 2001.

27. Bertha Henson, "PAP eases up to let MPs debate more freely," *The Straits Times*, 21 March 2002.

28. The scale of the victory (75.3 percent of the vote compared to 65 percent in 1997) was achieved partly because the three main opposition parties—the Singapore People's Party (SPP), the Workers' Party (WP), and the Singapore Democratic Party (SDP)—had weak platforms and the Malay voters supported the PAP.

29. Cho-Oon Khong, "Singapore: Political Legitimacy Through Managing Conformity," p. 135.

30. For details of Vietnam following China's economic path, see Margot Cohen, "Chinese School for Success," *FEER*, 18 January 2001, pp. 28–29. Introduced at the Sixth Party Congress in December 1986, *doi moi* was a policy designed to arrest the economy's decline by replacing the central planning apparatus with a market-oriented approach. It was essentially Vietnam's version of the USSR's perestroika policy.

31. Samuel P. Huntington, *The Third Wave: Democratization in the Late Twentieth Century* (Norman: University of Oklahoma Press, 1991), p. 41.

32. Saitip Sukatipan, "Thailand: The Evolution of Legitimacy," in Muthiah Alagappa (ed.), *Political Legitimacy in Southeast Asia: The Quest for Moral Authority* (Stanford: Stanford University Press, 1995), p. 212.

33. Richard Lloyd Parry, "A nation descends into anarchy," *The Independent*, 15 May 1998; Nick Cumming-Bruce, "Suharto returns to war zone," *The Guardian*, 14 May 1998.

34. Demonstrations over the slow pace of political reform returned to Indonesia in November 1998, leading to running battles between students and the military; the students feared the military would assume power. See John Aglionby, "Student protests come to violent head in Jakarta," *The Guardian*, 13 November 1998; John Aglionby, "Crackdown ordered as bloody riots drag Indonesia back to the brink," *The Observer*, 15 November 1998; and John Gittings and John Aglionby, "Jakarta awaits showdown," *The Guardian*, 16 November 1998.

35. Matt Frei, "Sinking tiger clings to the fattest cat of them all," *The Sunday Telegraph*, 1 March 1998.

36. For a quantitative account of Indonesia's poverty, see Shafiq Dhanani and Iyanatul Islam, "Poverty, Vulnerability and Social Protection in a Period of Crisis: The Case of Indonesia," *World Development* 30/7 (July 2002), pp. 1211–1231.

37. For a detailed account of the political maneuverings that took place, see Bilveer Singh, *Succession Politics in Indonesia: The 1998 Presidential Elections and the Fall of Suharto* (Basingstoke, UK: Macmillan, 2000), Ch. 5. Also see Olle Törnquist, "Dynamics of Indonesian Democratisation," *Third World Quarterly* 21/3 (2000), pp. 383–423.

38. Dewi Fortuna Anwar, "Indonesia: Domestic Priorities Define National Security," in Muthiah Alagappa (ed.), *Asian Security Practice: Material and Ideational Influences* (Stanford: Stanford University Press, 1998), p. 501.

39. Figures from Mochtar Pabottingi, "Indonesia: Historicizing the New Order's Legitimacy Dilemma," in Muthiah Alagappa (ed.), *Political Legitimacy in Southeast Asia: The Quest for Moral Authority* (Stanford: Stanford University Press, 1995), p. 251.

40. For details see Margot Cohen, "Days of Rage," *FEER*, 28 April 1994, pp. 14–15.

41. See John McBeth, "Social Dynamite," *FEER*, 15 February 1996, pp. 20–22.

42. For a detailed account of the political machinations that took place in 1998, see Singh, *Succession Politics in Indonesia;* Kevin O'Rourke,

Reformasi: The Struggle for Power in Post-Soeharto Indonesia (Crows Nest, Australia: Allen & Unwin, 2002), Ch. 8; and Stefan Eklöf, *Indonesian Politics in Crisis: The Long Fall of Suharto, 1996–98* (Copenhagen: Nordic Institute of Asian Studies, 1999), Chs. 8, 9.

43. For details of Indonesia's progress toward democratization before Megawati became president, see Abubakar E. Hara, "The Difficult Journey of Democratization in Indonesia," *Contemporary Southeast Asia* 23/2 (August 2001), pp. 307–326.

44. John Aglionby, "Indonesia takes a giant step down the road to democracy," *The Observer*, 11 August 2002.

45. John McBeth and Michael Vatikiotis, "An About-Turn on the Military," *FEER*, 25 April 2002, pp. 12–15.

46. Sadanand Dhume, "Holding on to Megawati," *FEER*, 18 July 2002, p. 22.

47. Salim Osman, "Indonesia's moderate Muslims back terror crackdown," *The Straits Times*, 30 October 2002.

48. John Aglionby, "Barricades burn in Malaysia riot," *The Guardian*, 26 October 1998.

49. The "extremists" was a reference to an obscure Islamic sect, Al-Ma'unah, that had stolen a variety of weapons from two army depots. The leaders of the sect were found guilty of sedition in November 2001 and sentenced to death. See Frances Harrison, "Malaysian forces lay siege to jungle hideout," *The Guardian*, 6 July 2000; and Patricia Martinez, "Malaysia in 2001: An Interlude of Consolidation," *Asian Survey* 42/1 (January/February 2002), p. 135.

50. For more on the Memali incident, see Kamarulnizam Abdullah, "National Security and Malay Unity: The Issue of Radical Religious Elements in Malaysia," *Contemporary Southeast Asia* 21/2 (August 1999), pp. 271–272.

51. William Case, "Malaysia: Aspects and Audiences of Legitimacy," in Muthiah Alagappa (ed.), *Political Legitimacy in Southeast Asia: The Quest for Moral Authority* (Stanford: Stanford University Press, 1995), p. 76.

52. John Sweeney, "Battered Anwar in court," *The Guardian*, 30 September 1998; John Gittings, "Interrogators 'abused Anwar speechwriter,'" *The Observer*, 22 November 1998. A royal commission of inquiry concluded in March 1999 that Anwar had been beaten by police chief Rahim Noor and that his detention under the ISA was to conceal his injuries.

53. John Gittings, "Mattress aired in Anwar trial—but alleged 'DNA evidence' still in lab," *The Guardian*, 16 December 1998.

54. John Gittings, "Anwar lawyer faces jail," *The Guardian*, 1 December 1998; Zakaria was later freed from the contempt of court conviction in June 2001.

55. John Gittings, "Anwar victim of smear campaign, says police report," *The Guardian*, 7 November 1998.

56. Russell Barling, "Anwar trial restarts as Mahathir's critics pay price," *The Guardian*, 25 January 2000.

57. Nick Hopkins, "Mahathir cracks down on protests," *The Guardian*, 22 September 1998.

58. For a detailed coverage of the events leading up to the 1999 election

and the election itself, see John Funston, "Malaysia's Tenth Elections: Status Quo, *Reformasi* or Islamization?" *Contemporary Southeast Asia* 22/1 (April 2000), pp. 23–59. Also see Meredith L. Weiss, "The 1999 Malaysian General Election: Issues, Insults, and Irregularities," *Asian Survey* 40/3 (May/June 2000), pp. 413–435.

59. S. Jayasankaran and Michael Vatikiotis, "Mahathir's Long Goodbye," *FEER*, 4 July 2002, pp. 12–15.

60. For details of Thailand's financial crisis, see William H. Overholt, "Thailand's Financial and Political Systems: Crisis and Rejuvenation," *Asian Survey* 39/6 (November/December 1999), pp. 1009–1035.

61. Michael Vatikiotis, "People's Putsch," *FEER*, 18 September 1997, pp. 14–16.

62. Michael Vatikiotis and Rodney Tasker, "Holding On," *FEER*, 28 August 1997, pp. 14–16.

63. When it became clear that the military junta, which had removed Chatichai's government to much popular acclaim, were intending to hold on to power, the people turned against them. Demonstrations took place in many urban areas and led to violent clashes with the army. When the confrontation ended, 52 protestors had been killed, 697 protestors and 284 police and military officers were injured, and the repair bill for damages was estimated at 31.1 billion baht. Figures quoted from Panitan Wattanayagorn, "Thailand: The Elite's Shifting Conceptions of Security," in Muthiah Alagappa (ed.), *Asian Security Practice: Material and Ideational Influences* (Stanford: Stanford University Press, 1998), p. 427.

64. Edward Tang, "Politicians now call the shots in Thailand," *The Straits Times*, 5 October 2002.

65. For indications that Thaksin's administration is weakening democratic governance, see Shawn W. Crispin, "Thaksin at a Crossroads," *FEER*, 7 February 2002, pp. 18–22; Michael Vatikiotis and Rodney Tasker, "Prickly Premier," *FEER*, 11 April 2002, pp. 14–18; Rodney Tasker, "Fighting Back," *FEER*, 30 May 2002, p. 21; Shawn W. Crispin, "Thaksin's New Deal," *FEER*, 1 August 2002, pp. 36–38; and "Thaksin rapped for Cabinet reshuffle," *The Straits Times*, 5 October 2002.

66. Duncan McCargo, "Security, Development and Political Participation in Thailand: Alternative Currencies of Legitimacy," *Contemporary Southeast Asia* 24/1 (April 2002), p. 64.

4

Traditional and
Nontraditional Security

While Chapters 2 and 3 were concerned with security problems within individual states, the remaining chapters analyze security issues within the Southeast Asian region. Internal problems will remain prevalent though, for they are an important element in understanding the international security relations of Southeast Asia. This chapter concerns the broadening of the concept of security to capture the multifaceted security issues facing the states and peoples of the region.

In this chapter the traditional military concept of security is complemented by environmental and economic security. While this division is useful to highlight the region's different types of security issues, they do overlap, and it is erroneous to assume they are separate. Broadening security ensures that nonmilitary security matters are analyzed, thus providing a comprehensive or holistic account of the security problems facing Southeast Asian states.

The broadening of the concept of security has enabled analysts to look beyond the state as the referent object of security (that is, the unit to be secured). For environmental security, the referents range from the local to the planetary biosphere, while economic security concerns include, among others, maintenance of the liberal international economic order. Here however, because interstate relations are being analyzed, the state will be the primary though not the only referent object. The chapter considers three aspects of security: military security, which examines the interplay between arms procurement and a state's perceptions of its neighbors' intentions; environmental security, which is concerned with a causal link between environmental degradation, resource scarcity, and conflict; and economic security, which examines access to resources, finance, and markets, seeking to maintain and increase levels of welfare and prosperity.

Military Security

The use of and threat of using military force to secure the state are the traditional concern of national security. In developed states, the threat is external, and military force is distributed among the three branches of the armed forces (army, navy, air force) to achieve security. The primary concern within this sector is therefore the military's capability to fulfil this goal. Credibility of the state's forces depends upon the capabilities of other powers; thus keeping a careful watch on those capabilities becomes an important nexus in the state's security calculations. It is self-evident why military security includes such concepts as deterrence, defense, arms races, arms control, and the security dilemma.

In developing states, however, the threat to state security emanates more often than not from within. In Southeast Asia, this led to the state elite concentrating their resources in the army and using it to crush internal rebellion, whether from ethnic separatist groups or communist insurgency. This is not to suggest that external concerns did not exist or do not remain. Thailand's army engaged Vietnamese forces along the Cambodian border in 1987 and the Laotian army between November 1987 and February 1988; throughout the 1990s, border skirmishes arose with Burmese forces. The latter remains a problem, and in February 2001, Thai and Burmese forces engaged in heavy fighting after Burmese troops took over a Thai border outpost. This particular external threat to Thailand is tied to a variety of security issues, including border demarcation, ethnic minority guerrilla forces, and drug trafficking, which are examined below. The key point, however, is that most resources devoted to the army were largely to suppress internal security threats.

Prior to the 1997 economic crisis, the states of Southeast Asia began to increase their defense budgets in line with the economic growth they were enjoying. There was a real increase in expenditure between 1985 and 1996, as follows: by Indonesia of U.S.$1,402 million; by Malaysia, $1,133 million; by the Philippines, $810 million; by Singapore, $2,337 million; and by Thailand, $1,653 million. From 1989 to 1996, delivery of arms to East Asia rose from 11.9 percent to 23 percent of all weapon transfers in the world. In 1996, only the Middle East received more weapons.[1] The difference in defense expenditure was not purely in terms of quantity; more significantly, these states spent their resources on new types of equipment, especially those that enhanced air and naval power. Fighter aircraft from the United States (F-16s/F-18s), Great Britain (Hawks), France (Mirages), and Russia (MiG-29s/SU-30Ks), as well as frigates and submarines, were added to the arsenals of Southeast Asian states.[2] Even the Philippines, where internal security problems remained the primary concern, showed interest in air and naval forces.[3]

By acquiring such power-projection weapons, the states of Southeast Asia were equipping their armed forces with weaponry capable of attacking their neighbors' territory. This gave rise to security concerns usually more prevalent in developed states. The early 1990s thus witnessed concerns about an East Asian arms race,[4] and although by the middle of the decade these had waned,[5] analysts warned that arms buildups could still worsen state relations, as the potential exists to do harm.[6] David Denoon noted that when defense forces are increased with contingency planning in mind, "there is no obvious boundary between taking prudent steps to prepare for future challenges and taking actions that could be perceived as threatening others and thus stimulate hostile responses."[7] Malcolm Chalmers likewise cautioned that even "where, as is the case at present, ASEAN political leaders have no reason to fear their existing counterparts, they still harbour concerns about future political trends. Signs of arms builds in neighbouring states will, therefore, tend to encourage precautionary build-ups in response."[8]

The economic crash in the summer of 1997 stopped the arms spending in its tracks.[9] Indonesia and Thailand were hit particularly hard, and this severely curtailed their procurement programs. Indonesia postponed indefinitely its procurement plans, while the Thai government cancelled its order of the F/A-18 Hornet jet fighters from the United States and deferred plans for other military equipment.[10] Thailand's 1999 defense budget cut spending by 4.4 percent in local currency, and the armed forces commander in chief, General Surayud Chulanont, stated that Thailand would make no major military purchases "for the next five years."[11] Malaysia suspended several procurement plans including submarines, AEW (airborne early warning) aircraft, and attack helicopters, although it did proceed with its order of twenty-seven patrol vessels and purchased two frigates.[12] The economic slowdown in the Philippines raised doubts over the long-term viability of its fifteen-year, U.S.$13 billion modernization program. Indeed, the only country to emerge with its plans still in place was Singapore, which has taken delivery of advanced F-16 fighters from the United States as part of its order of thirty planes, and its defense budget in February 1998 raised spending from 4.4 percent of GDP to 4.6 percent.[13]

As the region recovers from its bout of "Asian flu," there are signs that weapon procurement is rising again. Projects mothballed because of the crisis have been reinstated. Thailand purchased eighteen F-16 fighter planes from the United States in September 2000, while Indonesia announced plans to buy Russian aircraft and antisubmarine capabilities.[14] Malaysia has also announced its intention to revive orders for fighter planes (F/A-18s from the United States; SU-30s from Russia); helicopters (Lynx from Britain); tanks (Poland); patrol vessels from Germany; and submarines from France.[15] One key concern in the military sector is why have the states of Southeast Asia embarked upon a buildup of naval and air power-projection capabilities in the post–Cold War world?

Writing in 1993, Desmond Ball noted thirteen factors behind the arms buildup in East Asia: economic growth and increasing resources for defense spending; the requirements of enhanced self-reliance; the drawdown of the U.S. presence and capabilities; fears about Japan and China; regional conflict among Southeast Asian states; requirements for protecting exclusive economic zones (EEZs); broadening regional security concerns; prestige; technology acquisition; corruption; supply-side pressures; pre-emption of international restraints on arms transfers; and arms race dynamics.[16] It is possible to group these factors into four causes. The first is a permissive cause because it enabled the arms buildup to occur. The factors here include the economic growth that increased resources for defense spending and arms manufacturers seeking new markets after the end of the Cold War (supply-side pressures). Hence, when the "tiger economies" were humbled by the economic crisis, the states' procurement programs were postponed, deferred, or cancelled.

The second cause concerns the changing global circumstances that arose from the end of the Cold War. This cause groups together the requirements of enhanced self-reliance; the drawdown of the U.S. presence and capabilities; fears about Japan and China; and regional conflict among Southeast Asian states. Here the argument is that with Cold War concerns waning, the U.S. presence would decline, leaving a power vacuum to be filled by either China or Japan, and with the Cold War overlay removed, intraregional disputes frozen during the Cold War would thaw and resurface. In either case, so the argument goes, it would be in their best interest for Southeast Asian states to acquire power-projection weaponry.

The third cause relates to new security problems and includes requirements for protecting EEZs, broadening regional security concerns; and arms race dynamics. The buildup of arms, according to this cause, arose when the 1982 International Law of the Sea came into force after the required number of states ratified it on November 16, 1994. This law brought into effect two hundred nautical-mile EEZs for coastal states, thereby providing them with considerable natural resources for exploitation. It also created overlapping sea claims, especially in the South China Sea, hence the need for power-projection capabilities to provide surveillance over this new territory. These overlapping sea claims have proven troublesome in the South China Sea, especially with regard to gas/oil concessions. The need to protect resources from other states exploiting them has also been evident with regard to fishing; this is examined below under environmental security. Although not particularly evident, there was a concern that the procurement of weapons for resource protection would generate a security dilemma and a regional arms race.[17] With the return of arms expenditure after the financial crash, concerns about a regional arms race have resurfaced. Sheldon Simon has argued that the impetus behind Thailand's and Indonesia's fighter plane procurements was Singapore's commitment to continue with its military expenditure program during the financial crisis, while Carlyle Thayer notes that the arms race in Northeast Asia has spilled over to Southeast Asia and the South China Sea.[18] Analysts also note that Malaysia's arms procurements can be partly explained by the need to "catch up" with Singapore.[19]

The final cause has a myriad of domestic sources, which range from prestige to the acquisition of technology to corruption. This final cause can help explain not only why the region's states increased spending on the navy and air force at the expense of the army but also the reasoning behind specific procurements, such as Thailand's aircraft carrier, the *Chakri Naruebet*. Acquiring it gives the Thai navy the prestige of being the only Southeast Asian navy to have a carrier, albeit a small one. In Thailand, corruption is also evident in that the opportunity for personal enrichment is estimated to have added commissions as high as 15 percent to the price of military equipment. The result has been an inventory largely built up haphazardly, causing logistical problems for defense planning.[20]

A more general domestic cause of enhancing the navy and air force relates to the increasing level of democracy and accountability in some Southeast Asian states, in particular Thailand and to a lesser extent, Indonesia.[21] The argument here is that because of the internal nature of the security threats, the armed forces of these particular countries became politicized; indeed, Thailand has a history of military rule and the Indonesian armed forces (TNI) performed a dual role (political and military) known as *dwi fungsi*. In the 1990s, both countries witnessed increased democracy, which at least initially brought a determination to improve the army's professionalism by redirecting its focus to external threats and improving police and other law enforcement bodies to resolve internal problems. This has led to a decline in the role of the army vis-à-vis the other branches of the armed forces. For example, the return of civilian government in Thailand in 1992 led to increased accountability, although corruption remained prevalent. The appointment of General Surayud to army commander in chief in September 1998 coincided with restructuring the army so that it is better suited for conventional warfare and international peacekeeping duties. Hence Huxley writes that this restructuring "is likely to reinforce the military's depoliticisation by enhancing the standing of the navy and airforce at the expense of the traditionally more politically minded army."[22]

In Indonesia, profound changes have not yet come from the democratic transformation since 1998; indeed, increased incidents of intercommunal violence and fighting in Aceh have kept the armed forces deeply entrenched in Indonesian society. Even some initially encouraging developments seem to have failed to have the hoped-for impact. For example, on March 14, 2002, an ad hoc committee began the first of a series of trials against eighteen military officers, civilian officials, and militiamen for "crimes against humanity" committed in the appalling acts of violence in East Timor in 1999. While this is an important step forward, those further up the chain of command seem unlikely to face trial.[23] There was an attempt during Abdurrahman Wahid's presidency to improve the military's professionalism by restructuring the TNI and giving it a more outward-looking orientation, although financial pressures are likely to prevent substantial change. Increased emphasis on the navy and air force, coupled to the fact that unlike the army these branches of the armed forces were not tainted with human rights abuses, was seen in the appointment in November 1999 of Admiral Widodo Adisutjipto as chief of the armed forces—the first time a navy man has held the top job.[24] However, when he was replaced in June 2002, President Megawati Sukarnoputri overlooked the air force commander next in line and installed General Endriartono Sutarto, who had commanded former dictator Suharto's bodyguards.[25] Finally, although the decision in April 1999 to separate the police (Polri) from the army—in July 2000, the Polri came under the direct control of the president rather than the defense minister—was a positive move in redirecting the military's attention to external concerns, this separation did not indicate that the TNI's internal role was diminishing. The former defense minister, Juwono Sudarsono, predicted that the Polri would not be strong enough to maintain law and order until 2010 or 2015. Indeed, the March 2001 defense bill referred to TNI as the body to safeguard Indonesia's sovereignty and territorial integrity from internal as well as external threats.[26]

The acquisition of power-projection weapons does not signify that Southeast Asia is an unstable region. Territorial disputes, while not inconsequential in number, are largely quiescent and unlikely to be resolved through the use of force. Indeed, in recent times some disputes have been submitted to the International Court of Justice (ICJ) at The Hague. Indonesia and Malaysia referred their overlapping claims to the islands of Ligitan and Sipadan off the Sabah/Kalimantan (on the island of Borneo) coast to the ICJ, as have Malaysia and Singapore with regard to the rocky outcrop off the Straits of Johor that houses the Horsburgh Lighthouse. The ICJ granted sovereignty of Ligitan and Sipadan to Malaysia on December 17, 2002.

Military actions are not inconceivable, as evidenced in early 2001, when Burmese and Thai troops clashed. Although this was the most serious of a number of border skirmishes between the two states in the last decade, it was not over territory but rather a conjunction of Burma's civil war and drug trafficking. In the tri-border region of Thailand, Burma, and Laos, trade in heroin and methamphetamines has increased rapidly in recent years. The most powerful growers and manufacturers of these narcotics are the Wa, an ethnic minority that lives in Burma's Shan state. The Wa have reached an agreement with the Burmese authorities that effectively gives them self-rule in return for ending their rebellion. The result has been the strengthening of the United Wa State Army (UWSA), which protects an increasingly sizable narcotics production. These narcotics are exported throughout Asia, but in neighboring Thailand they are having such a detrimental impact that since 1999, the Thai government has identified the narcotics trade as the number-one threat to national security. Thailand's Narcotics Control Board estimated that 100 million amphetamine tablets were smuggled into Thailand in 1997; by 2000 that had risen to 600 million and an estimated one million Thais had become regular abusers.

The Shan, another ethnic minority, continues to wage a rebellion against the military authorities in Rangoon. In recent years the Shan have sought international support for their cause by showing that not only are the Wa responsible for the drug trafficking but that the Burmese authorities are complicit in this trade. Such accusations confirmed the Thai perception that their neighbor was not seeking to curb the drug trade and indeed was profiting from it. In April 2000, the Thai deputy foreign minister, Sukhumbhand Paribatra, revealed that Thailand had been conducting regular clandestine operations across the border against Wa-controlled areas in Burma.[27] These operations reportedly include using Shan forces to target the UWSA's methamphetamine factories.[28] In May, Sukhumbhand declared that Thailand would do what it could to stem the flow of drugs, even if those efforts "affect our good relations with some of our neighbours."[29] Burmese authorities regard such operations as evidence of Thailand's support for the ethnic minorities that continue to resist Rangoon's rule.

In February 2001, Thai-Burmese relations reached their nadir when Burmese forces took over a Thai border post. This was part of an effort to clear a Shan-controlled area for the Wa, which according to Kusuma Snitwongse, "would create an unencumbered drug highway [for the UWSA] into Thailand."[30] The immediate effect was to create a refugee problem for Thailand, with more than three hundred thousand Shan crossing the border. Thai troops quickly repelled the Burmese forces after an extensive exchange of fire. The commander of the Thai Third Army, General Wattanachai Chaimuanwong, accused Burma of using the UWSA to wage a proxy war against Thailand and linked Burmese commanders to the drug trade. Thai-Burmese relations are problematic and will remain so while the UWSA continues to flood Thailand with narcotics, unencumbered by the Burmese authorities.

Thai-Burmese relations, therefore, reveal that the use of force by the states of Southeast Asia cannot be ruled out as a means of conducting policy. This is also true with regard to Malaysia and Singapore, as examined below. What becomes evident, though, is that the cause of conflicts in the region lies not in the machinations of revisionist elites but in the concurrence of other variables. In the Thai/Burmese case, the Burmese military regime's attempts to defeat the Shan rebels, coupled with the Wa's narcotics industry, have created *the* national security problem for Thailand. I now explore environmental and economic factors to highlight the concurrence of these variables with not only the military sector but others as well, and thus provide a holistic assessment of interstate security issues in Southeast Asia.

Environmental Security

Broadening security to encompass sectors additional to that of the military raises important conceptual questions: What is being secured?

From where does the threat emanate? What makes something a security issue? And in this particular sector, is environmental degradation a security issue? Is it states, people, or the globe itself that is being threatened? Are environmental problems security issues in Southeast Asia, and if they are, what are those problems? This section is concerned primarily with the last question, but in order to address it, we must examine the others as well.

Environmental problems range vastly in scope from the local (soil erosion) to the regional (acid rain) to the global (global warming) and include issues as diverse as resource scarcity and urbanization. Not all of these are likely to be security issues, though, which begs the question: what makes some of them matters of security? The first step in finding the answer is appreciating that the environment itself is not the referent object—the thing to be secured—but instead it is human civilization. The threat is from human activity, which it is feared will have such a detrimental impact on the environment that our ecosystems or biosphere will be incapable of sustaining civilization. Hence Barry Buzan's statement that environmental security "concerns the maintenance of the local and planetary biosphere as the essential support system on which all other human enterprises depend."[31] This also points to the next step in determining what makes an environment problem a security issue.

The second step is to appreciate it is not the *causes* of environmental degradation, but rather its impact or *effect* that makes it a security issue. This becomes easier by utilizing the Copenhagen School's politicization and securitization terminology explained in Chapter 1.[32] In short, a problem within the politicization category can be managed through public policy, but a problem that is securitized can be dealt with only by extraordinary means. Jon Barnett and Stephen Dovers add an interesting rider to this formulation, noting that a state's capacity to react to environmental problems also determines whether securitization occurs. With regard to developed states they write:

> In these places land degradation is not a security issue in that there is the wherewithal to prevent real risks to human well-being and economic systems, perhaps even ecosystems. However, in other parts of the world [developing states] . . . land degradation undermines those most basic biophysical resources which support marginal communities who have limited ability to address the problem. So, in these places land degradation qualifies as a national and sometimes regional security issue. Wealth is therefore a critical factor in the delineation of environmental security issues.[33]

In other words, the lack of state capacity within developing states ensures that their response to environmental problems will require extraordinary actions. Since Southeast Asia is dominated by developing states with limited capacity to respond to environmental degradation, securitization rather than politicization can be expected to occur. As shown below, the region has environmental security problems.

Returning to causes and effects, in responding to the causes of environmental problems a considerable range of policies have been pursued to change how we live so as to limit and then reverse the damage of human activity on the environment. Although environmentalists urge us to act before it is too late, the general view is that the danger will occur in some unspecified and relatively remote future and that the problem is not an urgent one requiring an immediate response and extraordinary measures, but rather one that can be resolved through legislation. For example, air quality, waste management, and water protection all are important issues, but they are regarded not as security matters but as issues to be dealt with through political means.

When analysis focuses on the effects of environmental degradation, however, security issues are raised, because such degradation could lead to interstate wars, ethnic conflict, and political disintegration. For example, soil infertility, which could be caused by desertification, deforestation, or overcultivation, can lead to such severe economic deprivation that existing state institutions would be unable to cope. As Barnett and Dovers note, this is more likely to occur in states with developing institutional capacities. Such economic deprivation might lead to health problems from malnutrition and disease, which in turn could generate social problems such as riots and possibly rebellion. Soil infertility could also increase societal tension if it caused people to migrate. Migrations to fertile soil areas could lead to resentment from indigenous people and possible incidences of violence. Although noting that links between environmental degradation and unregulated population movements (UPMs) are not well established, Alan Dupont argues, "[I]t is becoming more and more apparent that human-induced environmental degradation is stimulating UPMs by reducing incomes, especially in rural regions, or by rendering the environment so unhealthy and unpleasant that people feel compelled to move."[34] While not necessarily causing violence, environmental degradation and ongoing urbanization can explain the movement of millions of Chinese (estimated to be between 100 and 130 million) within present-day China.[35]

These problems may not simply be contained within a state. Since pollution does not recognize state borders, one state's economic activity can have a direct impact upon its neighbors' welfare. For example, China's coal-burning factories and power plants emit seven hundred thousand tons of sulphur dioxide a year, which has led to acid rain in neighboring North and South Korea and Japan.[36] There is also the prospect that competition over scarce resources such as fish stocks or water could lead to interstate conflict. However, what becomes immediately evident is that examining the impact of environmental degradation raises security issues that are not in themselves environmental. Although soil infertility can lead to security problems, they are societal or health security problems. Likewise, where conflict over resources occurs, it manifests in the exchange of weapon fire (military) and/or heated diplomacy.

When thinking in terms of environmental security, therefore, it is best to think of environmental issues as secondary causes of insecurity. Environmental problems can give rise to security issues when other factors are also present, such as societal tension or military capability. Hence Richard Matthew's claim that there "is little doubt that [environmental factors] are a part of the network of variables that generate insecurity within and between states. The conditions under which they play a key or decisive role is far less clear."[37] Nevertheless, Matthew concludes that to "ignore the role of environmental change in fostering conflict and regional instability would be foolish, even if it is rarely the primary cause of such problems."[38]

The broadening of security to encompass environmental concerns, however, has not been without its critics, foolish or otherwise. In general, three criticisms are leveled, all of which can be countered by thinking of the environment as a secondary cause of insecurity. The first criticism is that security is concerned with organized violence, which has little to do with environmental degradation. If environmental issues should be regarded as security issues because people die, then the critics state, what of disease, crime, and natural disasters that routinely destroy life? If security relates to everything, then it loses its clarity and means nothing. The term *security* is sufficiently contested itself without the "environment" muddying the waters even more.[39] This, though, is not the argument; while environmental degradation may itself not be responsible for organized violence, it can aggravate tensions by interacting with other causes that in turn lead to it.

The second criticism concerns resource scarcity. Here the criticism is that the availability of substitutes for raw materials, plus a world trading system that has lessened resource vulnerability, coupled to changing state norms that make acquiring resources through military conquest unattractive, have weakened the nexus between resource scarcity and conflict. The problem with this criticism is that the resources in question have changed; environmental security is less about nonrenewable resources like oil and gas[40] and more about the pressures on "renewable" resources such as food stocks and water resources. Hence Alan Dupont's claim that what "differentiates the resource scarcity of this era from the past . . . is the assault on the planet's primary renewable resources."[41] Although pressures on renewable resources might not lead directly to conflict, they are prompting governments to protect their resources from exploitation by others. Thereby increasing the likelihood of clashes.

The final criticism is that the evidence linking environmental degradation and conflict is anecdotal and at best inconclusive. It is certainly true that conflicts arising directly from environmental degradation are rare, but the issue here is determining whether environmental factors, as secondary causes, have led to conflict. To do this, we must examine the specifics of Southeast Asia, and the analysis now turns to this to determine the importance of environmental concerns to the region's security dynamics.

The key to many of Southeast Asia's environmental pressures is the increase of the region's population. With the exception of Singapore, the other states are all experiencing high demographic growth. The population for the whole of Southeast Asia rose from 457.6 million in 1992 to 520 million in 1999, a rise of 14 percent. It is estimated that by 2025, the population of the region will be 722 million, a rise of 39 percent from 1999.[42] This rising population will place increasing pressures on the region's energy, food, and water resources, which has the potential to generate domestic and international strife. Chapter 2 showed how some of the internal security problems of Indonesia—which has the region's largest population—arise from the migration of people from the overcrowded islands of Java, Bali, and Madura to the Outer Islands.

With increasing populations to feed, an issue that has brought ever-increasing incidents of conflict is fishing. Over half the world's fish catch is caught in Asian waters, and the Pacific Ocean has aptly been called the region's "rice bowl" for the twenty-first century.[43] Thailand has the largest fishing fleet in Southeast Asia, and after its traditional fishing grounds were exhausted in the 1970s, Thai trawlers encroached upon other states' exclusive economic zones (EEZs) during the 1980s and 1990s. In the 1990s, this became a source of friction, especially with the neighboring states of Burma, Malaysia, and Vietnam. In late 1998 and early 1999, two clashes occurred in the Andaman Sea when the Burmese sought to intercept Thai fishing vessels and engaged Thai naval vessels; several Thai and Burmese sailors died. In the 1999 incident, Thailand considered deploying a squadron of F-5 fighter aircraft to the area.[44]

Thailand has also clashed with Vietnam. On May 31, 1995, there was an exchange of fire when Thai naval vessels tried to protect Thai trawlers from being seized by the Vietnamese navy; two Vietnamese sailors were killed and five of the six fishing boats were impounded. In April and May 1999, six Thai trawlers were impounded and eighty fishermen were arrested for illegal fishing in Malaysia's territorial waters. Although Thailand is the worst offender, it is not the only culprit. Vietnamese vessels have fired on fishing boats from Malaysia and from countries farther afield, such as China and Taiwan. Indeed, the Philippines has not only seized Chinese fishing vessels, but in July 1999 a Philippine naval boat collided with a Chinese fishing boat off the island of Palawan, causing the latter to sink. Relations already were poor between Beijing and Manila following evidence of continued Chinese construction work at Mischief Reef in the Spratly Islands, and they dipped further with China accusing the Philippines of deliberately ramming the Chinese vessel.

States have enacted legislation to protect their marine resources from foreign poachers. The Philippine senate in August 1997 passed legislation imposing heavy fines for poaching, and in the same year Indonesia banned foreign fishing vessels from its 6.5 million square kilometers of territorial waters; the law came into force in 2000. In 1999, President Abdurrahman Wahid created a new ministry for marine exploration and fisheries and highlighted illegal fishing as a governmental priority.[45] Between 1996 and 2001, Indonesia and Palau, a South Pacific island nation, captured four hundred Philippine fishing boats.[46] As noted above, the need to protect marine resources is a significant factor in explaining the acquisition of naval vessels by Southeast Asian states.

Another environmental factor that aggravates state relations in the region is access to fresh water. In interstate relations there are two particular areas where water access can exacerbate tensions: Singapore/Malaysia and the Mekong River Basin. In addition to these two particular cases, there is also general concern over the availability of water for all the region's population. This might seem odd given that the region experiences frequent flooding during the wet season, as devastatingly shown in October 2000, when between 350 and 400 people died in Vietnam's worst floods in seventy years.[47] However, the combination of increasing population, degradation of existing reserves of fresh water, and destruction of water tables because of deforestation, urbanization, and agricultural policies has resulted in a decline in the availability of fresh water. The World Bank estimates that by 2025 most states in the region will face severe water shortages. This has already led to domestic problems in Malaysia; in March 1998, there were protests in the state of Selangor over water shortages, and in June the government imposed water rationing on two million people.

To what extent the unavailability of fresh water can cause conflict in East Asia is unknown.[48] In the Singapore-Malaysia case, the problem arises because Singapore is not self-sufficient in water and relies upon Malaysia for just under 50 percent of its needs. In 1961 and 1962, Singapore and Malaysia signed two water-sharing arrangements. The 1961 agreement allows Singapore's public utilities board (PUB) to draw unlimited amounts of water from the Tebrau and Scudai Rivers and also from the Pontian and Gunong Pulai catchment areas in Malaysia's Johor state. This agreement expires in 2011. The 1962 agreement, which expires in 2061, allows the PUB to draw some 1.12 billion liters from the Johor River. Under the terms of the Separation Act of August 9, 1965, when Singapore left the Malaysian Federation, neither agreement can be unilaterally abrogated.

Singapore has sought to reduce its reliance on Malaysia by signing an agreement with Indonesia in 1991 to develop the Riau province in Sumatra; the earliest that water is expected from this source is 2005. Singapore also plans to build three desalination plants, the first expected to be operational by 2005. Nevertheless, Singapore for the foreseeable future will remain dependent upon Malaysia for its fresh water supply.[49] The potential for conflict arises because Singapore-Malaysia relations are beset with difficulties arising from their merger between 1963 and 1965 and their political, religious, and ethnic differences, as well as economic competition. Since 1965, Singapore has thus lived with the threat that Malaysia, despite its legal obligations, might cut off its water supply.[50] These threats emerge when relations are at a low ebb. Hence in 1986, when President Chaim Herzog of Israel visited Singapore, there were calls from anti-Zionist Malaysian politicians to end the water ties because of Singapore's lack of sensitivity toward its Muslim neighbor. In 1998, when relations were also poor, Malaysian Prime Minister Mahathir Mohamad, at a rally in Johor Bahru, referred to water when he publicly commented on the dispute over the relocation of Malaysia's customs, immigration, and quarantine (CIQ) facilities. He said, "[O]ur officers are asked to leave Singapore even while we supply them with water," to which the crowd responded by yelling, "Cut! Cut! Cut!"[51]

Although Malaysia has never cut the supply of water, the threat felt by Singapore is reflected in its military posture. Indeed, according to both Andrew Tan and Tim Huxley, this defense posture has deterred Malaysia from taking such action.[52] Huxley notes that all "the evidence points to the main focus of Singapore's defence policy—and the *principal* role of the SAF [Singapore Armed Forces] and the extensive civil defence programme—being the deterrence of military aggression or pressure, or political interference, from Malaysia [emphasis in original]."[53] Given Singapore's small size—and hence, lack of strategic depth—its defense would entail an advance into Johor of some eighty kilometers. According to Huxley, there "would be a clear rationale for halting the SAF's advance at this line. Such an operation would secure Singapore's water supplies and provide substantial strategic depth . . . , while not encumbering the SAF with the occupation of an area heavily populated with Malays."[54]

This does not mean that war is likely, although Malaysian former Defense Minister Syed Hamid Albar's assertion that "Malaysia has never considered such a possibility," is disingenuous.[55] Indeed, talks on supplying Singapore with water resumed following a meeting between Mahathir and Lee in September 2001.[56] A number of issues still require careful negotiation before the agreement is finalized, however, and these are affected by the prevailing condition of the Singaporean-Malaysian relationship. For example, in 2002 disputes over Singapore land reclamation; the Malaysian perception that Singapore was undermining its attempt to develop Johor into an international transit-cargo hub; the design of new road and rail links across the Johor Strait; differences over the price of water Singapore pays Malaysia and whether an increase can be backdated; and indeed, whether the water supply question should be considered separately from other outstanding issues, had brought the talks to a standstill.[57]

The second area of potential conflict over water is the Mekong River Basin. Such a conflict is not, though, one of interstate war, although relations between the riparian states could become tense; rather, the conflict is between economic imperatives and their impact on people who rely upon the river and its tributaries for their livelihoods.

The Mekong River, the largest in Southeast Asia, flows through six states: China, Burma, Thailand, Laos, Cambodia, and finally Vietnam. The river basin provides a habitat and sustenance for sixty million people. In Cambodia, the river sustains the world's largest freshwater lake (the Tonle Sap), providing two hundred thousand tons of fish, which in 1998 was worth U.S.$70 million. The river basin is also home to nearly half the Cambodian population and is responsible for an annual rice production of 2.4 million tons. In Vietnam, the Mekong Delta provides more than half the country's rice and about 40 percent of its total agricultural output. Thailand uses the river to irrigate its arid northeastern provinces and built the Pak Mun Dam in 1994 to generate hydroelectric power. Hydroelectric power generation is also underway in Laos, where the plan is to construct twenty-three dams, then sell the energy to neighboring Thailand and Vietnam. Laos's first dam was completed in the 1970s, and the Theun Hinboun Dam was completed in 1998. The proposed Nam Theun 2 Dam is expected to generate 900 megawatts and increase Laos's GDP by 15 percent. China also is building hydroelectric dams on the Mekong and its tributaries, the first of which was completed in 1993 (the Manwan Dam). China is considering building some thirteen dams, and in total, fifty-four dams are either built, being constructed or planned along the Mekong and its tributaries.[58]

The dams established upstream will not only generate hydroelectric power, they will also alter the flow of the river. Only eight of the fifty-four dams have had environmental impact studies, and there has been no serious attempt to investigate the effect of so many dams on the Mekong's flow. Alan Dupont writes that the "construction and operation of the dams will exacerbate soil loss, deforestation and land degradation in the Mekong basin, upsetting the river's ecological balance."[59] By changing the flow of the river, it is feared that reduction in water volume will clog the river's mouth, increase salinity as tidal effects reach further up the delta, and cause the rich deposits of silt—necessary for maintaining the basin's agricultural productivity—to disappear. Since the Manwan Dam and the Pak Mun Dam have become operational, fishermen downstream, especially in Cambodia and Vietnam, have claimed that catches are declining.

The importance of the Mekong to the region's economic development was recognized as far back as 1957, when the Mekong Committee was established. A product of the Cold War, it was essentially designed to limit communist influence in the Mekong River Basin, and even though it continued to exist in skeletal form, successive wars in Indochina prevented significant progress. In April 1995, however, it was reconstituted with the establishment of the Mekong River Commission. All the riparian states are members with the exception of China and Burma, who have elected not to join. The commission is designed to promote and coordinate sustainable management and development of water and related resources for the members' mutual benefit. To accomplish this, the commission has initiated a series of programs known as core, support, and sector.[60] However, the commission suffers from significant shortfalls that hamper its ability to achieve sustainable development of the Mekong Basin.

First, states can divert water flow without seeking the approval of other members, and second, China, the state with the greatest capacity to affect water flow, is not a member. The first shortfall can be seen in the Kok-Ing-Nan water diversion project planned in Thailand. The aim is to draw some 2,200 million cubic meters of water from three rivers, which has aroused local opposition and caused concern in downstream Cambodia. This is not the first time Thailand has done this. The much larger Kong-Chi-Mun project will, when completed, draw some 6,500 million cubic meters of water from the Mekong.[61] It too has aroused local opposition and caused concern in neighboring states. The second problem (China) is currently insurmountable; its need for hydroelectric power makes it unlikely the dam projects will be cancelled. China questions whether their dams will have the impact critics claim, pointing out that only 20 percent of the Mekong's volume comes from China.[62] The Chinese also note that whatever action China takes, it is an internal matter.

While the likelihood of creating conflict between the downstream and upstream riparian states is slight, damming the Mekong is very likely to have a major environmental impact on human security for people who rely on the Mekong Basin for their livelihoods. The flooding in Vietnam in 2000 was largely due to man-made problems. Deforestation has reduced the land's capacity to retain water, while creating concrete river banks so that buildings can be erected near the Mekong has increased the volume of water arriving downstream. In addition, damming leads to a sudden release of water when reservoirs are emptied. This impact on the natural flow of the Mekong is likely to have a devastating affect on the freshwater fishing industries in Cambodia and Vietnam. Milton Osborne concludes that the major environmental problems likely to arise in the near future "will be impossible to reverse short of demolishing the dams that China has built."[63]

When examining environmental security, it becomes apparent that incidents of interstate conflict are low, although clashes over fishing are on the rise and, as Robert Karniol claims, with the new capabilities sought by the region's actors, "conflicts in the region will no longer be a couple of guys with machine guns on a fishing boat. We're now talking about surface-to-surface missiles on naval ships."[64] The current level of command and control capabilities, though, limits the likelihood of major naval clashes. Although the prospect of interstate conflict is low, the impact of environmental degradation is enormous for the peoples of Southeast Asia. Some fifteen million Vietnamese rely on the Mekong for fish. Deforestation of the region's rainforests by illegal and legal logging operations has had a huge impact on indigenous populations, as has copper mining in Irian Jaya/West Papua.[65]

An environmental problem widely covered because of its international impact was the smog that enveloped Southeast Asia in late 1997 and early 1998, euphemistically referred to as "haze."[66] It was caused by forest fires in Indonesia that resulted in health problems and economic losses not just for that country but also neighboring Singapore and Malaysia. The fires occurred because since 1985 Indonesia has increased its palm-oil production; land given to palm plantations has increased from six hundred thousand hectares to five million hectares, and the cheapest and quickest way to clear land is by burning the forests. Fires lit by plantation owners in Kalimantan in 1994 caused smog, which forced airports on Kalimantan and Sulawesi to close for several weeks, and high levels of pollution in Singapore and Malaysia.

The 1997 forest fires were caused by large landholders controlled by business conglomerates with close ties to the Suharto family,[67] which coupled to the El Niño weather phenomenon, resulted in the worst smog in Southeast Asia to date. The economic damage in log and timber destruction was estimated at U.S.$912 million. It affected the health of twenty million Indonesians, impeded navigation through sea-lanes, and resulted in intramural tension in the Association of Southeast Asian Nations (ASEAN). The fires burned out of control and prevailing winds spread the smog as far as Thailand and the Philippines, while neighboring Singapore and Malaysia recorded their highest-ever levels of atmospheric pollution. The Wildlife Fund for Nature estimated that the health costs to Singapore were $8.8 million, while the impact on Singapore's tourist trade was some $8.4 million.[68] In Kalimantan and Sumatra, factories, schools, air and seaports, and government officer were closed, and on September 19, Sarawak declared a state of emergency. The cost of increased health-care provision and loss of tourism for Indonesia, Malaysia, and Singapore was initially estimated at $1.4 billion, but later assessments have calculated total losses at $4.4 billion.[69]

The reaction from Indonesia's ASEAN colleagues was sufficiently abrasive to require Suharto to make two unprecedented apologies for the smog; this reaction is examined in Chapter 5. Although the "haze" did not initiate a conflict, it was a source of health insecurity for the people and economic insecurity for the states of Southeast Asia. Thus while environmental factors may be secondary causes of insecurity, they clearly deserve to be part of the region's security calculus.

Economic Security

This sector differs from the others in that the general condition is one of insecurity, and the goal of achieving security does not include changing this. The reason for this paradox is the capitalist economic system, which is designed to create winners and losers; it is a Darwinian environment in which states compete to increase their material well-being. Security is not about making this environment less threatening—they are "*supposed* to feel insecure" (emphasis in original); instead, economic security seeks to ensure that the state can compete effectively.[70] Hence Barry Buzan's statement that one "particular characteristic of economic security under liberalism is that it is about the creation of stable conditions in which actors can compete mercilessly."[71]

In all other respects, economic security is similar to the military and environment sectors, and in particular, the evident overlap between them. As noted above, food scarcity has led to fishing disputes that have in turn produced an increasing number of clashes between naval vessels. The overlap between the environment and military can also be seen in the action-reaction dynamic of Singapore and Malaysia's arms procurement plans. This arms competition reflects their suspicion of one another; concern that Malaysia might interrupt the flow of water to Singapore has led to the procurement of SAF capabilities necessary to secure water resources held in Malaysian territory. This interaction of sectors also occurs with the economic sector.

A state rich in natural resources could become a target for a neighboring state, with Iraq's invasion and annexation of Kuwait a clear example of this; thus military threats can arise from the economic sector. A political security threat can also arise from the economic sector. Where an economy is failing, an international institution such as the International Monetary Fund (IMF) could impinge upon the state's sovereignty by demanding structural changes to the economy. This was graphically demonstrated when Michel Camdessus, IMF's managing director at the time, stood over President Suharto of Indonesia as he signed the IMF bailout agreement in January 1998.[72] A failing economy can also interact in the societal sector, leading to the emergence of disaffected segments of society. Such concerns lay behind the articulation of ASEAN's primary security concerns in the language of economic and social well-being.[73] This also explains why examining the security implications of the financial and economic crash of 1997–1998 tends to focus on the internal security problems faced by the region's regimes. This was certainly true in Indonesia and Malaysia where the cries of reformasi, calling for an end to corruption, collusion, and nepotism, were most vociferous. While the economic crises clearly did have such security implications—see Chapter 3, which examines the impact of cronyism on Southeast Asian security—these security issues are not economic but political.

Economic security is concerned with a state's ability to provide sufficient capacity to survive in what is a hostile, competitive, capitalist environment. Traditionally, survival has meant using economic capacity to maintain military capabilities in order to forestall potential aggressors, and this remains important. But economic capacity also includes, among other things, access to markets, finance, and supplies. The first aspect of economic security is thus concerned with protecting the state's current economic capacity. Survival in such an insecure environment, however, demands constant economic progression, in order to not only maintain a comparative advantage vis-à-vis the state's competitors but also to protect the state from shocks in the international economic system. Therefore economic security is concerned with maintaining a state's economic capacity, as well as its ability to increase economic growth and prosperity.[74] This is the second aspect of economic security—the ability to create propitious conditions for continued economic development. Such improvement is what Christopher Dent refers to as an "insurance policy" to protect the state from future challenges.[75] We can therefore use Robert Mandel's definition that "economic security is the extent to which a nation's goods and services *maintain* and *improve* a society's way of life through performance at home and in the international marketplace" (emphasis added).[76] I now analyze the threats to the economic well-being of Southeast Asian states and how they have sought to enhance their economic prosperity.

Creating propitious conditions for enhancing economic prosperity will be examined later, when I analyze free trade. First, we examine a factor that has raised concern, not only in Southeast Asia but also elsewhere in Asia—the rising incidence of piracy. The economic concern is that this criminal activity will disrupt states' supply routes. This issue also highlights the overlap between the sectors, in this instance where military resources are deployed to meet economic security concerns.

Although piracy has been endemic in Southeast Asia for hundreds of years, pirate attacks have increased markedly since the end of the Cold War. By the end of the 1990s, Asia saw an increase in piracy of more than 70 percent. The greatest numbers of attacks are reported in the waters of Southeast Asia, and Indonesia has become the most piracy-prone state in the world. In the first six months of 2002, of the 171 incidents reported worldwide, the highest number (44) came from Indonesia. The next, India, recorded only twelve, with nine incidents reported in the Malacca Straits.[77] The attacks vary from stealing valuables from the merchant vessels' crews to seizing a ship's entire cargo or even the ship itself. These attacks also show an increased willingness by pirates to use violence; the death toll rose from twenty-six crewmembers in 1996 to sixty-seven in 1998. In one particularly brutal incident, pirates killed twenty-three Chinese crewmen when they boarded their cargo vessel, the *MV Cheung Son,* on November 16, 1998.[78] In the wake of the Bali bombing on October 12, 2002, and the attack on the French oil tanker *Limburg* off Yemen earlier, on October 6, the International Maritime Bureau warned of the possibility of terrorist attacks on shipping in the Malacca Straits.[79]

The economic security threat raised by piracy and terrorism concerns their disruption to commercial transportation. The waters of Southeast Asia are home to some of the busiest shipping lanes in the world, and the free flow of commerce through these sea-lanes is vital to the economies of East Asia. For example, a substantial proportion of imported South Korean and Japanese oil is transported through these waters. In the wake of an attack on a Japan-bound freighter carrying U.S.$20 million worth of aluminum ingots in October 1999, Japan offered to join its Asian neighbors in joint antipiracy patrols.[80]

For Malaysia and Singapore, in particular, one of the greatest fears is the possibility of a massive oil spill in the vicinity of the Malacca Straits. A 1992 report from the International Maritime Bureau noted that an oil spill in the Phillip Channel (50–60 percent of the 150–200 ships that enter the Straits of Malacca and Singapore each day are oil tankers) could completely surround Singapore and many Indonesian islands. The report noted that "apart from the pollution consequences, there is every possibility that the seaway would have to be temporarily closed to shipping and the fishing in the area would be ruined for many years if not permanently."[81] In September 1992, a collision did occur between the supertanker *Nagasaki Spirit* and a container ship, *Ocean Blessing*; the

Ocean Blessing was apparently a "rogue ship," possibly under the control of pirates, that was zigzagging across the shipping lanes. The collision caused a fire that killed all aboard the *Ocean Blessing,* and although thirteen thousand tons of oil were spilled, favorable weather conditions allowed much of that to evaporate.

Pirate attacks on merchant vessels have noticeably shifted from one area of Southeast Asia to another. Between 1991 and 1992, half of all piracy attacks in Southeast Asia occurred in the vicinity of the Malacca and Singapore Straits. However, from 1993 to 1995, the attacks changed location and the hot spot became the Hong Kong–Luzon–Hainan triangle, known colloquially as the "terror triangle." Since 1997, the attacks have shifted again, and in 1998, there were no reported pirate attacks in the terror triangle. At that time the rising incidents of piracy were in the waters around Indonesia, where the number of reported attacks increased from 47 in 1997 to 113 by 1999.

The shift away from the Malacca and Singapore Straits to the "terror triangle" can be explained by four factors. First, Singapore, Malaysia, and Indonesia embarked upon unilateral means to control piracy, which included improved surveillance equipment and dedicated antipiracy commando units. Second, a number of bilateral initiatives have been undertaken, such as initiating joint antipiracy patrols between Malaysia and Singapore, Indonesia and Malaysia, and Singapore and Indonesia. Third, Peter Chalk and Jon Vagg note Indonesian complicity in the pirate attacks, highlighting the decline in piracy in the Malacca and Singapore Straits after Indonesian authorities ordered a crackdown.[82] Fourth, the increase in piracy in the terror triangle can also be explained by state complicity, in this case China. The circumstantial evidence supporting this comes from ships being stopped or seized by patrol craft manned by Chinese-speaking seamen, carrying Chinese weapons, and wearing Chinese military uniforms.[83] The increase in pirate attacks in Indonesian waters since 1997 is most likely a consequence of the economic crisis, weak law enforcement capabilities and the natural cover afforded by the country's many islands.

Combating piracy is a graphic manifestation, therefore, of the states' attempts to protect supply routes crucial to their economic growth. However, while combating piracy captures the overlap between the different sectors of security, ultimately the focus becomes concentrated on the states' military capabilities to combat pirates. Another factor that has a major impact on the states' economies, and remains in the economic sector, is the issue of free trade.

Not until January 1992 did ASEAN members accept the idea that free trade would benefit their economies by agreeing to form an ASEAN Free Trade Area (AFTA). Although originally scheduled to come into effect by 2008, this was subsequently brought forward to 2003. At the Hanoi Summit in 1998, it was agreed to bring forward the completion date, where possible, to 2002, but the formal deadline remained 2003.[84] By the end of the 1990s, ASEAN membership had expanded to include all ten states of Southeast Asia; implementation of AFTA has been extended for these members—for Vietnam it is 2006, for Laos and Burma, 2008, and for Cambodia, 2010. In September 1999, ASEAN economic ministers agreed that zero tariffs should be the ultimate AFTA goal—AFTA originally committed the members to reducing tariffs between 0 and 5 percent—to be accomplished by 2015 for the original ASEAN members plus Brunei, and by 2018 for the four members that joined in the 1990s.[85]

Before 1992, only Singapore favored free trade. This is primarily because, unlike its neighbors, Singapore has no natural resources but is an export-based entrepôt economy. It has always championed the idea of removing trade barriers, and thus, not surprisingly, Singapore has been the region's most vocal and ardent supporter of AFTA, the Asia-Pacific Economic Cooperation (APEC) forum, and the World Trade Organization (WTO). The other states of Southeast Asia, however, have sought to increase their economic capacity by protecting their infant industries from external competition and creating domestic monopolies. This policy also discouraged regional specialization according to each state's comparative advantage and minimized intraindustry trade. Consequently, pre-1992 ASEAN attempts to increase intra-ASEAN trade, such as the Preferential Trading Arrangement (PTA) in 1977, had only a marginal impact on liberalizing such trade.

By 1992, though, four factors changed this approach to maintaining economic growth. The first was political. With the end of the Cambodian conflict, ASEAN was seeking a new primary function, and the creation of AFTA demonstrated that it remained a relevant regional organization. The other factors were economic. Since the 1980s, the more protectionist ASEAN-4 states (Indonesia, Malaysia, the Philippines, and Thailand) had begun to adopt new outward-looking strategies and had therefore initiated unilateral reductions of tariffs. Thus a convergence began between ASEAN tariff levels and greater acceptance of regional market integration schemes.[86] In addition, the influx of investments by multinational companies was leading to an increase in intraindustry trade in the ASEAN region. Indeed, the importance of attracting foreign investment was a primary reason behind the creation of AFTA.[87] This raises the third reason why AFTA was adopted in 1992: the ASEAN membership was concerned that the creation of other trading blocs, such as the 1992 European Single Market and the North American Free Trade Agreement (NAFTA), would attract investment, and ASEAN members could compete with these only by establishing an equivalent free trade area. The final factor was fear that if the Uruguay negotiations on the General Agreement on Tariffs and Trade (GATT) failed, the world trading system could be replaced with competing trading blocs; thus AFTA represented a fallback position for such an eventuality.[88]

Despite the agreement in 1992 that free trade was the best means of maintaining and increasing the states' economic growth and thus prosperity, AFTA has run into problems. The underlying reason for this is that while AFTA seeks to attract foreign investment, for domestic political reasons some ASEAN elites have sought to protect their home industries. The AFTA project has been described by Helen Nesadurai as a developmental form of regionalism, as opposed to open regionalism, which is an attempt to embrace globalization, and resistance regionalism, which seeks to protect economies from globalization.[89] Developmental regionalism attempts to protect home industries and nurture them before they become internationally competitive. Once this has been achieved, these industries are then exposed to the global environment. Developmental regionalism thus lies halfway between open and resistance regionalism, although ultimately it is closer to open since it has a commitment to engage the global market. Development regionalism can be seen in Malaysia and Indonesia, which have political commitments to develop, respectively, an ethnic Malay and an indigenous Indonesian business class to offset the dominance of ethnic Chinese capital. In order to do this, they have resisted opening their markets to much foreign investment; indeed, both Malaysia and Indonesia objected to including investment on the inaugural World Trade Organization agenda in 1996. This reluctance can be best seen in the ASEAN Investment Area (AIA), which gave market access privileges to foreign (non-ASEAN) investors ten years later than to domestic or ASEAN national investors. Nesadurai writes that "[p]referential market access and national treatment privileges for ASEAN investors was aimed at providing domestic (ASEAN) firms space to grow and become internationally competitive before trans-national corporations were allowed full investment privileges in the regional market."[90]

In view of these domestic prerogatives, it is not surprising that as the timetable for implementing AFTA grew closer, so backsliding on agreements occurred. However, initial fears that the 1997–1998 economic crash would lead to a nationalist backlash and presage the end of regional interest in a liberal economic order have not been fulfilled.[91] What has emerged is that ASEAN members—although accepting the need to create a free trade area—are not prepared to put home industries with important economic or national status at risk. Thus a number of "highly sensitive" products "have some flexibility on the ending of tariff rates."[92] These include rice in Indonesia, Malaysia, and the Philippines and sugar in Indonesia and the Philippines. As Mohamed Ariff argues, because rice is the staple diet in these states, it is "an issue of economic and human security," and thus it is understandable why these ASEAN members are not prepared to bring tariff levels in line with other AFTA products.[93] In September 2002, for example, the Philippines and Indonesia were granted a deferral on tariff reductions for sugar imports until 2010.[94]

A particularly high-profile industry that could suffer without tariff protection is the automobile industry. Tariffs as high as 300 percent protected Malaysia's two car companies, Proton and Perodua, from foreign competitors. These tariffs were to be dropped in 2003 as part of Malaysia's AFTA commitments, but concerns that Proton, a symbol of national pride, would struggle to compete against such giants as Ford and Toyota built in Thailand, resulted in the tariffs being extended until 2005.[95] For AFTA to be effective, the countries of Southeast Asia will have to focus more acutely on their comparative advantages. Hence Nick Freeman's assertion that "the days of automobiles being assembled in each and every ASEAN-6 country are probably numbered, with perhaps just one or two countries performing this role in the future."[96] To what extent ASEAN members will fully embrace AFTA depends upon whether they perceive it will create greater prosperity and thus economic security. In Chapter 5 I analyze AFTA in the wake of the 1997–1998 economic crash to show that opt-out provisions in AFTA enable members to follow the Malaysian example.

Singapore has the most to lose from ASEAN's reticence to implement AFTA. With Southeast Asia accounting for 30 percent of its exports, Singapore's support for free trade is obvious. This is evident not only in AFTA but also in its backing of APEC, which is committed to creating a free trade and investment zone for all its twenty-one members by 2020, and at the global level, in its support for the World Trade Organization. Singapore's support of the WTO was acknowledged when it hosted the WTO's first inaugural ministerial meeting in December 1996; it was active in restarting the stalled negotiations after the Seattle meeting; and by 2001, it had concluded negotiations with forty other WTO members eliminating tariffs on information technology products.[97] In light of the stalled progress toward trade liberalization in APEC, the WTO (although talks were re-launched at the November 2001 ministerial meeting at Doha), and AFTA, Singapore has begun to establish bilateral free trade agreements. By March 2002, Singapore had signed free trade agreements with New Zealand and Japan, and by the end of the year they were finalizing agreements with the United States and Australia and also negotiating similar ones with Mexico, Canada, and the European Free Trade Area group.

For Singapore these agreements are designed first, to ensure protection for its own economy, but second, to prod or give momentum to regional attempts to create free trade. Although a perception exists that Singapore's bilateral agreements are undermining AFTA, most notably in Malaysia, given the importance of intraregional trade for Singapore, AFTA remains an important project for the Lion City.[98]

Another area where economic interests have a security role is in the creation of growth triangles, also known as natural economic territories or subregional economic zones. Four such growth triangles have emerged in the 1990s: the Singapore-Johor-Riau (SIJORI) triangle; the Indonesia-Malaysia-Thailand Growth Triangle (IMT-GT); the East ASEAN Growth Area (EAGA)—comprised of Sabah, Sarawak, and Labuan in Malaysia; North Sulawesi, and East and West Kalimantan in Indonesia; Mindanao in the Philippines; and Brunei—and the growth quadrangle of mainland Southeast Asia, consisting of Yunnan province in China, Laos, Thailand, and Burma. Designed to increase economic activity, these growth triangles play an additional security role in two mutually reinforcing ways. First, they link the participating states' economies so they develop a stake in one another's economic development and prosperity, and second, they lessen political tensions since they have an interest in maintaining stability within the triangles. Amitav Acharya refers to these security functions when he writes, regarding the stabilizing effect of the IMT-GT and EAGA, that "the states involved in the growth triangles had been bitter enemies in the not-too-distant past."[99] The former deputy prime minister for Malaysia, Anwar Ibrahim, also refers to their security function when he claimed, "Instead of talking about border disputes, we are now promoting economic cooperation through growth triangles and other cross-border linkages."[100] Acharya warns, however, that the growth triangles have "remained underdeveloped and their management was plagued by intramural differences."[101] This is true even for the most successful of the triangles, SIJORI. Singapore-based companies have been lured away to other low-cost locations, such as China, and the links between Johor and Riau have remained underdeveloped. The 1997–1998 economic crisis further constrained SIJORI's momentum.

In the economic sector, security issues relate to policies designed to maintain and enhance the state's economic prosperity. Therefore it is not just about protecting current economic activity, as illustrated by the actions to meet the piracy challenge, but also ensuring the state can continue to weather the storms of an insecure and hostile economic system. Since 1992, ASEAN members, with varying degrees of enthusiasm, have sought to accomplish this through free trade. The importance of the regional and global economic institutions that support free trade can be seen in Singapore's approach not only to AFTA, APEC, and the WTO, but also its support for the IMF during the 1997–1998 crisis. This support was manifest in its lukewarm reaction to the Japanese proposal to create an Asian monetary fund and also Singapore's support for conditions the IMF attached to loans provided to Indonesia and Thailand. In the wake of the economic crisis, some tariff reductions on "sensitive" products have been delayed, but overall the reaction has been to strengthen this momentum. In the following chapter I consider the impact of this on ASEAN, and in Chapter 6 I examine the involvement of extraregional powers (such as the ASEAN Plus Three talks). For now, though, economic security issues are those that impinge on a state's economic growth and thus can include policies designed to create propitious conditions for future prosperity.

Conclusion

This chapter has presented a holistic overview of security issues facing the states of Southeast Asia by looking at military, environmental, and economic issues. It complements the political and societal security sectors examined in Chapters 2 and 3. The broadening of security to encompass environmental and economic issues also entailed providing evidence that these factors can be regarded as security issues. The military issues are unambiguously security ones because they involve defense of the state's territory. It was noted that the states' arsenals in the post–Cold War era have increased in air and naval capability. While this would give states a capability to attack one another, this was an unlikely explanation for the increase. Instead, the reasons behind their acquisition lay more with the need to protect newly acquired marine resources and to safeguard passage through pirate-infested waters. It was also noted that a decreasing role for the army might assist the momentum toward democratization in the region, although this is still at an early stage and, in Indonesia, has been reversed.

Although the outbreak of interstate war is unlikely, the Thai-Burmese clash in 2001 provides evidence of other factors that can initiate conflict; in this instance a combination of Burma's civil war and the Wa's narcotics trade. An examination of environmental factors revealed that Southeast Asia is likely to suffer from resource scarcity because of a growing population. Where the resource is fresh water, this has the potential to cause conflict, especially between Singapore and Malaysia, whose relationship is beset with suspicion. Weapons fire has also been exchanged in fishing disputes, and with an increasing strain on water resources and improved weapon capabilities, such outbreaks of violence could get worse. However, while the level of command and control is rudimentary, a naval engagement as serious as the Thailand-Burma border clash is unlikely. Nevertheless, environmental concerns can be secondary causes of conflict, and in the Mekong River Basin, they can have a devastating impact on human security.

In the economic sector it was noted that while it is a competitive environment and Southeast Asian states are competitors, which explains the low level of intra-ASEAN trade, there is a complementary approach to creating propitious conditions for continued economic growth and prosperity—the establishment of a free trade area (AFTA). While there has been some reticence to do so, nevertheless the recognition that free trade creates economic security has been maintained. For example, at the East Asia economic summit in October 2002, Goh Chok Tong, the Singaporean prime minister, urged his ASEAN colleagues to deepen regional integration in order to to increase economic prosperity. He even suggested that a goal for the future should be to establish an "Asean Economic Community not unlike the European Economic Community of the 1950s."[102] In the following chapter I return to AFTA; for now, however, I contend that to understand the security dynamics at work in Southeast Asia requires a holistic overview.

Notes

1. The data are from *The Military Balance 1997/98* (London: International Institute for Strategic Studies, Oxford University Press), pp. 295, 267.

2. For details see Amitav Acharya, "An Arms Race in Post–Cold War Southeast Asia? Prospects for Control," Pacific Strategic Paper 8 (Singapore: ISEAS, 1994), Ch. 2.

3. In the Philippines, though, continuing problems with separatist forces in Mindanao, coupled to the economic crisis, have prevented Manila from implementing a modernization program first formulated in 1991.

4. See Gerald Segal, "Managing New Arms Races in the Asia/Pacific," *The Washington Quarterly* 15/3 (Summer 1992), pp. 83–101; Douglas M. Johnson, "Anticipating Instability in the Asia-Pacific Region," *The Washington Quarterly* 15/3 (Summer 1992), pp. 103–112; Michael T. Klare, "The Next Great Arms Race," *Foreign Affairs* 72/3 (Summer 1993), pp. 136–152; Susan Willet, "Dragon's Fire and Tiger's Claws: Arms Trade and Production in Far East Asia," *Contemporary Security Policy* 15/2 (August 1994), pp. 112–135.

5. See, for example, J. N. Mak and B. A. Hamzah, "The External Maritime Dimension of ASEAN Security," *Journal of Strategic Studies* 18/3 (September 1995), pp. 123–146; and Chien-pin Li, "Fear, Greed, or Garage Sale? The Analysis of Military Expenditure in East Asia," *Pacifica Review* 10/2 (1997), pp. 274–288.

6. See Julian Schofield, "War and Punishment: The Implication of Arms Purchases in Maritime Southeast Asia," *Journal of Strategic Studies* 21/2 (June 1998), pp. 75–106.

7. Mak and Hamzah, p. 134.

8. Malcolm Chalmers, *Confidence-Building in South-East Asia,* Bradford Arms Register Studies No. 6 (Boulder: Westview, 1996), p. 104.

9. For a concise account of the various defense programs halted because of the financial crisis, see Graeme Cheeseman, "Asian-Pacific Security Discourse in the Wake of the Asian Economic Crisis," *The Pacific Review* 12/3 (1999), pp. 339–342.

10. Thailand was relieved of the commitment to purchase the aircraft, and the United States waived the 7 billion baht fine. Indonesia postponed indefinitely its order of twelve SU-30s and eight Mi-17 helicopters from Russia in January 1998.

11. Tim Huxley and Susan Willett, "Arming East Asia," Adelphi Paper 329 (London: IISS, 1999), p. 17.

12. See "Defence purchases in the year 2000," *New Straits Times,* 22 April 1998; "Buying of attack copters being re-evaluated," *New Straits Times,* 23 April 1998; and "Navy will spend $600M on frigates," *The Straits Times,* 28 April 1998.

13. "RSAF receives advanced F-16 jet," *The Straits Times,* 10 April 1998; S. Jayasankaran, "Under the Gun," *Far Eastern Economic Review,* 3 September 1998, p. 20; Hereafter the *Far Eastern Economic Review* is referred to as *FEER*.

14. Shawn W. Crispin, "On Their Marks," *FEER,* 5 October 2000, pp. 29–30.

15. S. Jayasankaran, "Call for Arms," *FEER,* 16 May 2002, p. 20. Also see "Malaysia's new weapons 'not a threat,'" *The Nation* (Thailand newspaper), 8 April 2002; and "Work begins on Sabah submarine base," *The Straits Times,* 12 October 2002. For the region's interest in submarine procurement,

see David Lague, "We All Live for Another Submarine," *FEER*, 15 August 2002, pp. 12–14.

16. Desmond Ball, "Arms and Affluence: Military Acquisitions in the Asia-Pacific Region," *International Security* 18/3 (Winter 1993/94), pp. 78–112.

17. See Alan Collins, *The Security Dilemmas of Southeast Asia* (Basingstoke, UK: Macmillan, 2000), Ch. 4.

18. Crispin, "On Their Marks," pp. 29–30.

19. Jayasankaran, "Call for Arms," p. 30. Also see Lague, "We All Live for Another Submarine," p. 14.

20. Tim Huxley, "Reforming Southeast Asia's Security Sectors," *The Conflict, Security & Development Group Working Papers* (London: Centre for Defence Studies, King's College, 2001), p. 30.

21. For details of this, see ibid., Ch. 2.

22. Ibid., p. 33.

23. For details of radio interceptions providing evidence of a covert chain of command extending from then political coordinating minister, Feisal Tanjung, to officers on the ground in East Timor, see John McBeth and Murray Hiebert, "Calling the Shots," *FEER*, 11 April 2002, pp. 19–20. Also see John Aglionby, "East Timor trial farce lets real killers stay free," *The Guardian*, 15 March 2002.

24. See John McBeth, "Wiranto's Way," *FEER*, 25 November 1999, pp. 18-19.

25. Slobodan Lekic, "Suharto loyalist installed as Indonesia's new armed forces chief," *The Associated Press*, 18 June 2002.

26. Huxley, "Reforming Southeast Asia's Security Sectors," p. 47.

27. Alan Dupont, *East Asia Imperilled: Transnational Challenges to Security* (Cambridge, UK: Cambridge University Press, 2001), p. 207.

28. Bertil Lintner and Rodney Tasker, "Border Bravado," *FEER*, 8 March 2001, p. 19.

29. Kusuma Snitwongse, "Thai Foreign Policy in the Global Age: Principle or Profit?" *Contemporary Southeast Asia* 23/2 (August 2001), p. 200.

30. Ibid., p. 201.

31. Barry Buzan, *People, States and Fear: An Agenda for International Security Studies in the Post–Cold War Era,* 2nd ed. (Boulder: Lynne Rienner and London: Harvester Wheatsheaf, 1991), pp. 19–20.

32. For specifics on securitization and the environment, see Barry Buzan, Ole Wæver, and Jaap de Wilde, *Security: A New Framework for Analysis* (Boulder: Lynne Rienner, 1998), Ch. 4.

33. Jon Barnett and Stephen Dovers, "Environmental Security, Sustainability and Policy," *Pacifica Review* 13/2 (June 2001), p. 162.

34. Dupont, *East Asia Imperilled*, p. 165.

35. David Hsieh, "120 million and rising," *The Straits Times*, 8 October 2002.

36. M. Shamsul Haque, "Environmental Security in East Asia: A Critical View," *Journal of Strategic Studies* 24/4 (December 2001), pp. 214, 217.

37. Richard A. Matthew, "Integrating Environmental Factors into

Conventional Security," in Miriam R. Lowi and Brian R. Shaw (eds.) *Environment and Security: Discources and Practices* (Basingstoke, UK: Macmillan, 2000), pp. 40–41.

38. Ibid., p. 47. Karin Dokken makes the same point when writing that the "impact or weight of environmental issues on security will vary and, in some cases they may play no role at all. The *kind* of link is therefore uncertain. But that there *is a link* is quite obvious" (emphasis in original). K. Dokken, "Environment, Security and Regionalism in the Asia-Pacific: Is Environmental Security a Useful Concept?" *The Pacific Review* 14/4 (2001), p. 518.

39. The seminal piece on clarifying the meaning of security is Barry Buzan's *People, States and Fear.*

40. Although even with nonrenewable resources conflict is far from negligible, despite changing state norms. The potential oil and gas resources under the South China Sea have led to military clashes and caused deterioration in state relations among the claimant states. The potential for conflict in the South China Sea is examined in Chapter 7.

41. Dupont, *East Asia Imperilled*, p. 17

42. Figures from ibid., p. 40.

43. The phrase is from Rear Admiral R. M. Sunardi, senior adviser to Indonesia's minister of defense, quoted in Alan Dupont, "Indonesian Defence Strategy and Security: Time for a Rethink?" *Contemporary Southeast Asia* 18/3 (December 1996), p. 280.

44. Dupont, *East Asia Imperilled*, p. 105.

45. Ibid., p. 106.

46. Deidre Sheehan, "Losing It All in the Tuna Belt," *FEER*, 13 September 2001, pp. 24–25.

47. Owen Bennett-Jones, "Mekong takes its revenge for man's ravages along river," *The Guardian*, 18 October 2000. In 2002, the floods killed 200 Vietnamese. See "Death toll rises to 200 after two months of rain," *The Straits Times*, 27 September 2002.

48. Most works on "water wars" are concentrated in the arid Middle East. Even here, for all the dire warnings of conflict, Natasha Beschorner concludes there is little evidence of a Middle East conflict "directly and exclusively related to the control and exploitation of water resources." Natasha Beschorner, "Water and Instability in the Middle East," Adelphi Paper 273 (London: IISS, 1992), p. 6.

49. Not all commentators agree. Joey Long argues that the desalination plants plus the Riau water project will enable Singapore to be self-sufficient in water. He argues that Singapore "will thus be unaffected by any Malaysian threat to cut the water supply, and even a premature termination of the Malaysian water links then will not jeopardise the city-state's survivability, or be considered serious enough to trigger war between the two countries." Joey Long, "Desecuritizing the Water Issue in Singapore-Malaysia Relations," *Contemporary Southeast Asia* 23/3 (December 2001), p. 509.

50. On the day of separation (August 9, 1965) the Malaysian prime minister, Tunku Abdul Rahman, told the British high commissioner in Kuala Lumpur, Anthony Head, "that if Singapore's foreign policy was prejudicial to Malaysia's interests, we could always bring pressure to bear on them by threat-

ening to turn off the water in Johor." Lee Kuan Yew, *The Singapore Story: Memoirs of Lee Kuan Yew* (Singapore: Prentice Hall, 1998), p. 663.

51. Long, "Desecuritizing the Water Issue in Singapore-Malaysia Relations," p. 506–507.

52. Andrew Tan, *Intra-ASEAN Tensions*, Discussion Paper 84 (London: Royal Institute of International Affairs, 2000), Ch. 2; Tim Huxley, *Defending the Lion City: The Armed Forces of Singapore* (London: Allen & Unwin, 2000), pp. 58–63.

53. Tim Huxley, "Singapore and Malaysia: A Precarious Balance?" *The Pacific Review* 4/3 (1991), p. 208.

54. Ibid.

55. S. Jayasankaran, "Under the Gun," *FEER*, 3 September 1998, p. 20.

56. Details of these can be found in Long, "Desecuritizing the Water Issue in Singapore-Malaysia Relations," pp. 522–523.

57. Trish Saywell and S. Jayasankaran, "Dire Straits," *FEER*, 18 April 2002, pp. 22–23; "Singapore's concessions for a water deal are off," *The Straits Times*, 16 October 2002; Tan Tarn How and Reme Ahmad, "Singapore questions KL's sincerity over water talks," *The Straits Times*, 18 October 2002; Reme Ahmad, "Water: KL to take 'patient' approach in talks," *The Straits Times*, 19 October 2002.

58. Details of the Mekong River Basin can be found in Dupont, *East Asia Imperilled*, pp. 126–130; and Milton Osborne, "The Strategic Significance of the Mekong," *Contemporary Southeast Asia* 22/3 (December 2000), pp. 429–444.

59. Dupont, *East Asia Imperilled*, p. 129.

60. Details of these programs and the Mekong River Commission can be found at the Internet site http://www.mrcmekong.org.

61. For details see Evelyn Goh, "The Hydro-politics of the Mekong River Basin: Regional Cooperation and Environmental Security," in Andrew T. H. Tan and J. D. Kenneth Boutin (eds.), *Non-Traditional Security Issues in Southeast Asia* (Singapore: Institute of Defence and Strategic Studies, 2001), pp. 478–479.

62. Although it is true that 20 percent of the Mekong's total volume flows from China, at Vientiane, the capital of Laos, 60 percent of the water comes from China.

63. Osborne, "The Strategic Significance of the Mekong," p. 439. For a concise overview of the problem, see James Borton, "'Mother of Rivers'; China's dams pose threat to way of life for nations downstream," *The Washington Times*, 6 September 2002.

64. Quoted in Crispin, "On Their Marks," p. 30.

65. See John McBeth, "Bull's-Eye," *FEER*, 4 December 1997, pp. 22–23.

66. For a detailed account of the forest fires, see James Cotton, "The 'Haze' over Southeast Asia: Challenging the ASEAN Mode of Regional Engagement," *Pacific Affairs* 72/3 (Fall 1999), pp. 331–351.

67. Although small freeholders were initially blamed, satellite evidence did not support this accusation.

68. Figures from Robin Ramcharan, "ASEAN and Non-interference: A Principle Maintained," *Contemporary Southeast Asia* 22/1 (April 2000), p. 69.

69. Dupont, *East Asia Imperilled*, pp. 53–55.

70. Buzan et al., *Security: A New Framework for Analysis*, p. 95.

71. Ibid., p. 98.

72. For criticisms of and reaction toward the IMF, see Michael Vatikiotis and Salil Tripathi, "Fund Under Fire," *FEER*, 14 May 1998, pp. 60–65. For Camdessus's view, see his interview in *FEER*, 16 December 1999, pp. 50–51.

73. In the ASEAN declaration of August 8, 1967, the first aim of the association is "[t]o accelerate the economic growth, social progress and cultural development in the region . . . [and thereby] strengthen the foundation for a prosperous and peaceful community of South-East Asian Nations." The ASEAN Declaration, Bangkok, 8 August 1967.

74. Christopher Dent captures the "prosperity' aspect of security in the following definition of economic security: "Safeguarding the structural integrity and prosperity-generating capabilities and interests of a politico-economic entity in the context of various externalised risks and threats that confront it." The term *politico-economic entity* instead of state is designed to show that a state has extraterritorial economic interests and thus its concerns are not tied to its own territory. See Christopher M. Dent, "Singapore's Foreign Economic Policy: The Pursuit of Economic Security," *Contemporary Southeast Asia* 23/1 (April 2001), pp. 6–7.

75. Ibid., p. 7.

76. Robert Mandel, *The Changing Face of National Security: A Conceptual Analysis* (Westport, CT: Greenwood, 1994), p. 61.

77. "Indonesia remains pirates playground, Somali waters increasingly risky," *Agence France Presse*, 23 July 2002.

78. William M. Carpenter and David G. Wiencek, "Maritime Piracy in Asia," in William M. Carpenter and David G. Wiencek (eds.), *Asian Security Handbook 2000* (New York: M. E. Sharpe, 2000), p. 90.

79. Lawrence Bartlett, "Malacca Strait seen as prime terrorist target," *Agence France Presse*, 27 October 2002.

80. Nayan Chanda, "Foot in the Water," *FEER*, 9 March 2000, pp. 28–29.

81. Peter Chalk, "Contemporary Maritime Piracy in Southeast Asia," *Studies in Conflict & Terrorism* 21 (1998), p. 91.

82. Ibid., p. 95. For Indonesian complicity, also see Jon Vagg, "Rough Seas? Contemporary Piracy in South East Asia," *British Journal of Criminology* 35/1 (Winter 1995), pp. 63–80.

83. See Carpenter and Wiencek, "Maritime Piracy in Asia," pp. 93–94; also see Chalk, "Contemporary Maritime Piracy in Southeast Asia," pp. 92–95.

84. Helen E. S. Nesadurai, "Cooperation and Institutional Transformation in ASEAN: Insights from the AFTA Project," in Andrew T. H. Tan and J. D. Kenneth Boutin (eds.), *Non-Traditional Security Issues in Southeast Asia* (Singapore: Institute of Defence and Strategic Studies, 2001), p. 200.

85. Mohamed Ariff, "Trade, Investment, and Interdependence," in Simon S. C. Tay, Jesus P. Estanislao, and Hadi Soesastro (eds.), *Reinventing ASEAN* (Singapore: ISEAS, 2001), pp. 47–48.

86. For details of why the ASEAN-4 adopted outward-looking strategies, see Chia Siow Yue, "Trade, Foreign Direct Investment and Economic Development of Southeast Asia," *The Pacific Review* 12/2 (1999), pp. 252–258.

87. Shaun Narine, "ASEAN into the Twenty-first Century," *The Pacific Review* 12/3 (1999), p. 366.

88. Chia Siow Yue, "The ASEAN Free Trade Area," *The Pacific Review* 11/2 (1998), pp. 217–218.

89. Helen E. S. Nesadurai, "Attempting Developmental Regionalism Through AFTA: The Domestic Politics–Domestic Capital Nexus," IDSS Working Paper 31 (Singapore: Institute of Defence and Strategic Studies, August 2002).

90. Ibid., p. 14. In September 2001, this restriction was lifted and foreign investors were granted full market access by 2010 instead of 2020.

91. See Danny Unger, "A Regional Economic Order in East and Southeast Asia?" *Journal of Strategic Studies* 24/4 (December 2001), pp. 187–191.

92. Ibid., p. 221.

93. Ariff, "Trade, Investment, and Interdependence," p. 50.

94. Gil C. Cabacungan, Jr., "RP sugar sector gets reprieve," *Philippine Daily Inquirer*, 23 September 2001.

95. See Lorien Holland, "Moment of Truth," *FEER*, 23 November 2000, pp. 64–66.

96. Nick J. Freeman, "Regional Economic Trends," *Regional Outlook: Southeast Asia 2002-2003* (Singapore: ISEAS, 2002), p. 45. Add Singapore and Brunei to ASEAN-4 to get ASEAN-6. Also see Edward Tang, "Major carmakers rev up Thai operations," *The Straits Times*, 12 September 2002.

97. Christopher M. Dent, "Reconciling Multiple Economic Multilateralisms: The Case of Singapore," *Contemporary Southeast Asia* 24/1 (April 2002), pp. 153–154.

98. By the end of 2002, Malaysia's position had changed, and it began to see bilateral free trade agreements as a positive development. See Reme Ahmad, "Malaysia changes stance, now open to FTAs," *The Straits Times*, 26 October 2002.

99. Amitav Acharya, *The Quest for Identity: International Relations of Southeast Asia* (Singapore: Oxford University Press, 2000), p. 153.

100. Quoted from Amitav Acharya, *Constructing a Security Community in Southeast Asia: ASEAN and the Problem of Regional Order* (London: Routledge, 2001), p. 144.

101. Acharya, *The Quest for Identity*, p. 154.

102. "The road for ASEAN," *The Straits Times*, 12 October 2002.

5

Achieving Security
the "ASEAN Way"

This chapter focuses on the Association of Southeast Asian Nations (ASEAN), which was formed on August 8, 1967, in Bangkok. By the end of the twentieth century, this regional body had achieved the goal of an ASEAN-10, with ten of the eleven states of Southeast Asia as members.

The key features of ASEAN, including the "ASEAN Way," are discussed, as well as the challenges ASEAN faces at the beginning of the twenty-first century—challenges that have led some commentators to question its continuing validity. The chapter also examines a variety of security concepts, including security communities and regimes, and comprehensive, cooperative, and common security.

National Resilience, Regional Resilience, and the ASEAN Way

ASEAN originally consisted of five states (Indonesia, Malaysia, Thailand, Singapore, and the Philippines), and it represented the third attempt by the states of Southeast Asia to form a regional multilateral body. The previous two—the Association of South-East Asia (ASA) and MAPHILINDO, comprised of Malaysia, the Philippines, and Indonesia—foundered on territorial disputes. In 1984 Brunei became ASEAN's sixth member, and it plus the original five comprise the ASEAN-6; these members have the more developed economies within ASEAN. In 1995 Vietnam joined, while Burma and Laos were admitted in 1997. Cambodia's admission was postponed in 1997 because of internal unrest, but it was "welcomed" as a member during the Hanoi summit in December 1998 and officially joined in April 1999. The four new members that joined in the 1990s are collectively known as the CMLV and have less developed economies.

From its inception ASEAN has provided a security function, although it was implicit because the founders were aware that an explicit security function could lend credence to the charge that ASEAN was a replacement for the defunct Western-inspired military alliance, SEATO (South-East Asian Treaty Organization). It was feared that creating a military alliance would invite countermeasures from the communist states and thereby generate greater insecurity for the ASEAN ones. In addition, a military alliance among states with few capabilities to aid one another was unlikely to help solve the security threats the founders faced.

ASEAN was specifically created to stabilize the region after Konfrontasi and the Malaysian-Philippine dispute over Sabah. It is no coincidence that ASEAN's inaugural meeting was in Bangkok; Thailand had not become involved in Konfrontasi and had tried to mediate between Malaysia and Indonesia and also between Malaysia and the Philippines over Sabah. Konfrontasi, also referred to as Confrontation, was the coercive strategy adopted by the Sukarno regime in Indonesia toward the newly created Malaysian state between 1963 and 1966. It wrecked the prospects of MAPHILINDO and came to an end only when the new Suharto regime in Indonesia renounced the policy in favor of a regional order based on the non-use of force. The Sabah dispute between Malaysia and the Philippines arose when the former British colony of North Borneo (Sabah) opted to join the Malaysian federation in September 1963 instead of the Philippines. This caused the collapse of ASA and later in the decade Sabah also proved to be the first major test for ASEAN. The Sabah dispute is examined below, under the means by which ASEAN manages intramural tensions.

Beyond these immediate threats to the region's stability, ASEAN was designed to be first and foremost an association of states engaged in nation building. Since nation building is often a brutal business, the elite wanted to be able to implement their policies knowing that neighbors would not interfere in their domestic affairs. ASEAN was therefore established to ensure sovereignty remained firmly located at the national level. It was not intended to be a supranational institution that would provide a legal framework for enhancing cooperation among members, and it was never intended to be an Asian equivalent of the European Union. This desire not to pool sovereignty and make ASEAN more than just a sum of its parts lies behind much of the criticism directed at the organization after the financial/economic crisis of 1997–1998. This is not to suggest there was no interest in developing a strong region, but that regional strength would emanate from strong states, not from a strong regional institution. This can be seen in the language of national and regional resilience adopted by ASEAN members in the association's formative years.

With the exception of Thailand, the members of ASEAN had been colonies, and the security problems they faced were typical for newly decolonized states. With a diverse ethnic mix of peoples within territorial boundaries created by the colonizers, the security problems facing the elite were internal and were concerned with challenges to the state's territorial integrity from ethnic secessionist demands and to the regime from communist insurgency. The solution lay in economic development and prosperity. A state that enjoys economic growth, it was reasoned, will bring prosperity to its people, increasing their association with the country and also reducing the appeal of communism. Thus the primary functions of ASEAN are "to accelerate the economic growth, social progress and cultural development in the region."[1] It is immediately evident therefore that security issues in Southeast Asia are comprehensive in nature. That is, security is broadly conceived to encompass the multitude of threats that arise in the economic, cultural, social, and political fields, as well as military. This comprehensive approach to security problems was captured in their inward-looking conception of security and was called national resilience.

The term *national resilience* refers to the security of the nation emerging from the strength of national development. Thus national resilience covers all aspects of nation building—ideological, political, economic, social, cultural—and the security of the state is dependent upon the population's loyalty to that state. By focusing on internal issues and addressing the dangers of subversion, the state remains a viable entity and prevents the contagion of communist insurgency and ethnic separatism from infecting neighboring states. Consequently, if all states adopted national resilience, they would provide regional stability. Regional stability was called regional resilience; this has been likened to a chain that derives its strength from its constituent parts.[2] Regional resilience would likewise support national resilience by creating stable external relations that would enable the regimes to concentrate on national development. Michael Leifer expresses the logic of the process when he writes: "By cultivating intra-mural accord and so reducing threats among themselves, the ASEAN states would be able to devote themselves through the instrumentality of economic development to the common cause of political stability."[3] In practice this meant that state elites could engage in what were often brutal policies against their own people with the knowledge that their neighbors would not interfere. Political stability was thus achieved for the regime by removing alternative sources for the people's loyalty. ASEAN publicly endorsed regional resilience in the 1976 Treaty of Amity and Cooperation in Southeast Asia (TAC) and the 1971 Zone of Peace, Freedom and Neutrality (ZOP-FAN).[4]

Regional resilience is accomplished via the states' adherence to a set of agreed-on norms of behavior, noted below. Confidence that others will abide by such norms creates security because it makes state actions more predictable. ASEAN, however, does not bind its members to agreements that specify various punishments for transgressors. ASEAN persuasion comes not through the threat of sanctions against members if they refuse to abide, but rather, as Leifer notes, "peer-group pressure underpinned by an assumption of self-interest."[5] This is worth repeating. The agreement to abide by the norms of behavior does not come from fear of punishment, and neither does it mean that the states are being altruistic; instead, it signifies awareness that their own security is best achieved in concert with others. Leifer refers to this as cooperative security, an ambiguous term that encapsulates the achievement of security through dialogue, inclusivity of participants and subject matter, and a belief that security is gained in concert with others rather than through unilateral action.[6]

There are two security concepts that are frequently applied to ASEAN: comprehensive and cooperative security. The former arises because security is conceived in terms of nation building (national resilience) and thus relates to a wide range of issues. It therefore follows that achieving security must be conceived of as comprehensive in nature. Comprehensive security thus captures the ASEAN members' internal, holistic approach to achieving security. Security in the ASEAN context relates to much more than concern over military issues and external threat scenarios. In order to create regional stability (regional resilience) the members adopted the second security concept—cooperative security. Stability from this approach comes because member states agree to act within norms of behavior that make their actions more predictable. By acting in conjunction they are achieving security not unilaterally, but in concert. The importance of security with, as opposed to against, each other is seen when we examine common security below. First, we analyze the norms of behavior of ASEAN's cooperative security approach.

The behavioral norms for ASEAN members—whether they actually abide by them or not is contentious—are the principles and processes collectively known as the "ASEAN Way." Amitav Acharya has divided these into codes of conduct that govern their interaction and "the *process* through which such interactions are carried out" (emphasis in original).[7] The codes of conduct are the principles enshrined in the 1967 Bangkok Declaration: mutual respect for political independence, territorial integrity, and national identity; noninterference in the internal affairs of one another; peaceful settlement of disputes; renunciation of the threat or use of force; and effective cooperation. The processes are noted below, but in brief the ASEAN Way refers to the informal, consensus decisionmaking approach of ASEAN and the importance of public unity. Acharya has subsequently referred to the codes of conduct or principles as legal-rational norms and the process of decisionmaking as sociocultural norms.[8]

The existence of these norms raises the prospect that the Southeast Asian security complex exhibits the characteristics either of a security regime or possibly, a security community. The term *security complex* was coined by Barry Buzan to refer to a region where states' "primary security concerns link together sufficiently closely that their national securities cannot realistically be considered apart from one another."[9] Although N. Ganesan refers to two security complexes in Southeast Asia—in Indochina and in the Malay Archipelago—the interaction among the members of both complexes enables us to talk of a Southeast Asian security complex.[10] This is especially so since the end of the Cold War, when all Southeast Asian states (except East Timor) have become members of ASEAN, as well as in the economic field, where they are all members of the ASEAN Free Trade Area (AFTA). Within a security complex, relations between its members can be plotted along a spectrum depending upon the levels of amity and enmity exhibited. For Buzan, amity refers to the "expectation of protection or support," while enmity refers to relationships beset "by suspicion and fear."[11] Where the states' security interdependence is marked by enmity, Buzan refers to the security complex at this extreme end as Raimo Väyrynen's conflict formation. Toward amity lies a security regime, while at the extreme end of the spectrum toward amity is Karl Deutsch's security community.[12]

In a security regime the key element is that the norms and rules that constrain and guide state behavior entail more than following short-term interests. Statesmen are prepared to accept short-term losses with the understanding that in moments of relative weakness: they will not be taken advantage of (that is, other states will be restrained); other states will also endure moments of relative weakness (that is, the roles will be reversed and reciprocation will occur); and ultimately, their security will improve. A security regime can operate on specific subissues in the states' security relationship. For example, the relationship might be adversarial, such as that of the United States and the USSR during the Cold War, but the states have agreed to a series of norms and rules that constrain their actions over a particular issue, such as an arms control agreement. Alternatively, the regime might be all-encompassing, and the norms might operate and guide state practice over a range of different issues. An example of the latter would be the Concert of Europe and, as will be shown, ASEAN.

A security community arises when norms are established that abolish the use of force to settle disputes between members of the regime. In a security community there exists "a real assurance that the members of that community will not fight each other physically, but will settle their disputes in some other way."[13] In this respect, the members of the European Union form a security community since it is inconceivable that force would be used to settle disputes among its membership. In the case of ASEAN, the use of force to resolve member disputes is not inconceivable. In Chapter 4, for example, the conflicts that periodically flare between Burma and Thailand over drug trafficking and the activities of ethnic minorities fighting the Burmese army, plus Singapore's defense strategy being predicated on invading Malaysia, were noted. In this sense Ganesan is right to state that the presence of "bilateral tensions within . . . ASEAN disproves the hypothesis that ASEAN constitutes a security community."[14] Ganesan is in good company; both Tim Huxley and Amitav Achaya concur. Huxley asserts, "Such a degree of optimism is almost certainly misplaced, as at least one ASEAN member (Singapore) bases its defence strategy primarily on the deterrence of one or more ASEAN neighbours (Malaysia and Indonesia)."[15] While Acharya notes that although "ASEAN has come a long way to reducing tensions between its members, it has not yet reached the stage of a 'security community.'"[16]

If not a security community, is ASEAN a security regime? To address this question, it is necessary to determine what norms exist, if they are peculiar to ASEAN, and whether the members abide by them. The norms must be peculiar to ASEAN, otherwise members would have to apply them toward non-ASEAN members as well, thus undermining their usefulness in proving the existence of an ASEAN regime. In this respect the principles enshrined in the Bangkok Declaration are not ones to use to determine if ASEAN is a security regime, since they replicate those in the UN Charter. The noninterference norm, however, is an exception because it has a particular meaning in the ASEAN context. The norms to evaluate are instead those that form the process through which ASEAN manages intramural tensions.

There are at least three norms that in combination create an informal, discreet dialogue style that values consensus decisionmaking and avoidance of adversarial bargaining strategies. Often explained as distinct from the ASEAN practice of *musyawarah*, it is possible, nevertheless, to see these various principles emanating from it (Musyawarah, an Arabic word, means making decisions via discussion and consultation). The three norms are: first, decisionmaking is achieved through consensus; second, if a compromise cannot be found, then the issue is adjourned; and third, members are prepared to defer their own interests to the interests of the association.

The consensus norm, known as *mufakat*, is associated with village politics in Indonesia and to a lesser extent in Malaysia and the Philippines. Discussion begins at an informal level where differences can be aired and a compromise sought. Once a general consensus is reached on the issue, this acts as the starting point for discussions, with unanimous agreement the desired outcome. In ASEAN, the informal stage manifests in the close personal relationships that have developed among the statesmen. Hoang Anh Tuan quotes former foreign secretary of the Philippines, Carlos Romulo: "I can pick up the telephone now and talk directly to Adam Malik or Rajaratnam [former Indonesian and Singapore foreign ministers, respectively]. We often find that private talks over breakfast prove more important than formal meetings."[17] The informal stage is important because a member can raise objections knowing that should a decision be made despite its concerns—which could only occur because the member dropped its objection—it will not need to explain its policy reversal. The process of musyawarah thus allows ASEAN members to "save face" because none will be shamed by the decision reached. This informal bargaining occurs long before ASEAN convenes, with members contacting one another about proposals and ascertaining their likely degree of support. After some manipulation, if the proposal is acceptable to the other members, it is placed on the ASEAN agenda; if not, it is likely to be dropped. This does not mean that consensus equates to unanimity. If one member disagrees with a proposal but finds itself in a minority, and if the issue itself will not have negative repercussions when implemented, then even though the member does not support the issue, it will not prevent others from proceeding: a consensus is said to have been reached via the "Minus X" principle. Lee Kuan Yew says:

> So long as members who are not yet ready to participate are not dam-
> aged by nonparticipation, nor excluded from future participation, the
> power of veto need not be exercised . . . when four agree and one does
> not object, this can still be considered a consensus, and the four
> should proceed with a new regional scheme.[18]

In addition to saving face, consensus also maintains good relations by producing a united ASEAN position on an issue, and thus the members' interests are seen to be complementary and supportive of one another. Indeed, the informal approach encourages the attitude that negotiations are conducted among friends, not opponents.

The second norm is closely related with the consensus approach. If it is not possible for members to reach a compromise, the issue is adjourned in order to prevent it from undermining the states' relationships and ASEAN as a whole. An example of ASEAN members adjourning discussions because no compromise can be reached is the Malaysia-Philippine dispute over the state of Sabah. Although the dispute dates to 1961, a report in March 1968 of a secret army being trained on the island of Corregidor sparked the crisis.[19] With diplomatic relations curtailed between the two countries a few months later, and Malaysia refusing to attend ASEAN meetings where the Philippines could raise the matter, ASEAN was faced with its first serious security problem. Thailand and Indonesia urged restraint, and in December 1968, at a meeting of ASEAN foreign ministers, both sides were persuaded to limit the public airing of their grievances. By March 1969, the Philippines had agreed not to raise the Sabah issue in ASEAN meetings, and when diplomatic relations resumed in December 1969, "both countries . . . agreed to avoid bringing up the topic in discussion and dialogues, citing the interests of ASEAN."[20] This adjournment of issues is colloquially described as "sweeping controversial issues under the carpet"; when discussions are held, they take place outside the ASEAN framework.

Sometimes adjourning the issue results in a later outcome. The decision to place security on the agenda of the ASEAN foreign ministers' meeting and to create the ASEAN Regional Forum (ARF) is an example of a sensitive issue that eventually was accepted by the ASEAN membership. Mely Caballero-Anthony, who refers to adjournment as "agreeing to disagree," writes that "the importance of adopting such a mechanism yet again emphasizes ASEAN's basic approach that until members can actually get comfortable with each other and elements of distrust can be reduced, if not eliminated, to build confidence and trust, the slow, incremental, low-risk, flexible style is still the effective way forward."[21] While this might be true, the willingness to adjourn sensitive issues rather than confront them has led ASEAN to manage but not resolve security problems, as seen in the case of Sabah. In November 1998, when Philippine President Joseph Estrada established a task force to review the Sabah issue, Kuala Lumpur sought assurances from Manila that the administration would not revive the Philippine claim.[22] While the Philippines stated the claim was not a priority, Manila was clearly signaling that Sabah remained a disputed territory. A consequence of this "management" of the dispute is that the Sabah issue can complicate Malaysian-Philippine relations when problems arise over other issues. In September 2002, Philippine President Gloria Arroyo reconvened an advisory council on Sabah that had been established in 1993, when Malaysian-Philippine relations worsened over the mistreatment of illegal Filipino immigrants in Sabah.[23] Manila has not abrogated its claim to Sabah and it remains a disputed territory.

Therefore, the adjournment of problems, while it might build confidence, has ensured that ASEAN has not become a conflict resolution body. The ASEAN High Council provides tangible evidence of this. Established in the TAC to arbitrate intramural disputes, the High Council has never been convened. Indeed, as noted in Chapter 4, ASEAN members have instead used the International Court of Justice to settle territorial disputes.

The third norm, the willingness to suffer short-term losses for long-term gains, is extremely important since this indicates member states are prepared in certain circumstances to defer their own national interests to the interests of the association as a whole. This is a critical element in the operation of a security regime because it highlights the perception that other regime members will act with restraint and not take advantage of a state's short-term loss. The willingness to defer state interests to the interests of ASEAN was a feature of Indonesia's actions during the Suharto era. Arnfinn Jørgensen-Dahl writes that with the arrival of the New Order regime, "[r]eliance on more conventional diplomatic methods and mores, eschewal of abrasive behaviour, and consciousness of the need to accommodate the interests of its regional partners came in the years that followed to characterise much of Indonesia's involvement in Southeast Asian affairs."[24] This willingness was most marked during the Vietnamese occupation of Cambodia.[25] ASEAN's role in resolving the conflict is examined in Chapter 6; for now, our interest is in Indonesia's deference to Thailand's interests. Thailand—which traditionally sought to balance Vietnamese influence in Indochina and, after the Vietnamese invasion of Cambodia had become the "front-line" state—steered ASEAN toward a confrontational stance with Vietnam. Indeed, Thailand established a de facto alliance with China as it sought to undermine Vietnam's occupation of Cambodia.

The ASEAN approach led by Thailand was not in the Indonesian interest because Jakarta viewed Vietnam as a buffer against Chinese influence in Southeast Asia. In addition, Jakarta feared that a confrontational stance would increase Vietnamese reliance on the USSR, thus increasing Soviet influence in the region. Initially, Indonesia sought a compromise allowing Hanoi to retain de facto domination of Cambodia. However, response to this initiative from Indonesia's ASEAN partners was not supportive and proved highly divisive. Thus in a speech on August 16, 1980, Suharto, "concerned with this disruptive effect within ASEAN," was more critical of Hanoi than he had been the previous year and emphasized Indonesia's support for the Thai position.[26] Throughout the Vietnamese occupation, Indonesia attempted a number of diplomatic solutions, as would befit a major regional actor. However, whenever these approaches were deemed not to be in ASEAN and specifically, Thai interests, Jakarta halted their progress. While Vietnamese intransigence was often cited as a reason for Indonesia's solutions faltering, the major factor was the need to maintain ASEAN unity and support Thailand, because Indonesia saw ASEAN as the best vehicle through which it could influence international affairs. Therefore throughout the occupation, Jakarta was prepared to subordinate its concerns regarding China's long-term threat to Thailand's desire to balance Vietnam's Soviet-sponsored communist expansion. The Sabah case also highlights the willingness of ASEAN members to exercise restraint in their relationships; for example, the Philippines did not take advantage of the racial riots in Kuala Lumpur in 1969 to pursue its claim.

Some, however, dismiss the ASEAN Way as a myth. Referring to the norm of consensus decisionmaking during the Vietnamese occupation of Cambodia, Tobias Ingo Nischalke argues that Thailand's de facto alliance with China did not involve consultation with its ASEAN colleagues. Even the Thai's changed approach to the conflict in 1988, when Chatichai Choonhavan became prime minister and announced a desire to turn Indochina "from a battlefield into a marketplace," is seen as breaching ASEAN's procedural norms. Nischalke writes: "Chatichai had made no efforts to consult his ASEAN partners and seek consensus for a new ASEAN policy on Indochina. Instead he pursued unilaterally an initiative that represented a volte-face from the previous ASEAN position."[27] Nevertheless, as Nikolas Busse writes, during Vietnam's occupation of Cambodia the "ASEAN foreign ministers made 80 per cent of their important decisions during a series of informal meetings."[28] Indeed, the ASEAN peace initiative of 1988—the Jakarta Informal Meetings—arose from a round of cocktail parties. This, Busse concludes, is "a true reflection of regional political culture."[29] Contention over the existence of the ASEAN Way is also seen regarding the adjournment norm. The Kuantan Statement of 1980 can be interpreted as either supporting or undermining this norm. The statement from Indonesia and Malaysia called on the USSR and China to stay out of the conflict, which was not the Thai position. For Nischalke, to make such a public declaration knowing it opposed the Thai position is clearly at odds with keeping one's own counsel when compromise cannot be found. Yet an alternative interpretation would be that Jakarta and Kuala Lumpur allowed the Kuantan Statement to lapse because Thai Prime Minister Prem Tinsulanond found it unacceptable. Indonesia and Malaysia therefore did not pursue a policy publicly that would prejudice ASEAN solidarity.

Whether ASEAN members strictly abide by the norms of the ASEAN Way is questionable. However, when members see these norms as a means to achieve national and regional resilience a picture emerges of them conceiving of their security as indivisible. Certainly prior to the Vietnamese invasion of Cambodia, nation building was the prime security goal for ASEAN members and arguably remains the priority today. The practice of musyawarah enables members to reach agreement without undermining one another. This support for neighboring regimes is inherent in ASEAN's cardinal principle: noninterference. Together the principles and process reveal a supportive network of state leaders (cooperative security) who are assisting one another in their pursuit of national resilience (comprehensive security), which also creates regional resilience (regional stability). It reveals an appreciation that the members' security is inextricably tied to one another; it is indivisible. It reveals that ASEAN has pursued a form of common security.

Common Security via Noninterference

The Palme Commission first coined the term *common security* in 1982; its core tenet is that because security is indivisible, attaining lasting security can be achieved only when all states feel secure—common security is mutual security.[30] The Palme Commission was concerned with the threat of nuclear war between the two Cold War superpowers, but Richard Smoke highlights the value of common security in the ASEAN context. He writes that

> if the other side were to be threatened by, for instance, severe economic collapse, large-scale continuing terrorism, or societal breakdown, such dangers could not help but diminish the first side's security. To protect its own security, the first side has an interest in taking action to forestall such threats to the other side. This idea represents one version of mutual security because the extent the first side helps forestall the emergence of such dangers the security of both is enhanced.[31]

In ASEAN the "action" Smoke refers to is the ASEAN Way and its cardinal principle of noninterference, which despite recent challenges remains the modus operandi of ASEAN. In the ASEAN context it means that members will refrain from publicly criticizing one another. It does not mean that members are indifferent to one another; indeed, state elites have aided other elites. This support for elites as they seek to consolidate positions of power and generate legitimacy for the regime is seen in a variety of forms.

First is the refusal to criticize publicly. During the "people power" revolt in the Philippines in 1986, ASEAN members initially ignored the revolution taking place, and they dropped their implicit support for Ferdinand Marcos's regime only after the United States had withdrawn its support. During 1992, ASEAN members did not respond to the military crackdown in Thailand, and when Indonesia annexed East Timor and was subject to a hostile resolution in the UN General Assembly in December 1975, ASEAN members supported Indonesia's position.[32]

Second, ASEAN members have assisted each other in their internal conflicts, with both military and political support. Indonesia provided military transport aircraft to assist the Marcos regime in the Philippines in its conflict against communist insurgents. Bilateral defense cooperation arrangements between Malaysia and Indonesia and Malaysia and Thailand were established to help fight insurgency movements. Indeed, despite Malaysian and Thai relations being strained because of the activities of the Communist Party of Malaya (CPM) operating out of Thailand, and Muslim separatists in southern Thailand operating from Malaysia, Thailand granted Malaysia the right to pursue guerrillas across the border.[33] In the aftermath of the terrorist attacks against the

United States on September 11, 2001, counterterrorism agreements were made; in December, Indonesia, Malaysia, and the Philippines began joint naval interdiction operations, while in February 2002, foreign ministers from the three countries signed a comprehensive agreement to facilitate counterterrorism cooperation and interoperability. ASEAN members have also conducted joint military operations with the United States, which in some cases were exercises, but in the Philippines the United States has supported the government in its campaign against the terrorist group Abu Sayyaf.

Political support from ASEAN members has come in the form of strong backing. When Corazon Aquino replaced Marcos in the Philippines, her position was threatened by both the communists and disgruntled military officers. Despite security concerns, the other ASEAN members attended the Manila summit in December 1987, and thereby showed their willingness to endorse President Aquino's authority. ASEAN has provided support to a number of Cambodian governments as well. During Vietnam's occupation of Cambodia, ASEAN supported a coalition of opposition groups (the Coalition Government of Democratic Kampuchea, CGDK) to the Vietnamese-installed regime, and again in 1997, ASEAN sent a troika of foreign ministers to Cambodia to mediate between the parties when intrafactional conflict arose.

A third means by which noninterference supports nation building has been ASEAN members' willingness to criticize acts of interference. The Vietnamese invasion of Cambodia in December 1978 is a good example of this. Although the invasion resulted in the replacement of the despotic Pol Pot regime, ASEAN criticized the invasion on the grounds that it breached Cambodia's territorial integrity and threatened its political system.

The principle of noninterference links together the concepts of comprehensive, cooperative, and common security. Hence it can be asserted that noninterference coupled to the ASEAN Way of consultation and consensus decisionmaking, which creates the perception of public unity by not shaming another member, have been the principal means by which ASEAN members have assisted each other's pursuit of security via nation building. Confident they could resolve their internal security threats because their neighbors would not intervene, the region's elites were able to devote their resources, often in a brutal fashion, to national resilience. Hence Malcolm Chalmers's statement that "common security took the form of a strong norm of non-interference in each other's internal affairs."[34] It should be noted, however, that the

ASEAN elite does not acknowledge ASEAN's implementation of common security, unlike comprehensive and cooperative security. The reason? Although it is not unusual for the elite to refer to the indivisibility
of members' security, the term *common security* is associated with the
Palme Commission. The commission's recommendations for implementing common security were diametrically opposed to the means
adopted by ASEAN. For the Palme Commission, common security
required transparency in matters relating to security in order to build
confidence about neighboring states' intentions; it most certainly did
not endorse a noninterference approach. Nevertheless, my position here
is that ASEAN and the commission share the view that security is indivisible, and this notion lies at the heart of common security.[35]

Developments since the end of the Cold War have, however, questioned whether ASEAN members can continue to achieve security the
same way. At the turn of the twenty-first century, the Singaporean foreign minister, S. Jayakumar, called on ASEAN to reinvent itself at the
ASEAN ministerial meeting in Bangkok.[36] What has gone wrong?

ASEAN in the Post–Cold War Era

Far from being a "sunset" organization, ASEAN was regarded as a success story prior to 1997.[37] It could boast a membership of "tiger
economies" that were courted by the major powers. Confidence was
high, with outspoken leaders such as Malaysia's prime minister,
Mahathir Mohamad, and Singapore's senior minister, Lee Kuan Yew,
preaching the virtues of "Asian values." ASEAN had assumed the primary role in the new regional security body (ARF), analyzed in Chapter
6, and it was committed to economic developments both within
Southeast Asia (ASEAN Free Trade Area, AFTA) and the wider Asia-
Pacific (Asia-Pacific Economic Co-operation forum, APEC). Finally,
ASEAN had expanded to incorporate its erstwhile opponent, Vietnam,
in 1995. By the end of the decade, all Southeast Asian states would be
members of ASEAN; the goal of an ASEAN-10 would be accomplished.[38]

Eighteen months later, at the end of 1998, this picture of ASEAN
was hardly recognizable. The combination of an economic collapse
with its political and social consequences, the difficulties of membership expansion, and intramural tensions caused by environmental pollution, drug trafficking, and backsliding on economic commitments,
fueled doubts about the practicality of the principles and processes

behind ASEAN's success, and indeed raised doubts about the continuing viability of the association itself. At the end of December 1998, at the Sixth ASEAN Summit in Hanoi, ASEAN produced its Hanoi Plan of Action (HPA). In order to assess ASEAN's response to the challenges it is facing, it is necessary to look at how the cardinal principal of noninterference has weathered the storm, and in particular, to determine why Robin Ramcharan wrote that at "the Hanoi Summit in 1998 . . . a consensus seemed to have been reached on a clear differentiation of politico-security issues and issues on political economy: in the former case, the ASEAN way applies; in the latter it no longer does."[39] Why does Ramcharan see this division, and is it possible to operate with the ASEAN Way in some areas and not in others?

Noninterference, as noted above, does not mean that ASEAN members are indifferent to one another, nor does it mean they never become involved in each other's domestic affairs. It simply means that one elite supports another by not publicly criticizing the other and by providing support, both tangible and nontangible, if an elite is threatened by internal rebellion. Hence John Funston's statement that "helping neighbouring governments and countries—acting as a mutual support group—is very much the essence of ASEAN."[40] In practice this means that security becomes synonymous with maintaining domestic stability. However, in the 1990s a number of incidents occurred that highlight the interdependency of ASEAN members' security. This interdependence has meant that security problems emanating from one member impact directly on others, which has led to pressure being applied on the incumbent regime. The smog that engulfed parts of Southeast Asia in 1997 is a good example of this.

The smog or "haze" was caused by smoke created by burning agricultural land to clear it for new palm-oil plantations (see Chapter 4). Winds carried it beyond Indonesia's borders, blanketing Singapore, Brunei, Malaysia, and parts of Thailand. The haze was a concern not only for environmental and health reasons, but it also caused a drop in tourism revenue. It also challenged the ASEAN members' commitment to noninterference. According to James Cotton, "the haze has been among Southeast Asia's biggest internal challenges . . . since Vietnam's invasion of Cambodia in 1979."[41]

The initial response of ASEAN members was in line with the ASEAN Way, despite an unhelpful nonchalant approach to the problem by the Indonesian government; the haze had not affected Jakarta. The Singapore government raised its concerns through private diplomacy, and ASEAN strengthened its joint environmental efforts by adopting a regional haze action plan in December 1997. This built upon earlier environmental protocols and established a procedure for pooling resources for regional fire fighting, which in April 1998, resulted in establishing two subregional fire-fighting arrangements in Indonesia. Public criticism of the Indonesian government, although not nonexistent,[42] was limited, and even Malaysia restricted news coverage of the haze.[43]

The impact of these measures was limited, however, and the perception was that the Indonesian regime was more interested in supporting the business conglomerates responsible for the forest fires than in immediately resolving the problem and preventing a reoccurrence. Exasperation over this, especially from Singapore, was noticeable. The Centre for Remote Imaging, Sensing and Processing (CRISP) at the National University of Singapore had been providing the Indonesian government, via Singapore's Ministry of the Environment, with satellite imagery of the fires in Indonesia. Frustrated by the lack of progress by the Indonesian authorities, the center decided to publish these images on the Internet. This was a clear attempt to bypass the regime and influence the Indonesian public directly. It was also notable that at the Fourth ASEAN Ministerial Meeting on Haze held in Singapore in June 1998, the final communiqué praised the involvement of nongovernmental organizations (NGOs) in helping to resolve the haze problem. Given the Indonesian government's suspicious and uneasy relationship with NGOs, such official recognition of their role indicated ASEAN's willingness to praise domestic actors within an ASEAN member state that were not part of the governing regime—to praise alternative recipients of the people's loyalty.

The haze problem thus indicated a departure from the noninterference principle; however, it would be wrong to overstate this. In 1998, both the Philippines and Malaysia were hostile to NGO-sponsored conferences on East Timor. Amitav Acharya writes that this manifests a "continued reluctance of ASEAN states to provide a platform to the dissidents and critics of the governments of fellow members."[44] Noninterference would though receive its most serious challenge in 1998 in the guise of Thai foreign minister, Dr. Surin Pitsuwan, and his call for flexible engagement.

Surin's proposal for flexible engagement built upon the notion of "constructive intervention" suggested in July 1997 by the deputy prime minister of Malaysia, Anwar Ibrahim. Flexible engagement was a proposal for adjusting the members' economic and political development in the aftermath of the 1997–1998 economic crisis. At the June 1998 Asia-Pacific roundtable in Kuala Lumpur, Surin argued:

> ASEAN members perhaps no longer can afford to adopt a non-committal stance and avoid passing judgement on events in a member country, simply on the grounds of "non-interference." To be sure, ASEAN's respect for the sovereignty of fellow members is one reason why the grouping has come this far and enjoyed such longevity. However, if domestic events in one member's territory impact adversely on another member's internal affairs, not to mention regional peace and prosperity, much can be said in favour of ASEAN members playing a more proactive role. Consequently, it is obvious that ASEAN countries have an overriding interest in the internal affairs of its fellow members and may, on occasion, find it necessary to recommend a certain course of action on specific issues that affect us all, directly or indirectly. Or, to be explicit, we may need to make intra-ASEAN relations more dynamic, more engaged, and, yes, more "constructive" than before.[45]

Surin was therefore proposing to alter the principle of noninterference to make it appropriate for the interdependent environment in which ASEAN members were operating. This interdependency was not only manifest in the regional impact of the haze, but also the speed with which the financial crisis had spread from Thailand to the other ASEAN members, and this in a region with low intraregional trade. The traditional noninterference element of assisting one another remained, but now Surin was arguing that since contemporary problems facing the membership were having regional consequences, and that "delays and setbacks in one country can affect the recovery of the region as a whole," this assistance required intervention.[46]

The proposal came from Thailand not only because of the economic crisis but also because Thailand had been practicing constructive engagement for much of the 1990s with its neighbor, Burma. It matters that Thailand proposed flexible engagement because it reflects, first, the failure of Thailand's engagement policy, and second, where flexible engagement calls for changes to the ASEAN Way.

Thailand had sought to bring about political change in Burma ostensibly to improve Thai security concerns and economic interests. In particular, it would end the clashes between Burmese, Thai, and Burma's ethnic minorities that lie along the Burma-Thailand border. Constructive engagement would also deflect criticism from Western nations aimed at Thailand's cooperative approach toward Rangoon's military regime, which was guilty of appalling human rights abuses. In 1991 constructive engagement was adopted by ASEAN at its ministerial meeting.

The notion that engineering political change in Burma is in accordance with noninterference, even if it is via ASEAN's quiet diplomacy, may seem incompatible. Yet the achievement of stability and security through private consultation and consensus is very much the essence of the ASEAN Way. A difficulty arises, however, if the recipient of this "constructive engagement" does not want to change; indeed, by 1996 it had become clear that constructive engagement had failed. Border skirmishes had not diminished and human rights abuses were increasing. The response from ASEAN members has not been to disengage from Burma but to maintain engagement and strengthen their ties by admitting the country into ASEAN. Indeed, at the Fourth ASEAN Regional Forum (ARF) held in Kuala Lumpur in 1997, ASEAN was tasked with reforming Burma. The Western view was that improving conditions in Burma was ASEAN's responsibility. U.S. Secretary of State Madeleine Albright stated: "Burma's future and ASEAN's future are now joined. And now, more than ever, Burma's problems need an ASEAN solution."[47]

The failure of constructive engagement to bring about change in Burma and the regime's human rights record, which tarnishes the association as a whole, led to Surin's flexible engagement proposal. Flexible engagement challenges noninterference in that it raises the prospect of members not just intervening in the affairs of others but also publicly criticizing them in order to achieve change. Public criticism of neighboring states over an issue as sensitive as human rights, for example, also helps distance the member and the association from the negative image created by regimes that abuse human rights. This mattered to Thailand because it had been criticized by Western nations for its constructive engagement of the military regime during the 1990s, and in the aftermath of the 1997 financial crisis, it needed to convince the United States and European Union that it merited financial support because of its democratic credentials. It was not alone in this since the economic crisis made good relations between other ASEAN members and Western states imperative. Such thinking led Mahathir Mohamad, the Malaysian prime minister, to inform his hosts when he visited Burma in March 1998 that "you have to understand that Europe is very important to us."[48]

The notion of public criticism led to the rejection of flexible engagement when it was proposed to members in July 1998 at the

Thirty-first ASEAN Ministerial Meeting. ASEAN instead adopted enhanced interaction. This change of name, though, was not enough to stop public, critical comments being made by the presidents of the Philippines and Indonesia, Joseph Estrada and B. J. Habibie, respectively, over the arrest and detention of Malaysia's deputy prime minister, Anwar Ibrahim, in late 1998. Estrada made a series of public comments about Malaysia's political and judicial procedures, and he raised the prospect of boycotting the APEC summit that was held in Kuala Lumpur. Habibie also refused to rule out boycotting the summit and only agreed to attend after Anwar was released from detention. Both presidents met Anwar's daughter Nurual Izzah, who led protests against Mahathir, and stated their support for Anwar, with Estrada exhorting her to tell her father "not to waver, because he is fighting for a cause, the cause of the Malaysian people."[49] Such actions were clearly at odds with the principle of noninterference. Not only were ASEAN members criticizing another member over its handling of an internal problem, but they were also giving tacit support to the opposition. Habibie also drew protests from Singapore in early 1999 when he accused the island state of racism for not promoting or appointing Malay officers within the Singapore Armed Forces.[50]

Clearly, the notion of avoiding public criticism of another member's domestic affairs was threatened. The ASEAN Way also appeared under threat at the Hanoi summit in December 1998, when there was an un-ASEAN-like squabble over admitting Cambodia to the association. Despite differences over whether the timing of Cambodia's entry was propitious, it was nevertheless "welcomed" as ASEAN's tenth member. According to Michael Vatikiotis, the negotiations that led to breaking the impasse were conducted in an uncompromising fashion that reminded delegates of Hanoi's stance during its occupation of Cambodia—"the experience has left a bad aftertaste."[51] The negotiations were not conducted according to the tried and tested ASEAN approach of consensus building and compromise. In the summer of 1998, Ali Alatas, the Indonesian foreign minister, warned that if public criticism was allowed, the region would return to the tension and mutual suspicion that existed before ASEAN was formed.[52] By the end of the year, "ASEAN's reputation as a zone of peace, stability and progress" was being questioned.[53]

The Hanoi summit marked a turning point for ASEAN. Since the summit, the issue of public criticism has declined as ASEAN has distanced itself from flexible engagement, a term that not only does not appear in ASEAN documentation but was not used by Surin in early

2000 when he argued the merits of intensive interaction and closer coordination of ASEAN members' policies.[54] Instead, enhancing interaction is the preferred term, with the communiqué from the Thirty-fourth ASEAN Ministerial Meeting (AMM) held at Hanoi in July 2001, frequently referring to enhancing ASEAN cooperation. However, this same communiqué reaffirms the central role of private and informal meetings to accomplish goals—in other words, the traditional ASEAN Way of consensus decisionmaking. Enhanced interaction is therefore a rejection of flexible engagement and marks an attempt to maintain non-interference. This can be witnessed in four events, all of which fall within the politico-security framework that Ramcharan correctly argues is a continuation of the ASEAN Way.[55]

The first event concerns the initiation of an ASEAN foreign ministers' retreat in July 1999. This has become an annual event in which the ministers can broach any topics that have an impact on their state or the association as a whole. There is no set agenda and topics have included the establishment of a troika (noted below), international criminal activities, and the status of East Timor. Foreign ministers have used the occasion as a means to keep fellow ASEAN members informed of developments. The Burmese foreign minister apparently used the retreat to inform his counterparts as to the status of the dialogue between the Burmese government (State Peace and Development Council, SPDC) and opposition leader Aung San Suu Kyi. In this sense it is a robust form of enhanced interaction, and it does indicate a willingness to discuss internal topics previously considered taboo in exchanges among foreign ministers. It does not, though, mark a sudden departure from the ASEAN Way. It continues the practice of quiet diplomacy conducted behind closed doors, and there is no suggestion that topics can be discussed against the wishes of those directly involved.

The second event concerns ASEAN's involvement in East Timor. The willingness to provide support for incumbent regimes, an essential element of the ASEAN Way, helps explain ASEAN members' involvement in the Australian-led peacekeeping force sent to East Timor in 1999—the International Force for East Timor (INTERFET). Four ASEAN members (Thailand, the Philippines, Singapore, and Malaysia) contributed to INTERFET, with a Thai general holding deputy command. Invited to contribute by Jakarta—without such consent they would not have become involved—their presence was designed to support Indonesia in two ways. First, Indonesian President B. J. Habibie had come to resent Australia's leading role in the unfolding East Timor crisis, thus the presence of "friendly" ASEAN states was welcomed. In this sense ASEAN was responding to a request for assistance by a fellow member. Second, ASEAN members were concerned that Indonesia's international standing, and by association ASEAN's image as a whole, was damaged by the violence in East Timor, especially given the complicity of Indonesia's army in that violence. By being seen to act, these four ASEAN members were thus seeking to limit the damage done to Indonesia's reputation and to their own. It is pertinent to note that ASEAN was sensitive to criticism of its record on human rights because only two years previously it had admitted Burma to membership.

Throughout the operation of INTERFET, ASEAN members were respectful of Indonesia's sensitivities, and none regarded the operation as endorsing the type of humanitarian intervention conducted in the former Yugoslavia. The intervention in East Timor should thus be seen as willingness to support a fellow ASEAN member—a continuation of the ASEAN Way.

The third event that shows a continuation of noninterference was the decision taken at the Thirty-third AMM in Bangkok in July 2000, to establish an ASEAN troika, an ad hoc body comprising three ASEAN foreign ministers. This builds upon the decision by ASEAN members to send a troika to assist in Cambodia's internal affairs in 1997. The troika was established to "address in a timely manner urgent and important regional political and security issues and situations of common concern likely to disturb regional peace and harmony," yet it was to accomplish this in accordance with "the core principles of consensus and non-interference."[56] Not surprisingly, the troika has not been activated for a host of issues that have disturbed the region's peace and harmony. It has had no role in assisting attempts to end violence in the Moluccas or problems in Mindanao. Despite UN Secretary-General Kofi Annan suggesting the troika could play a role in a confrontation between Aung San Suu Kyi and the SPDC in September 2000, over her right to travel outside Rangoon, it was not used. Finally, when Thai and Burmese troops clashed in 2001, the troika again was not implemented since, as Lee Kim Chew argued, "Theirs is a longstanding spat which ASEAN can do little to help. Nor do they welcome third-party intervention."[57]

The final event concerns the rules of procedure for the ASEAN High Council established in the TAC. The rules were adopted in 2001, and while this might indicate that ASEAN had decided to resolve rather than manage disputes between TAC signatories, this was not the case. If a member decides to call upon the High Council, then it must give, through diplomatic channels, fourteen days' notice to other parties to the dispute and try to reach an accommodation through diplomacy. The other parties must give their consent to the invocation and operation of the High Council, and finally, decisions taken by the council are based upon consensus.[58]

ASEAN's flirtation with tacit approval of public criticism has therefore, at least in the politico-security field, been brought to an end. The ASEAN Way's emphasis on consensual agreement through private negotiation remains the modus operandi of the association. Yet changes were afoot in late 1998, relating to Ramcharan's claim that where issues of political economy are concerned, the ASEAN Way no longer applies.

At the Sixth ASEAN Summit held in Hanoi in December 1998, ASEAN announced its Hanoi Plan of Action (HPA); in subsequent years ASEAN has introduced a bewildering number of programs to enhance economic cooperation among the association's membership. HPA committed ASEAN to implementing the ASEAN Free Trade Area a year ahead of schedule, and it proposed establishing an ASEAN surveillance process (ASP) in the financial sector, which was endorsed by ASEAN finance ministers on October 4, 1999. The ASP involves "exchanging information and discussing [the] economic and financial development of Member States in the region." It does this through "a peer review process" designed to prevent another crisis by "propos[ing] possible regional and national level actions."[59] Of particular importance was the May 2000 launch of the Chiang Mai Initiative. Launched by ASEAN members with Japan, China, and South Korea, it commits "the governments to exchange information and review each other's financial policies."[60] It also allows members to borrow currency from one another to fend off currency speculators; this was one cause of the economic crash in 1997–1998. By May 2002, six bilateral swap arrangements had been concluded, another four were either at an advanced stage or substantial agreement had been reached, while four more had been initiated.[61] ASEAN has also sought to entice foreign investment back to Southeast Asia through its ASEAN investment area (AIA) initiative. One of the main concerns after the economic crisis has been the slow return of foreign investment, which is due to the opening of the Chinese market to foreign direct investment (FDI), as well as suspicions that the structural problems leading to the crash have not been resolved. Thus the AIA is a measure to entice FDI back to Southeast Asia, which along with the ASEAN Framework Agreement on Intellectual Property Cooperation and the ASEAN Framework Agreement on Services, could— although this is not presently the case—complement AFTA. Hadi Soesastro refers to such an outcome as AFTA Plus.[62]

The commitment to enhancing economic prosperity is seen not only in the desire to increase intra-ASEAN trade and attract foreign investment; there is also an appreciation that the new members, the CMLV, need assistance to narrow the development gap between them and the other ASEAN members. Echoing concerns expressed by Anwar Ibrahim in 1997, that ASEAN was partly responsible for the collapse of national reconciliation in Cambodia because it had left it to fend for itself, ASEAN has adopted a series of measures to assist the region's less developed economies.[63] These measures are referred to as "bridging the development gap," and they include a wide variety of economic assistance. In free trade the CMLV members' deadlines have been extended before they implement tariff reductions.[64] ASEAN has also agreed to implement an ASEAN Integration System of Preferences for newer members that will enable them to gain tariff-free access to the more developed ASEAN markets earlier than previously agreed.[65] At the fourth informal summit, held in Singapore in November 2000, ASEAN adopted the Initiative for ASEAN Integration (IAI), and in July 2001, at the Thirty-fourth AMM, this commitment was reiterated with the "Hanoi Declaration on Narrowing Development Gap for Closer ASEAN Integration." This entails providing training by the older ASEAN members to the CMLV over a wide range of development issues, for example, from information technology and customs management to family planning and teaching English.[66] By the end of 2001, ASEAN agreed on the need for the Roadmap for Integration of ASEAN (RIA) to establish specific steps and timetables in order to realize ASEAN's Vision 2020, declared on December 15, 1997.[67] By the summer of 2002, in order to prevent a "two-tier" ASEAN, the association had established four IAI work plans in infrastructure development, human resource development, information and communication technology, and regional economic integration. Given a six-year timeframe, the IAI is guided by the principle of "prosper thy neighbour to prosper thyself."[68]

These economic measures, from the surveillance of the ASP to the assistance of the development programs, clearly will entail a degree of intrusiveness that sits awkwardly with the principal of noninterference. Ramcharan's claim that in this field the ASEAN Way no longer applies can thus be understood. Of course it could be argued that these measures reflect the indivisibility of the members' security—prosper thy neighbor to prosper thyself—and in this regard they do not breach the common security approach that underpins the noninterference principle. However, there is a critical difference between these measures and the type of assistance that ASEAN members have provided in the past. The more recent ones require members to coordinate actions within cooperative enterprises, which by their very nature demand transparency and dialogue about members' domestic policies, and they ultimately reject noninterference and establish rules and procedures that ensure ASEAN members fulfill their obligations.

There is little cause for optimism that this has occurred, however. Instead, the ASEAN Way is much in force and can be seen in AFTA, ASP, and the AIA. In AFTA, as noted in Chapter 4, there have been instances of backsliding on agreements, the most high-profile one being the Malaysian decision to seek deferment on tariff reductions for its automotive industry. Such deferments can occur because the regulations governing AFTA allow members to delay transferring a product to the Inclusion List (products to which tariff reductions between 0 and 5 percent will apply) or even withdraw it from the list. In light of this, the likelihood of fully implementing AFTA is questionable. Markus Hund argues, "AFTA invites the continuous reassessment, renegotiation, modification and, eventually, dissolution, of the original consensus . . . subjecting [AFTA] to the changing developments in, and power-play politics of, intra-ASEAN relations."[69] It can be expected in light of the decision in October 2000 to allow Malaysia to backslide on its automotive commitments that other members will also seek exemptions.[70] Indeed, by the end of 2002, Philippine President Gloria Arroyo openly stated that she intended to "slow the (tariff) liberalization program phase . . . to the minimum and take full advantage of all accepted loopholes allowed."[71]

The experience of the ASP likewise does not inspire much confidence that ASEAN will engage enough to make it function. Member states are not obliged to provide the necessary economic data for the ASP to function as an early warning system but instead agreed to submit the information voluntarily. Considerable details of each member's economy would be required in order for the ASP to act as a surveillance mechanism. In view of the sensitivity of such data, it is not surprising that progress on the ASP has been slow and disappointing. ASEAN's secretary-general, Rodolfo Severino, admitted this when he noted the "reluctance by some member economies to reveal 'too much' information and data."[72] Herman Kraft also makes this point, writing that, it is the ASP's "need for a degree of transparency that some members of the organisation have found objectionable. Malaysia and Singapore have opposed turning over the kind of macroeconomic data needed . . . Laos, Myanmar and Vietnam have likewise been reported as registering their misgivings about it. The plan bogged down before it had a chance to be tested."[73]

The ASP actually highlights the weakness of the ASEAN Way's informal procedures, which clearly are not compatible with an intrusive surveillance mechanism that, by scrutinizing members' economic data, could alert ASEAN to an impeding crisis. This reluctance to establish mechanisms that impinge upon members' sovereignty can also be seen in the AIA; it is intended to encourage foreign investment in ASEAN by obliging member states to open their industries to foreign and ASEAN investors by 2010. However, the institutional framework to ensure compliance reveals reluctance among ASEAN members to pool their sovereignty. The body that oversees the project is the AIA Council, which comprises the ministers responsible for investment and the ASEAN secretary-general. The AIA Council answers to the ASEAN economic ministers (AEM). Hund thus argues the "AIA Council is no independent body to oversee the unconditional implementation of the AIA, but merely represents the extended arm of the national governments."[74] He also notes that no measures exist for penalizing noncompliance.

What then can be expected of ASEAN? Is it unfair to criticize the association for not adopting measures that are alien to its modus operandi? The period after the financial crisis has essentially revealed ASEAN for what it is: a loose arrangement of states that have agreed not to make the difficult task of nation building harder by criticizing one another. Indeed, they have assisted each other where such assistance has not required them to pool or surrender their sovereignty. The various transnational problems they now face require much more coordinated action, and although this is recognized, there remains reluctance to adopt the overarching mechanisms to ensure state compliance, as can be seen in the economic field. It can be argued equally, though, that the public criticism directed at Mahathir by Estrada and Habibie over the Anwar affair provides insight into what could happen if noninterference is dropped. ASEAN is thus in a malaise, and while it is unlikely to be dissolved, it might become increasingly irrelevant. Shaun Narine rightly notes that "ASEAN's capacity to be assertive on the international stage and to be a major regional economic actor is contingent on its ability to reform its methods of interaction. Yet . . . without the ASEAN way, ASEAN would dissolve through internal conflict. ASEAN is as unified and coordinated a regional organisation as it can be, given the domestic interests and weaknesses of its members."[75]

At the beginning of the new century ASEAN has become incapacitated. The elite talk of greater economic integration—Singaporean

Prime Minister Goh Chok Tong has urged his counterparts to consider the 1950s' European Economic Community as a model to create an ASEAN Economic Community (AEC)—but they have been reluctant to adopt the necessary measures, including pooling their sovereignty, that would enable the association to respond to current challenges.[76] Instead, ASEAN has sought to maintain its traditional approach, and while dangers do exist in adopting the type of flexible engagement Surin called for in 1998, if rhetoric is to be matched by action, ASEAN will need to change or, in Jayakumar's words, reinvent itself.

One final development, while at an early stage, offers the prospect of ASEAN revitalizing itself. ASEAN's Vision 2020 calls for the association to create "caring societies" in which "all people enjoy equitable access to opportunities for total human development regardless of gender, race, religion, language, or social, and cultural background." It envisions "our nations being governed with the consent and greater participation of the people, with its focus on the welfare and dignity of the human person and the good of the community."[77] The ASEAN eminent persons group (EPG) reported at the fourth informal summit held in Singapore in November 2000, that "the peoples of ASEAN must themselves . . . *take ownership of the ASEAN Vision 2020*, and that ASEAN matters should not only be the prerogative of governments, but also of businesses, the civil society and ultimately, the people" (emphasis in original).[78] This stands in marked contrast to the traditional ASEAN emphasis of security articulated by the elite, for the elite—in other words, regime stability in each member state. Tentative steps have been taken toward increasing the participation of the region's people in decisionmaking with the creation in November 2000 of the ASEAN People's Assembly (APA) and a greater acceptance of nongovernmental organizations in what are increasingly referred to as track-III activities.[79] Whether track-III projects or the APA are proof that ASEAN will become more than a club for the elite remains to be seen.

Conclusion

Since the nadir of 1998, ASEAN has certainly agreed upon a series of programs in the spirit of the Bangkok Declaration, TAC, and ASEAN Concord. These programs emphasize that only by working in concert can the members provide common prosperity, stability, and ultimately, common security. Hence Etel Solingen's assertion that "all in all, ASEAN leaders responded to the worst economic and political debacle in thirty years by conforming to the premise that internationalist strategies compel helping—not undermining—the most ravaged partners, and that any attempt to take advantage of feebler neighbours would undermine the collective."[80] However, if the plethora of programs ASEAN has initiated are to have the desired economic impact, the noninterference principle will have to change. When Tobias Nischalke dismisses ASEAN initiatives, referring to the 2000 and 2001 AMMs as producing "meagre results" that have given "further impetus to the notion of ASEAN's progressive marginalization," his criticism is aimed at the ASEAN Way.[81] The attempt to implement these changes while continuing to use old procedures is simply not doable. Jusuf Wanandi writes:

> If ASEAN can overcome the financial and economic crisis as well as the divide between the old and new members in the medium term, then ASEAN will become stronger in facing its future challenges. In this regard, the long established practice of what has come to be known as the "ASEAN way" must be radically changed, if not completely done away with.[82]

ASEAN's rejection of flexible engagement, however, is strong evidence the elite are not prepared to abandon an approach that has served them well for the first thirty years of the association's existence. Noninterference enabled them to nation build without fear of neighboring states taking advantage of their internal weaknesses (namely ethnic separatist demands and communist insurgency); it was therefore regarded as providing a mutual support framework by which common security could be achieved among the region's elite.

The current transnational problems cannot be resolved without coordinated action, transparency, and dialogue over members' domestic affairs. Although there are few grounds for optimism that ASEAN will do this, it is worth noting that if ASEAN is going to continue to conceive of the security of its members as indivisible, transparency in decisionmaking is a key element in the Palme Commission's version of common security. Perhaps ASEAN's future lies in Vision 2020, with its emphasis on greater participation from the peoples of ASEAN states. The existence of alternative voices to member governments will perhaps enable ASEAN to fundamentally change from its concern with regime security to being concerned with the region's security, in all its manifestations. Albeit at an early stage, this could be seen in NGO activity during the haze problem and the establishment of the APA.

ASEAN therefore faces the difficulties of adapting to a new environment. These challenges are not only intramural, they also concern the association's relationship with states outside of Southeast Asia. The analysis now turns to the change from keeping extraregional powers at arms length to engaging with them in the security and economic field—and what this means for ASEAN.

Notes

1. "The ASEAN Declaration, Bangkok," Thailand, 8 August 1967. For details of the declaration, see the Internet site http://www.aseansec.org/1212.htm.

2. Jusuf Wanandi has written, "[I]f each member nation can accomplish an overall national development and overcome internal threats, regional resilience will automatically result in much the same way as a chain derives its overall strength from the strength of its constituent parts." Quoted in Amitav Acharya, *Constructing a Security Community in Southeast Asia: ASEAN and the Problem of Regional Order* (London: Routledge, 2001), p. 58.

3. Michael Leifer, *ASEAN and the Security of South-East Asia* (London: Routledge, 1990), p. 2.

4. The Indonesian concepts of national and regional resilience are enshrined in articles 11 and 12 of the TAC. Russell H. Fifield, *National and Regional Interests in ASEAN: Competition and Co-operation in International Politics*, Occasional Paper 57 (Singapore: Institute of Southeast Asian Studies, 1979), p. 16.

5. Michael Leifer, "The ASEAN Peace Process: A Category Mistake," *The Pacific Review* 12/1 (1999), p. 27.

6. David Capie and Paul Evans, *The Asia-Pacific Security Lexicon* (Singapore: ISEAS, 2002), pp. 98–107.

7. Amitav Acharya, "Ideas, Identity, and Institution-building: From the 'ASEAN Way' to the 'Asian-Pacific Way'?" *The Pacific Review* 10/3 (1997), p. 329.

8. Acharya, *Constructing a Security Community in Southeast Asia*, pp. 25–26.

9. Barry Buzan, *People, States and Fear: An Agenda For International Security Studies in the Post–Cold War Era,* 2nd ed. (Boulder: Lynne Rienner and London: Harvester Wheatsheaf, 1991), p. 190. For details of homogeneous and heterogeneous complexes, see Barry Buzan, Ole Wæver, and Jaap de Wilde, *Security: A New Framework for Analysis* (Boulder: Lynne Rienner, 1998), pp. 15–19.

10. N. Ganesan, *Bilateral Tensions in Post–Cold War ASEAN*, Pacific Strategic Paper 9 (Singapore: ISEAS, 1999), p. 3. Elsewhere Ganesan notes that because of the number of crosscutting issues between the two complexes, their utility is exaggerated; he also notes that both complexes had dissipated by the end of the Cold War. See N. Ganesan, "ASEAN's Relations with Major External Powers," *Contemporary Southeast Asia* 22/2 (August 2000), pp. 258–278.

11. Barry Buzan, "Third World Regional Security in Structural and Historical Perspective," in Brian L. Job (ed.), *The Insecurity Dilemma:*

National Security of Third World States (Boulder: Lynne Rienner, 1992), p. 168.

12. For conflict formation, see Raimo Väyrynen, "Regional Conflict Formations: An Intractable Problem of International Relations," *Journal of Peace Research* 21/4 (1984), pp. 357–359. For security community, see Karl Deutsch, *Political Community and the North Atlantic Area: International Organization in the Light of Historic Experience* (Princeton: Princeton University Press, 1957).

13. Deutsch, ibid., p. 5.

14. Ganesan, *Bilateral Tensions in Post–Cold War ASEAN*, p. 56.

15. Tim Huxley, *Insecurity in the ASEAN Region* (London: Royal United Services Institute Whitehall Paper, 1993), p. 11.

16. Amitav Acharya, "Regional Military-Security Cooperation in the Third World: A Conceptual Analysis of the Relevance and Limitations of ASEAN (Association of Southeast Asian Nations), *Journal of Peace Research* 29/1 (February 1992), p. 12.

17. Hoang Anh Tuan, "ASEAN Dispute Management: Implications for Vietnam and an Expanded ASEAN," *Contemporary Southeast Asia* 18/1 (June 1996), p. 67.

18. Quoted from Acharya, "Ideas, Identity, and Institution-building," p. 332.

19. Filipino Muslims were recruited and trained at a military base on Corregidor to infiltrate Sabah. In response to a mutiny in the camp, the recruits were killed. When this became public knowledge, the Malaysians were outraged, especially since this coincided with the arrest in Sabah of twenty-six armed Filipinos. To make matters worse, the Philippine government in an effort to cover up its actions—which were embarrassing if spread abroad and were alarming for Muslims in Mindanao—used the incident to revive its claims for Sabah. Saber rattling resulted between the two states, diplomatic staff were recalled from their respective capitals, and Malaysia even reported the incident to U Thant, the UN Secretary-General. For details see Leifer, *ASEAN and the Security of South-East Asia*, pp. 31–37.

20. Kamarulzaman Askandar, "ASEAN and Conflict Management: The Formative Years of 1967–1976," *Pacifica Review* 6/2 (1994), p. 67.

21. Mely Caballero-Anthony, "Mechanisms of Dispute Settlement: The ASEAN Experience," *Contemporary Southeast Asia* 20/1 (April 1998), p. 61.

22. "Malaysia asks RP not to revive claims over Sabah," *The Philippine Star*, 22 November 1998.

23. "Arroya revives 9-year-old council to study claim on Sabah," *The Sunday Times (Singapore)*, 8 September 2002; Luz Baguioro, "Manila-KL row just a 'minor irritant,'" *The Straits Times*, 10 September 2002.

24. Arnfinn Jørgensen-Dahl, "Indonesia as Regional Great Power," in Iver B. Neumann (ed.), *Regional Great Powers in International Politics* (London: St. Martin's, 1992), p. 85.

25. For an account of Indonesian initiatives during the Cambodian crisis, see Andrew J. MacIntyre, "Interpreting Indonesian Foreign Policy: The Case of Kampuchea 1979–1986," *Asian Survey* 27/5 (May 1987), pp. 515–534.

26. Ibid., p. 519.

27. Tobias Ingo Nischalke, "Insights from ASEAN's Foreign Policy Co-

operation: The 'ASEAN Way,' a Real Spirit or a Phantom?" *Contemporary Southeast Asia* 22/1 (April 2000), p. 94.

28. Nikolas Busse, "Constructivism and Southeast Asian Security," *The Pacific Review* 12/1 (1999), p. 50.

29. Ibid., p. 51.

30. The Report of the Independent Commission on Disarmament and Security Issues, under the chairmanship of Olof Palme, produced a book entitled, *Common Security: A Programme for Disarmament* (London: Pan Books, 1982).

31. Richard Smoke, "A Theory of Mutual Security," in Richard Smoke and Andrei Kortunov (eds.), *Mutual Security: A New Approach to Soviet-American Relations* (Basingstoke, UK: Macmillan, 1991), p. 82.

32. Singapore initially abstained but subsequently endorsed Indonesia's incorporation of East Timor. See Leifer, *ASEAN and the Security of South-East Asia,* p. 42.

33. Acharya, *Constructing a Security Community in Southeast Asia,* p. 60.

34. Malcolm Chalmers, "The Debate on a Regional Arms Register in Southeast Asia," *The Pacific Review* 10/1 (1997), p. 105.

35. For the applicability of common security to the Asia-Pacific region, see Geoffrey Wiseman, "Common Security in the Asia-Pacific Region," *The Pacific Review* 5/1 (1992), pp. 42–59; and Michael Leifer, "Debating Asian Security: Michael Leifer Responds to Geoffrey Wiseman," *The Pacific Review* 5/2 (1992), pp. 167–169; also see David Dewitt, "Common, Comprehensive and Cooperative Security," *The Pacific Review* 7/1 (1994), pp. 1-15.

36. Simon S. C. Tay, "Institutions and Processes: Dilemmas and Possibilities," in Simon S. C. Tay, Jesus P. Estanislao, and Hadi Soesastro (eds.), *Reinventing ASEAN* (Singapore: ISEAS, 2001), p. 244.

37. Not all commentators agreed. See M. L. Smith and D. M. Jones, "ASEAN, Asian Values and Southeast Asian Security in the New World Order," *Contemporary Security Policy* 18/3 (December 1997), pp. 126–156.

38. With East Timor gaining independence in the summer of 2002, ASEAN might again expand its membership.

39. Robin Ramcharan, "ASEAN and Non-interference: A Principle Maintained," *Contemporary Southeast Asia* 22/1 (April 2000), p. 81.

40. John Funston, "ASEAN: Out of Its Depth," *Contemporary Southeast Asia* 20/1 (April 1998), p. 27.

41. James Cotton, "The 'Haze' over Southeast Asia: Challenging the ASEAN Mode of Regional Engagement," *Pacific Affairs* 72/3 (Fall 1999), p. 348.

42. Simon Tay, a nominated member of Singapore's parliament, was outspoken and criticized Indonesia for: (1) failing to ensure compliance with its own laws by the conglomerates responsible for the haze; (2) failing to develop the capacity to cope with the fires; and finally (3) failing to change land use for sustainable development. Tay also questioned the validity of the ASEAN Way by stating it should be "reconsidered" and "adapted" and not treated as "something sacred and immutable." Simon S. C. Tay, "What Should Be Done About the Haze," *Indonesian Quarterly* 26/2 (1998), pp. 99–117.

43. Cotton, "The 'Haze' over Southeast Asia," pp. 347–348.

44. Acharya, *Constructing a Security Community in Southeast Asia*, p. 59.

45. Quoted from Jürgen Haacke, "The Concept of Flexible Engagement and the Practice of Enhanced Interaction: Intramural Challenges to the 'ASEAN Way,'" *The Pacific Review* 12/4 (1999), pp. 585–586.

46. Ibid., p. 586.

47. "Most successful ARF meeting since inception," *The Straits Times*, 28 July 1997.

48. Quoted in Bertil Lintner, "Lightning Rod," *Far Eastern Economic Review*, 12 November 1998, p. 29; hereafter the *Far Eastern Economic Review* is referred to as *FEER*.

49. John Aglionby, "Anwar's teenage daughter picks up baton of reform," *The Guardian*, 19 October 1998.

50. See Lim Seng Jin, "No Place for Discrimination," *The Straits Times*, 28 February 1999.

51. Michael Vatikiotis, "Awkward Admission," *FEER*, 24 December 1998, p. 17.

52. See Haacke, "The Concept of Flexible Engagement and the Practice of Enhanced Interaction," p. 593.

53. Berti Lintner, Shada Islam, and Faith Keenan, "Growing Pains," *FEER*, 28 January 1999, p. 26.

54. See Surin Pitsuwan, "Heeding ASEAN's Legacy," *FEER*, 17 February 2000, p. 29.

55. The four events are covered in detail in Jürgen Haacke, *ASEAN's Diplomatic and Security Culture: Origins, Development and Prospects* (London: Routledge/Curzon, 2003), Ch. 8.

56. "The ASEAN Troika." Internet site: http://www.aseansec.org/3637.htm.

57. Lee Kim Chew, "Distrust bedevils Thai-Myanmar relations," *The Straits Times,* 11 April 2001.

58. For the High Council's rules of procedure, see "Rules of Procedure of the High Council of the Treaty of Amity and Cooperation in Southeast Asia." Internet site: http://www.aseansec.org/3639.htm.

59. "Terms of Understanding on the Establishment of the ASEAN Surveillance Process." Internet site: http://www.aseansec.org/6309.htm.

60. Simon S. C. Tay, "ASEAN and East Asia: A New Regionalism?" in Simon S. C. Tay, Jesus P. Estanislao, and Hadi Soesastro (eds.), *Reinventing ASEAN* (Singapore: ISEAS, 2001), p. 206.

61. "The Joint Ministerial Statement of the ASEAN+3 Finance Ministers Meeting," 10 May 2002. Internet site: http://www.aseansec.org/5473.htm.

62. Hadi Soesastro, "Towards an East Asian Regional Trading Arrangement," in Simon S. C. Tay, Jesus P. Estanislao, and Hadi Soesastro (eds.), *Reinventing ASEAN* (Singapore: ISEAS, 2001), p. 234.

63. Anwar Ibrahim, "Crisis Prevention," *Newsweek*, 21 July 1997, p. 13.

64. For tariff reductions between 0 and 5 percent, which for the ASEAN-6 had a 2002 deadline, Vietnam's deadline is 2006, for Laos and Burma it is 2008, and for Cambodia, 2010. For items that are on the Sensitive List the deadline for the ASEAN-6 is 2010, for Vietnam, 2013, 2015 for Laos and

Burma, and 2017 for Cambodia. For details see Soesastro, "Towards an East Asian Regional Trading Arrangement," p. 227.

65. "Press Statement by the Chairman of the 7th ASEAN Summit and the 5th ASEAN + 3 Summit," 5 November 2001 at Bandar Seri Begawan, Brunei Darussalam. Internet site: http://www.aseansec.org/5317.htm.

66. Margot Cohen, "Reality Bites," *FEER*, 16 August 2001, p. 28.

67. "ASEAN Vision 2020"; for details see the Internet site: http://www. aseansec.org/5228.htm.

68. "ASEAN Forms Partnerships to Close the Development Gap Among Its Members"; for details see the Internet site: http://www.aseansec.org/11501.htm.

69. Markus Hund, "From 'Neighbourhood Watch Group' to Community? The Case of ASEAN Institutions and the Pooling of Sovereignty," *Australian Journal of International Affairs* 56/1 (2002), pp. 104–105.

70. Kamarul Yunus, "No delay in the implementation of AFTA," *Business Times (Malaysia),* 12 September 2002.

71. "Philippines leader calls for slowdown of her tariff reduction policy," *Agence France Presse*, 26 September 2002.

72. Quoted in Hund, "From 'Neighbourhood Watch Group' to Community?" p. 110.

73. Herman Kraft, "ASEAN and Intra-ASEAN Relations: Weathering the Storm?" *The Pacific Review* 13/3 (2000), p. 458.

74. Hund, "From 'Neighbourhood Watch Group' to Community?" p. 107.

75. Shaun Narine, "ASEAN in the Aftermath: The Consequences of the East Asian Economic Crisis," *Global Governance* 8/2 (2002), p. 189.

76. For the Singaporean initiative, see "The road for ASEAN," *The Straits Times*, 12 October 2002; and Chua Lee Hoong, "Singapore's plan for single ASEAN market," *The Straits Times*, 5 November 2002. ASEAN Secretary-General Rodolfo Severino's exasperation with progress on economic integration is revealed in his comment that such progress "has fallen short of being commensurate to the challenges confronting our region and carrying out the leaders' vision and resolve." See "More Commitment, Direction and Push Needed for ASEAN Economic Integration, Says ASEAN Sec-Gen," 4 November 2002. Internet site: http://www.aseansec.org/13151.htm.

77. Ramcharan, "ASEAN and Non-interference: A Principle Maintained," p. 83.

78. "Report of the ASEAN Eminent Persons Group (EPG) on Vision 2020: The People's ASEAN." See the Internet site: http://www.aseansec.org/5304.htm.

79. Track I refers to government-government forums; track II is supposedly where nongovernmental experts and government officials acting in a private capacity can discuss matters. However, the nongovernmental experts at the workshops are often from government-supported think tanks, and government officials remain constrained by their official position. Track III thus attempts to bring track-II participants together with NGOs and to allow greater participation in decisionmaking than track II provides. For an excellent coverage of NGO and track-III activities, see Amitav Acharya, "Democratization and the Prospects for Participatory Regionalism in Southeast Asia," *Third World Quarterly* 24, no. 2 (April 2003), pp. 375–390.

80. Etel Solingen, "ASEAN, Quo Vadis? Domestic Coalitions and Regional Co-operation," *Contemporary Southeast Asia* 21/1 (April 1999), p. 49.

81. Tobias Nischalke, "Does ASEAN Measure Up? Post–Cold War Diplomacy and the Idea of Regional Community," *The Pacific Review* 15/1 (2002), p. 90.

82. Jusuf Wanandi, "ASEAN's Past and the Challenges Ahead: Aspects of Politics and Security," in Simon S. C. Tay, Jesus P. Estanislao, and Hadi Soesastro (eds.), *Reinventing ASEAN* (Singapore: ISEAS, 2001), p. 29.

6

From Arms Length
to All in Together:
Managing Extraregional Powers

Internal security concerns and development issues lay behind the formation of ASEAN. The five founding members sought to create a stable external environment that would assist the regimes' internal fight against ethnic separatism and communist insurgency. Maintaining a stable region necessitated concern for the actions of extraregional powers, in particular, the potential for intervention by the two superpowers and China in Southeast Asia. Thus in the early period of ASEAN's existence, member states adopted a Zone of Peace, Freedom and Neutrality (ZOPFAN), which essentially seeks to limit extraregional intervention in Southeast Asia. However, the desire to keep extraregional powers at arms length is complemented, or perhaps contradicted by, the region's need and desire to involve the great powers for economic and security purposes.

This tension between warding off external actors and welcoming their presence has continued in the post–Cold War era with the adoption of the South East Asian Nuclear Weapons Free Zone (SEANWFZ), which is a means of implementing ZOPFAN, and the establishment of a security forum to engage extraregional powers. The latter, the ASEAN Regional Forum (ARF), is also complemented in the economic field by Southeast Asian states developing closer ties with China, Japan, and South Korea. In December 1997 at Kuala Lumpur, the first ASEAN Plus Three (APT) summit was held between heads of state from China, Japan, and South Korea and the ASEAN members. In 2002, the APT extended its remit to consider such security issues as transnational crime.

In this chapter our interest in Southeast Asian security addresses how ASEAN members have sought to manage the involvement of external powers in their region. We revisit ASEAN's early period to examine the paradox of needing the presence of external powers in the region while also seeking to limit it. We analyze ZOPFAN and ASEAN's involvement in the Cambodian conflict of the 1980s, then turn to the post–Cold War era and show that ASEAN has adopted a cooperative security approach toward extraregional powers by continuing to maintain defense agreements with Western powers while also engaging with China. ASEAN attempts to balance the power of extraregional states but not through traditional balance-of-power concepts such as alliances, arms buildups, and deterrence policies. The chapter concludes by examining Southeast Asia's latest means of engaging extraregional powers, the APT process, and what this might mean for ASEAN.

Extraregional Powers During the Cold War

The adoption of the Zone of Peace, Freedom and Neutrality (ZOPFAN) declaration at an ad hoc meeting of ASEAN foreign ministers at Kuala Lumpur in November 1971, provides a good starting point for understanding the association's almost schizophrenic approach to relations with extraregional powers. Even though the ZOPFAN declaration is a policy of nonalignment, it did not prevent ASEAN members from entering into defense agreements with extraregional powers, in particular, Malaysia and Singapore with Great Britain, Australia, and New Zealand in the Five Power Defence Arrangements, and the Philippines' mutual defense treaty with the United States. Indeed, only Indonesia pursued a policy of nonalignment during the Cold War.

The ZOPFAN proposal arose in the late 1960s and early 1970s as a consequence of what was an unsettling time for the region's states. In January 1968, the British government announced an accelerated timetable for withdrawing forces east of Suez. The deteriorating U.S. position in South Vietnam had been revealed by the Tet offensive in January-February 1968. In July 1969, President Richard Nixon delivered a speech at Guam stating that the United States would not continue to carry the burden of fighting conventional wars against communist guerrilla forces. This reduction in Western involvement was replaced by a more assertive presence by the communist states. The passage of a small Soviet naval flotilla through the Straits of Malacca into the Indian Ocean in March 1968 was widely perceived as the USSR moving in to replace British influence. The United States complemented its declining role in Vietnam by improving its relations with China. The secret meetings between U.S. national security adviser Henry Kissinger and Chinese Premier Zhou Enlai in 1971 led first, to the People's Republic of China (PRC) taking control of China's seat in the UN Security Council, and second, to Nixon's historic visit to China in February 1972. The early 1970s thus ushered in a period of U.S.-Chinese rapprochement.

With the reduced Western presence filled by the USSR and China emerging to create a period of tripolarity, ASEAN members faced a changed external environment. Malaysia responded by pursuing a policy of neutralism and opening diplomatic relations with China. Faced with a communist insurgency led by the Communist Party of Malaya (CPM), the regime in Kuala Lumpur hoped that creating diplomatic ties with the PRC would demonstrate to its Malaysian Chinese population and the CPM that its legitimacy was endorsed by Beijing. The policy of neutralism or nonalignment, while evidently not pro-China was nevertheless interpreted by other ASEAN members, and most especially Indonesia, as Malaysian acceptance of a Chinese interest in the region. Michael Leifer writes: "Malaysia's policy implied a regional power vacuum which could only be filled in an orderly manner through external involvement. Such thinking was an anathema in Jakarta."[1]

At the November 1971 meeting in Kuala Lumpur, Indonesia's foreign minister, Adam Malik, not only rejected Malaysia's neutralization proposal because it implied that Southeast Asia's stability would be determined by external powers, but according to Leifer, Jakarta was annoyed that Malaysia thought it could prescribe unilaterally for the region.[2] Indonesia is first among equals in ASEAN and Malik took the lead role in diluting Malaysia's neutrality and re-emphasizing the regional states' primary role in creating stability. In September 1971, Malik argued:

> I strongly believe that it is only through developing among ourselves an area of internal cohesion and stability, based on indigenous sociopolitical and economic strength, that we can ever hope to assist in the early stabilisation of a new equilibrium in the region that would not be the exclusive "diktat" of the major powers . . . In fact, I am convinced that unless the big powers acknowledge and the Southeast Asian nations themselves assume a greater and more direct responsibility in the maintenance of security in the area, no lasting stability can ever be achieved.[3]

The neutrality proposal also caused problems for the other ASEAN members because of their security ties with extraregional powers.

Thailand was fighting a communist guerrilla threat and thus was not willing to adopt nonalignment; the Philippines did not want to prejudice its defense treaty with Washington (the Manila Pact of 1954); and Singapore also feared that neutralism could result in U.S. disengagement. That neutrality appears in ZOPFAN's title should not be seen therefore as ASEAN's adoption of a nonalignment policy, rather it is ASEAN paying lip service to Malaysia's proposal. The ZOPFAN declaration refers to the neutrality provision as a desirable objective to achieve at some future point. In contrast, the declaration reiterates the Indonesian preference for ASEAN members to strengthen their own internal security through economic and social development and, in so doing, create a stable region free from external interference—in other words, the Indonesian notions of national and regional resilience. In essence, by strengthening their own states' legitimacy and eradicating the underlying social problems that give rise to internal threats to the regimes' hold on power—underdevelopment and poverty—Southeast Asia could become a "Zone of Peace."

Consequently, ZOPFAN has not been seen as a statement describing ASEAN's position in the 1970s, since quite patently, Southeast Asia did suffer from external interference and ASEAN members either were in no position to limit such influence or, in the case of U.S. involvement, they wanted it limited. Instead, ZOPFAN, which was also included in the Declaration of ASEAN Concord at the first heads of government meeting at Bali in February 1976, was regarded as a goal for ASEAN members to achieve. While neutrality was a long-term goal, the more immediate concern was for ASEAN to assume the primary role in creating a stable region. In the 1970s and 1980s, it was assumed that such a role required isolating Southeast Asia from the superpowers' rivalry; a rivalry that had revealed in the Vietnam War how much it could damage a state's development.

ASEAN's primary role came to the fore during the Vietnamese occupation of Cambodia (known as Kampuchea at the time) in the 1980s, although paradoxically the International Conference on Cambodia held at Paris in 1991, which ended the conflict, also started a process that has effectively ended ZOPFAN. However, ZOPFAN does officially remain an ASEAN declaration of intent.

The Soviet-sponsored Vietnamese invasion of Cambodia in December 1978 presented ASEAN with an opportunity to become the primary organization for achieving stability in Southeast Asia. The invasion violated ASEAN principles of national sovereignty and territorial integrity and thus forced it to take a stand. If ASEAN had failed to respond to Vietnam's actions, it is unlikely the organization would have survived. At the outset it was evident that Thailand, Malaysia, and Indonesia had different solutions to the problems the invasion raised. For Malaysia and Indonesia, the primary objective was to limit external involvement of the Soviet Union and China and essentially to prevent these two powers from using Southeast Asia as a battleground in their dispute. Kuala Lumpur and Jakarta feared that Vietnam would become a pawn in the Sino-Soviet conflict, with the inevitable result that it would be weakened; Vietnam would therefore either become subject to Chinese domination or be bound in a permanent client relationship to Moscow. In either case, ZOPFAN would remain an even more distant objective than before the invasion. This Malaysian-Indonesian concern was manifest in their Kuantan Statement in 1980, which envisaged Vietnam free from Soviet and Chinese influence but also recognized a legitimate Vietnamese security interest in Cambodia. Thailand, however, rejected the proposal since Bangkok was not prepared to accept that Hanoi had a legitimate security interest in Cambodia. Consequently, the Kuantan Declaration was discarded. What this revealed about the ASEAN Way was examined in Chapter 5; with regard to external relations, it signified that Malaysia, Indonesia, Thailand, Singapore, and the Philippines would use ASEAN for a diplomatic resolution to the conflict.

ASEAN was successful throughout the 1980s in keeping the Cambodian crisis on the international agenda and, even more important, in determining that the issue was Vietnam's invasion of Cambodia rather than the overthrow of the Pol Pot regime. The ASEAN members initiated the July 1981 International Conference on Kampuchea (ICK), convened under the auspices of the UN Secretary-General, and while the conference produced little of substance, its proposal for an interim administration and elections conducted by the UN was not too different from the one adopted in 1991. The ICK failed because Vietnam and the Soviet Union were not present. They objected to the ousted Khmer Rouge regime occupying Cambodia's seat in the UN, and thus the conference became one of states opposed to Vietnam rather than a forum for negotiation. Nevertheless, the ICK signified ASEAN's importance as a diplomatic vehicle by putting its five members at the heart of resolving the conflict.

ASEAN was also able to deny for the most part international legitimacy for the Vietnamese-installed regime (the People's Republic of Kampuchea, PRK), while making the overthrown Khmer Rouge administration acceptable by helping create a coalition of parties opposed to the PRK. ASEAN thought the Coalition Government of Democratic Kampuchea (CGDK) would be more acceptable not only to an international audience but also to Vietnam because it contained factions that were unlikely to present Hanoi with a security threat. Hanoi, however, was not swayed and remained convinced that the main actor in the coalition was China's client, the Khmer Rouge.

By the mid-1980s, ASEAN had kept the Vietnamese invasion of Cambodia on the international agenda; it had not been forgotten in two weeks as Ha Van Lau, Vietnam's permanent representative to the UN, had confidently informed his Singapore counterpart, Tommy Koh, in January 1979. Despite the despotism of the defeated Khmer Rouge regime, ASEAN maintained international support for it first, by ensuring that UN resolutions condemned the Vietnamese invasion rather than Pol Pot's indefensible human rights record, and second, by helping create the more acceptable CGDK. Despite ASEAN's diplomatic achievements, however, it was not able to overcome Vietnam's obduracy. The source of the peace agreement in 1991 came not from ASEAN, but rather the new political thinking implemented by Mikhail Gorbachev in the USSR.

The fundamental change in relations between the USSR and the West that would end the Cold War affected Vietnam in at least three ways. First, it ushered in an improvement in Sino-Soviet relations, which meant that Vietnam could not rely upon Soviet backing in the face of Chinese pressure. Second, Soviet material assistance to Vietnam, worth U.S.$3 billion a year, ceased. Finally, the changes underway in the Soviet economy—perestrioka—raised doubts over the viability of the Soviet economic model. These concerns coupled to the economic cost of the Cambodian occupation led in 1986 to Vietnam's adoption of doi moi, a policy of economic renovation. Because of concerns about their economy and worries of international isolation, Hanoi began to seek better regional relations.

In this regard, Vietnam was assisted by the advent of a new civilian government in Bangkok in August 1988. The new Thai prime minister, Chatichai Choonhavan, recognized the economic opportunities that Vietnam's doi moi policy was creating and declared that Thailand wanted to turn the battlefields of Indochina into marketplaces. It was an important policy reversal by Thailand and indicated that the two historic competitors for hegemony in Indochina could cooperate. The initial response by other ASEAN members was lukewarm, but as the Cambodian crisis reached a conclusion, relations between other

ASEAN members and Hanoi improved. Indonesian President Suharto visited Vietnam in November 1990, and a year later Vo Van Kiet became the first Vietnamese prime minister to visit an ASEAN capital since 1978 when he arrived in Singapore. In 1992, the prime ministers of Thailand, Malaysia, and Singapore all visited Hanoi.

In December 1987 and January 1988, there were face-to-face meetings between Prince Sihanouk, the nominal leader of the CGDK, and PRK prime minister, Hun Sen. These paved the way for two informal meetings in Jakarta in July 1988 and again in February 1989, which not only included the internal parties of Cambodia but also Laos, Vietnam, and the ASEAN-6 (Brunei had joined in 1984). The beginning of the dialogue process was followed in April 1989 by Hanoi's declaration to unconditionally withdraw its troops from Cambodia in September. This in turn was the incentive to convene a second International Conference on Cambodia in Paris in July 1989. It was co-convened by France and Indonesia, and unlike the 1981 conference, the participants included all internal and external parties to the conflict. Although progress was made at the conference, difficulties still remained over the composition of an interim administration that would govern Cambodia between signing a political settlement and holding a general election.

In 1990, the UN Security Council agreed to establish the United Nations Transitional Authority in Cambodia (UNTAC) to provide executive authority in the interim period. Differences still remained, however, over the powers of UNTAC, the status of the incumbent Cambodian government, and demobilization and disarmament of the Cambodian factions. Eventually the breakthrough came in July 1991, when Vietnam, desperately in need of better international relations, deferred to Chinese priorities in Indochina and withdrew its patronage of the incumbent Cambodian regime. On October 21, the International Conference on Cambodia reconvened in Paris and two days later signed a comprehensive political settlement ending Vietnam's occupation of Cambodia.

For ASEAN, the negotiations of 1990 and 1991 highlighted the shortcomings of the association. Despite the diplomatic achievements ASEAN had accomplished throughout the 1980s, the political settlement relied upon changes in the USSR, the intervention of the Security Council, and China. In other words, Southeast Asian stability was achieved by extraregional powers. Ultimately, the Cambodian experience was a salutary lesson for ASEAN; not only did it pave the way for an improvement in relations between ASEAN and Vietnam, which resulted in the latter joining the association, but it also initiated a new approach toward extraregional powers, one that is incompatible with ZOPFAN.

The early post–Cold War era witnessed not only a reduced Soviet presence in the region but also a reduced U.S. military presence. The Philippine decision to close the Subic Bay naval base in 1992, when the Philippine senate rejected the Treaty of Friendship, Cooperation and Security with the United States, was a prime example of this. The reduced involvement of the superpowers would seem to be in keeping with the goal of ZOPFAN, but the post–Cold War period has been marked by a realization that ZOPFAN is neither realistic nor desirable.

In the aftermath of the closure of the U.S. naval base and Clark Airfield in the Philippines, the other ASEAN members increased their defense ties with the United States, thus revealing their perception that a U.S. military presence in Southeast Asia was desirable. Singapore was the first to initiate such moves, and despite criticism from Malaysia that it contradicted the spirit of ZOPFAN, Singapore signed a memorandum of understanding with the United States in November 1990, which provided for the deployment of U.S. aircraft and personnel. In 1992, Singapore agreed to the relocation of logistic facilities from Subic Bay, which consisted of two hundred personnel to resupply U.S. warships and coordinate their activities. Despite Malaysia's criticism of closer U.S. defense ties, it was revealed in 1992 that Malaysia and the United States had been cooperating on military matters since 1984, and that such cooperation included joint exercises across the three branches of the armed forces. These exercises were complemented in the early 1990s by making the maintenance facilities at Subang airport and the Lumut naval yard available to the United States. Even Indonesia, the strongest ASEAN proponent of minimizing external involvement in Southeast Asia, offered the superpower facilities for ship repair at Surabaya. The official ASEAN position was that by not offering military bases, these agreements were not incompatible with ZOPFAN. However, it is evident that ASEAN members' willingness to enter into such arrangements testified to ZOPFAN's obsolescence as a desirable framework for regional security.

It was also evident in the early post–Cold War period that not only was a U.S. military presence desirable, but it was unrealistic to assume that in a world of increasing economic interdependence—globalization—Southeast Asia could engage in such cooperation while also insulating the region's security affairs from external influence. It was increasingly evident—as witnessed in the solution of the Cambodian crisis coming from outside the region—that security matters in Southeast Asia were part of a wider East Asian security complex. If ASEAN was to provide security for its members, it needed to engage in this wider security complex and take a leading role in establishing its security agenda.

ASEAN has sought to engage extraregional powers by adopting a cooperative security approach in order to achieve a balance of power among the main East Asian actors, ostensibly the United States, Japan, and China and to a lesser extent, Russia and India. Cooperative security is the pursuit of security with adversaries as well as allies.[4] It is thus an inclusive approach that seeks dialogue among like-minded states and also those with different perspectives on regional security issues. It achieves a balance of power by enmeshing the great powers in norms of acceptable conduct that (1) reduce uncertainty about another's intentions, thus producing stability, and (2) constrain their actions and lessen the prospect of one of them achieving hegemony.[5]

This change in ASEAN's approach is the focus for the remainder of this chapter. As an introduction, it is worth noting the attitude of ASEAN members to the South East Asian Nuclear Weapons Free Zone (SEANWFZ). The SEANWFZ proposal was first considered in 1984, and since none of the ASEAN members possess nuclear weapons, its value is in restricting the deployment and passage of nuclear weapons by the great powers. SEANWFZ is thus a means of implementing ZOPFAN because it is designed to limit extraregional involvement in Southeast Asia. During the Cold War, SEANWFZ was resisted by the United States since it covered only the ASEAN members and not Vietnam, and therefore not the Soviet Union. Likewise, those ASEAN members that were cooperating with the United States militarily—Thailand and the Philippines, plus Singapore, which viewed a U.S. presence as desirable—were at best ambivalent toward SEANWFZ, hence it became moribund.

SEANWFZ, though, was revitalized in the benign environment of the early post–Cold War period; this reflected growing confidence among ASEAN members that the organization was emerging as the central actor in Southeast Asian affairs. Although the signing of the SEAN-WFZ treaty in 1995 was seen as implementing ZOPFAN, the interpretation of its provisions by ASEAN members indicates that the involvement of nuclear-capable states in the region is recognized not just as unavoidable but also as desirable. For example, when the aircraft carrier *USS John C. Stennis* visited Malaysia in 2000, there was concern that its passage had contravened SEANWFZ. However, the ASEAN secretariat in Jakarta stated that because none of the nuclear powers had signed the protocol, SEANWFZ did not bar passage of nuclear weapons through the region. SEANWFZ, for now, prohibits only the ASEAN states from possessing nuclear weapons.[6] That SEANWFZ is out of step with the direction security relations between ASEAN and extraregional powers are heading is captured in the treaty's lack of coverage in the literature.

Extraregional Powers in the Post–Cold War Era

During the 1990s, ASEAN replaced its official notion of insulating Southeast Asia from the great powers to one of actively engaging them. This reflected both an acceptance that globalization meant Southeast Asia could not be insulated from the world market—and indeed, that for trade purposes it was preferable not to be—plus a growing concern among some ASEAN members that China might represent a threat to their sovereignty. In February 1992, the standing committee of China's National People's Congress had approved a law on territorial waters and contiguous areas, which appeared to extend China's sovereign jurisdiction over the entire South China Sea. Since ASEAN was militarily incapable of halting China's jurisdictional expansion, and it still wanted good relations with Beijing for trade purposes, it has pursued a combination of engagement and containment since the end of the Cold War.

Engaging with China would help lessen the threat by tying Beijing into cooperative undertakings, and keeping the United States involved would help balance China should such undertakings fail to contain it. This position was formalized at the first post–Cold War ASEAN summit in January 1992 in Singapore. ASEAN leaders stated that the organization should "intensify its external dialogues in political and security matters using the ASEAN Post-Ministerial Conferences."[7] In May 1993, the chairman of the meeting between ASEAN senior officials and postministerial dialogue partners in Singapore stated: "The continuing presence of the United States, as well as stable relationships among the United States, Japan, and China and other states of the region would contribute to regional stability."[8] The following year in Bangkok, a multilateral security forum—the ASEAN Regional Forum (ARF)—was convened for the first time. In keeping with the cooperative security approach of inclusivity, the ARF's membership, which began with eighteen and currently stands at twenty-three, is drawn from the Asia-Pacific region and includes all the great powers.[9]

Two factors contributed to the formation of the ARF. The first was the development of proposals for security dialogue at the Asia-Pacific level, and the second was a changing attitude among ASEAN members themselves. The initial proposal for security dialogue came from Soviet President Mikhail Gorbachev at Vladivostock in 1987, when he called for a Pacific version of the Conference on Security and Cooperation in Europe (CSCE). In July 1990, this was followed by an Australian initiative to create a Conference on Security Cooperation in Asia (CSCA). These proposals were rejected by ASEAN on the basis that a security forum covering the whole Asia-Pacific region would lessen ASEAN's relevance and consequently its ability to influence the agenda. In 1993, at the Twenty-sixth AMM, Singapore's prime minister, Goh Chok Tong, stressed that ASEAN must not allow its future to be decided by external powers, and at the Fifth ASEAN Summit held at Bangkok in 1995, Malaysia's prime minister, Mahathir Mohamad, warned against ASEAN becoming a "pawn" in global politics and that it should insist upon a role in the management of regional affairs.[10] It was also feared that Western members might use a CSCE-type regime to raise the contentious matter of human rights. These statements thus confirm the longstanding desire of ASEAN members not to be marginalized in issues pertaining to Southeast Asia. Given that these proposals were rejected by ASEAN, it might seem odd that they contributed to the formation of the ARF. However, it is necessary to distinguish between the rejected proposals and the general notion of a consultative mechanism for security dialogue, which was better received.

The second factor was the recognition that ASEAN states required the involvement of extraregional powers. With the end of the Cold War, the Philippines wanted to "share the burden" of the U.S. military presence with its ASEAN members. In order to achieve this, the former foreign secretary of the Philippines, Raul Manglapus, proposed that ASEAN hold consultations to forge a "consensus within the region about what it [ASEAN] wants for its security."[11] Malaysia and Indonesia publicly refused the initiative since neither wanted to be seen as supporting a U.S. presence. However, Amitav Acharya notes that the proposal "helped desensitise ASEAN states to the idea of multilateral consultations on regional security issues."[12] Both Manila and Thailand convened semiofficial meetings in 1991 that discussed security matters, and in 1990, Indonesia started what have become a series of informal workshops to discuss the South China Sea dispute. The latter, in which

the Chinese participate, is of great importance given Indonesia's preference for minimizing extraregional involvement. The explanation for
Indonesia engaging with an external power it regarded as the region's
long-term threat lies in President Suharto's first visit to China in
November 1990. He observed that China's economic development was
not only impressive but could also sustain a regional assertiveness.
Michael Leifer writes that as a result of this visit "Indonesia lent its
influential support to private discussions within ASEAN to promote a
wider framework for security dialogue beyond the limited bounds of the
Association itself."[13] Increasingly, security matters involving extraregional powers were being discussed by ASEAN states. This change in
approach was reaffirmed in 1996 by S. Jayakumar, Singapore's foreign
minister: "For ASEAN, the issue now is not how to avoid entanglement
in big power conflict. It is how to maintain a stable balance of the major
powers at a time of immense fluidity."[14]

The process began at the July 1991 AMM, where Japan's foreign
minister, Taro Nakayama, proposed that the ASEAN Post-Ministerial
Conference (ASEAN-PMC) could be used for "political discussions
designed to improve the sense of security among us."[15] The use of the
PMC framework offered ASEAN the advantage of having a controlling
influence over the agenda, thus placing the organization at the center of
the process. The PMC has been held after the annual meetings of AMM
since 1978, and they are comprised of ASEAN foreign ministers and
their counterparts from states known as dialogue partners.[16] Before the
January 1992 meeting, the ASEAN-PMC meetings had been confined
to matters of economic cooperation; they would now include dialogue
on political and security issues. The key difference between the
ASEAN-PMC and the ARF was that the former had been a means of
ASEAN gaining economic cooperation from Western-aligned states
during the Cold War; therefore, it did not include China or Russia during this period. Unlike the ASEAN-PMC, the ARF, which has included
China and Russia from the outset was a multilateral forum designed to
develop predictable and constructive relationships in the Asia-Pacific
region. In the post–Cold War period, the distinction between the
ASEAN-PMC and the ARF is not clear since all ten members of the
ASEAN-PMC are also ARF members. At the ASEAN-PMC in July
1996, the Japanese foreign minister, Yukihiko Ikeda, noted the need to
distinguish between these forums, and despite the Thai foreign ministry's claim that the PMC discusses global issues and the ARF regional
ones, the distinction does not exist in practice.[17]

Although ASEAN has changed its official approach to security relations with extraregional powers, the desire to control the region's security affairs remains. Whereas ZOPFAN sought to do this by trying to insulate the region from the great powers, ASEAN seeks to be the driving force behind the ARF. The ARF's agenda and the processes used to achieve its goals—the consensus and consultation approach of the ASEAN Way—are set by ASEAN. This does not mean the great powers have no influence over the direction of the ARF, for indeed they do; rather ASEAN has sought to ensure it will not be sidelined during security discussions in East Asia. This ASEAN role, and China's influence, is exhibited in the 1995 Concept Paper.

The Concept Paper established the ARF agenda. It proposed that the ARF provide security and stability in East Asia through a three-stage process. The first stage is the promotion of confidence-building measures (CBMs), the second is the development of preventive diplomacy mechanisms, and the final stage is the development of conflict resolution mechanisms. The term *conflict resolution* was unacceptable to the Chinese and thus the final stage was restated as "elaboration of approaches to conflicts." This was not the only influence the Chinese exerted. In keeping with the ASEAN principles of consultation and consensus decisionmaking, the Concept Paper noted that "the ARF process shall move at a pace comfortable to all participants." Since China wants the process to move at a slower pace than do other members—Chinese officials often refer to "incremental" progress or development—it gives China de facto control over the discussion and implementation of each stage.[18]

The evolution from stage to stage is accomplished via a two-track process (track I and track II). Track I involves government officials and is concerned with stage one, the promotion of CBMs, although in 1997 the decision was taken to move toward the second stage on preventive diplomacy (PD).[19] Track I has subsequently been subdivided into two: the intersessional support group (ISG), which is concerned with security perceptions and defense policy papers, and intersessional meetings (ISM), which deal with cooperative activities such as peacekeeping, search and rescue coordination, and disaster relief. At the Ninth ARF Summit held in July 2002 in Brunei, an ISM was established on counterterrorism and transnational crime. According to Leifer, the difference in name between the ISG and ISM was to accommodate Chinese concerns that CBM discussions might give the impression of continuous institutionalized activity. The same reason is given for using the term *inter,* which implies it meets on an ad hoc basis.[20]

These groups are co-chaired, with one of the chairs drawn from the

ASEAN members. In the 1996–1997 year, China and the Philippines co-chaired the ISG, with the meeting in Beijing in March 1997 marking the first time China had hosted an official multilateral conference on security issues. The ISG was not very productive, and Rosemary Foot suggests that the reason lay with the Chinese participants who felt it was necessary to be deliberately intransigent on home soil in the presence of the People's Liberation Army (PLA) officials.[21] At the 1997–1998 ISG, CBMs were subdivided into those that could be implemented in the near term (basket one) and those that would require more discussion (basket two). This subdivision was endorsed at the Fifth ARF Summit in the Philippines in July 1998.

Track II involves discussions by academics and nongovernmental security specialists to explore possible activities at the current and subsequent stages of the ARF process. The track-II process takes place under the auspices of the Councils for Security Cooperation in the Asia-Pacific (CSCAP), and there are currently five working groups that report annually to CSCAP.[22] A good example of how work conducted in track II came to be adopted by the ARF is in the concept and principles of preventive diplomacy. The initial ideas were formulated in the CSCAP working group on confidence- and security-building measures (CSBM WG), which were then forwarded to the co-chairs (Malaysia/South Korea) of the 2000–2001 ISG on CBMs for their consideration. The ISG endorsed the principles as providing an overlap between the ARF's stage one (CBMs) and stage two (PD), and they were adopted at the Eighth ARF Summit in July 2001. The four measures that provide this overlap are: an enhanced role for the ARF chair;[23] an ARF register of experts/eminent persons; the publication of the *Annual Security Outlook*; and the publication of voluntary background briefings on regional security issues.[24] Other examples of CSCAP influence on government decisionmaking can be seen with the prototype defense white paper crafted by the CSBM WG being used by Mongolia and Vietnam and partially applied by China.[25]

Has the ARF proven to be a successful means by which ASEAN has managed the impact of extraregional powers in Southeast Asia? In Chapter 7, the South China Sea dispute will be examined; for the ASEAN members, engaging China in the ARF has been an important element in trying to resolve this dispute peacefully. In this chapter we find the answer by looking at what ASEAN members hoped to achieve through the ARF and how extraregional powers have reacted to it.

For the small to medium powers of ASEAN, taking the leading role and becoming the primary driver behind an East Asian security forum that includes the region's great powers is a demanding task. The hope has been that ASEAN can persuade the United States, Japan, and China to conduct their relations through norms and rules of diplomacy established in the ARF, rather than through arms races, alliances, and the pursuit of deterrence and containment. Yet at the same time, ASEAN has not wanted the great powers to set the ARF agenda and essentially create a concert of great powers that relegates ASEAN members to a second tier—in other words, making decisions that impact Southeast Asian affairs with the region's states having little influence over those decisions. Although the latter has not occurred, this is largely because the United States and Japan are disappointed with the progress the ARF has made, and therefore, at best, they have considered it a complement to their defense alliance. Rather than be in concert with China, they have pursued a combination of engagement and containment with Beijing—what Gerald Segal refers to as "constrainment"; engagement through the ARF, and containment by strengthening the U.S.-Japanese defense agreement in 1997 and supporting the status quo in the China-Taiwan affair.[26]

If the enthusiastic involvement of the United States in the ARF has not been gained—and given Washington's wariness of multilateralism this is hardly surprising—the involvement of China, a state equally suspicious of the benefits of multilateralism, has been a more positive outcome for the ARF. In 1997 Chen Jian, the Chinese assistant foreign minister, stated that China would support the ARF "as a new approach to regional security, an approach different from Cold War mentality, an approach which seeks to strengthen peace through dialogue and cooperation."[27] Beijing chose the ARF and relevant track-II meetings to voice its concern over the strengthening of the U.S.-Japan defense alliance, and thus Acharya notes, "China has come to acknowledge the usefulness of the ARF."[28] Indeed, perhaps the ARF's greatest success has been acceptance by Chinese officials that defense transparency is a laudable goal. The debate within China has moved away from whether it is in China's interest to be transparent, to how transparent it should be to generate confidence in others about its benign intentions. As Rosemary Foot states, it is "doubtful that such a debate would have taken place at all within Chinese official circles in the absence of the ARF."[29] By April 1997, China had become sufficiently comfortable with the multilateral security body to allow the South China Sea dispute to be formally placed on the ARF's agenda.

Despite the engagement of China, the general assessment of the ARF is that it has been a disappointment.[30] Commentators who doubt the usefulness of a multilateral solution to East Asia's security problems are, not surprisingly, disdainful of the ARF. Robyn Lim dismisses the ARF as a means of improving security because it is hamstrung by the consensual procedures of the ASEAN Way; she also claims it undermines security by enabling China "to isolate the United States." Lim instead prefers the bilateral system of alliances created by the latter to maintain a balance of power and resist a "China bent on hegemony."[31] Even commentators more sympathetic to the ASEAN Way have raised doubts it can be transposed into the wider Asia-Pacific region. Shaun Narine notes that the type of states in the ARF is different from those in ASEAN, and thus what worked for creating intramural harmony in ASEAN is not likely to be appropriate for the ARF. Narine writes that unlike "the ASEAN member states, the great powers will not cooperate or make difficult compromises out of a sense of mutual weakness."[32] In addition, even those who place a less malign interpretation on Chinese intentions nevertheless note that the ARF cannot prevent China from taking a particular action. Ralf Emmers concludes that "the ARF seems so far to have failed to operate as a structure of constraint on China's regional foreign policy, at least as indicated by its sustained irredentist claims in the South China Sea."[33] Why then has the ARF proved to be a disappointment?

The main reason lies with ASEAN's centrality and in particular the cautious, slow-moving, consensus approach of the ASEAN Way and its cardinal principle of noninterference. The latter increasingly will prove problematic for the ARF as it tries to move through its three stages. The reason it took the ARF from 1997 until 2001 to adopt the principles regarding preventive diplomacy was primarily Chinese concerns that PD would allow a third party to become involved or interfere in a dispute. Even the ARF's official documentation notes that the "definition of PD has proven to be controversial." Among the eight key principles of PD the emphasis is on consensus and consultation; it is a voluntary exercise, it is noncoercive, and does not entail the use of military force, and since it only applies to conflicts between and among states, it cannot be applied to internal conflicts.[34] In its eight years of existence, the ARF has therefore only taken a tentative step toward stage two, and according to Simon, "CSCAP members . . . believe that the level of trust necessary for the implementation of preventive diplomacy has not been attained within the ARF."[35]

The ARF is thus hamstrung and cannot intervene in many key security matters that arise. This was particularly noticeable during the violence that marked East Timor's secession from Indonesia. The ARF is also incapable of becoming involved in the Chinese-Taiwanese dispute because Beijing regards it as an internal Chinese matter. ASEAN's centrality has also resulted in the security concerns of Northeast Asia, in particular the Korean dispute, receiving less attention than those of Southeast Asia. Indeed, progress in resolving the Korean dispute involves the Four-Party talks, the KEDO project, and South Korea's "sunshine" policy, which are all independent of the ARF.[36]

The ARF's stuttering progress with regard to PD should not be a surprise. At stage one, progress in those CBMs that impinge on sensitive security matters has been disappointing. A key feature in any CBM is transparency, and while many in the ARF no longer regard it with suspicion, the degree of transparency that provides security is certainly questioned. Thus it is far from evident whether all ARF members consider that providing details of their weapon systems—where and why they were acquired and the size of their inventory—equates to increased security. An important CBM proposed in the 1995 Concept Paper was a regional version of the UN conventional arms register; however, little progress has been made, with China in particular balking at the prospect of providing such details to a multilateral body that includes the United States and Japan. Even the defense white papers that have been published have given few details. Vietnam's paper said virtually nothing about its air or naval power, mobile forces, or organization.[37]

This halting progress has led to frustration with the slow-moving approach of the ASEAN Way, especially from the ARF's Western members such as Australia, Canada, and the United States. While this approach is well suited to China, and arguably was necessary to ensure Chinese membership, the Western members want to see quicker progress through the stages and the adoption of concrete proposals. Given Beijing's reticence to be tied to legally binding treaties, its fear that other members will gang up on China in the ARF, and its preference for bilateral agreements, it is likely that Western ARF members will remain frustrated. Indeed ARF documentation continues to reaffirm it will develop at a pace comfortable to all participants—in other words, the pace dictated by Beijing.

The ARF's limited effectiveness has meant that ASEAN members have sought to complement this multilateral process through continuing their defense ties with extraregional powers. Keeping a Western and specifically U.S. military presence in the region is seen among the ASEAN members as necessary to balance China and to a lesser extent, Japan. Thus Malaysia and Singapore continue to conduct military exercises with the UK, Australia, and New Zealand in the Five Power

Defence Arrangements (FPDA). Likewise, Thailand continues to hold annual military exercises with the United States, known as "Cobra Gold." Since 1995, the U.S. Navy has participated in a series of bilateral annual military exercises—Cooperation Afloat Readiness and Training (CARAT)—with Brunei, Indonesia, Thailand, Malaysia, Singapore, and the Philippines. In 1995, Indonesia broke from its traditional stance of minimizing external state involvement in Southeast Asia by signing a defense agreement with Australia. Although not a defense treaty, the combined military exercise conducted at the Natuna Islands—an area that has been within Beijing's claimed jurisdiction—revealed that China's ambitions in the South China Sea are an Indonesian concern. Likewise, Chinese activity in the South China Sea prompted the Estrada administration in the Philippines to apply pressure on the Philippine senate to pass a visiting forces agreement (VFA) with the United States in 1999. The VFA has led to the resumption of major military exercises with the latter, including ones held in the South China Sea. The general disquiet over China's actions in the South China Sea has also led Singapore and Australia to reaffirm the importance of a U.S. presence in the region.[38] Completion of the Changi Naval Base in Singapore in 2001, which provides the U.S. Navy with the type of port facilities it has not had in the area since the closure of Subic Bay, was specifically designed to facilitate the movement of the U.S. Seventh Fleet in the region.[39]

ASEAN Plus Three (APT)

Although there is some trepidation in the military security field regarding China's intentions, and lingering suspicion of the benefit of increased Japanese involvement in Southeast Asia (given the region's experience with Japan in World War II), in the economic field relations are much more positive. In December 1997, at ASEAN's second informal summit held in Kuala Lumpur, the heads of government from Japan, China, and South Korea met with their ASEAN counterparts, and the ASEAN Plus Three (APT) process was born. A year later at Hanoi it was agreed that these meetings should become annual, and in 2000, finance ministers met in May and foreign ministers met after the annual July ASEAN ministerial meeting; these meetings have also become annual. At the Thirty-fifth AMM held at Bandar Seri Begawan in Brunei in July 2002, the foreign ministers of Japan, China, and South

Korea held their first three-way meeting and agreed this too would become an annual event alongside the APT talks.[40]

The APT represents a nascent interest in the notion of East Asian regionalism—that is, an East Asian solution to East Asian problems. It arose in 1997 because of the financial crisis. The speed with which that crisis spread from Southeast to Northeast Asia had dramatically revealed—with the closure of Japanese banks and the failure of the giant South Korean conglomerates—the interdependence of the region's economies.[41] The Asian powers' disappointment at the ineffectiveness of the global economic institutions led to the formation of ASEAN Plus Three (APT). Thai deputy prime minister, Supachai Panitchpakdi, now director-general of the World Trade Organization, stated: "We cannot rely on the World Bank, Asian Development Bank, or the International Monetary Fund but we must rely on regional cooperation."[42] There was certainly frustration over the perceived failure of the conditions (tighter monetary controls, structural reforms) the IMF attached to its loans, as well as the ineffectiveness of APEC and the WTO. Tied to this feeling that Western-dominated institutions had failed them was disappointment over apparent U.S. indifference to the Asian plight. The prevailing view was that U.S. response to the three previous world financial crises (the 1982 debt crisis, the European monetary crisis of 1992–1993, and the 1994 Mexican financial crisis) had been immediate and appropriate. In addressing these reasons, the APT also enables the ASEAN members and Japan to integrate the increasingly powerful Chinese economy into the regional environment.

The first major accomplishment of the APT was the Chiang Mai Initiative launched in May 2000, as discussed in Chapter 5. As noted there, the initiative sought to curtail currency speculators by several means, especially the bilateral swap arrangements.[43] In addition to financial cooperation, a Chinese proposal for a China-ASEAN free trade area was endorsed by both parties in November 2001, and agreed to a year later; it is set to be operational within a decade.[44] The Japanese expressed interest in a Japan-ASEAN comprehensive economic partnership (CEP) when they concluded a bilateral free trade agreement with Singapore in January 2002; the CEP was agreed on in November 2002.[45] In May 2002, Japan also stated a preference for an East Asia free-business zone, linking the APT members with Australia and New Zealand.[46] More fanciful ideas of a common currency, an East Asian union, or an Asian monetary fund have also been voiced.

In 2002, the APT extended its area of cooperation beyond the economic realm to include issues of security more readily associated with the ARF. In November 1999, the Philippines proposed moving beyond economic concerns by establishing an East Asian security forum,[47] and while it was not agreed to establish such a forum at that stage, at the APT gathering in July 2002 in Brunei, participants agreed to examine security matters. In 2003, the APT will convene in Bangkok to discuss transnational crime. Although a Malaysian proposal to establish an APT secretariat in Kuala Lumpur was considered premature, the view of Singapore's foreign minister, S. Jayakumar, that the APT is "here to stay" and the question now "is how to nurture it," confirms that the APT is emerging as a key forum for ASEAN to monitor the involvement of extraregional powers.[48]

The APT represents a marked change for ASEAN, which at the beginning of the 1990s had coolly received Malaysia's call for an East Asian Economic Grouping (EAEG). At that time ASEAN reconstituted the proposal as the East Asian Economic Caucus (EAEC) to operate within the APEC framework, as opposed to outside it as the EAEG proposal had sought. The APT thus represents an attempt by ASEAN to achieve economic security with other East Asian, as opposed to Asia-Pacific partners. Not surprisingly, it was Malaysia that proposed establishing an APT secretariat. It is also not surprising that the emergence of the APT has raised doubts about the continuing validity of APEC and, since it is partly an East Asian solution to Southeast Asian problems, of ASEAN itself.[49]

Since the APT process is itself at an early stage of development, and various challenges exist to its continuing development, it would be imprudent to claim it will lead to ASEAN's decline. Nevertheless, the encouragement ASEAN members have given this process indicates a belief that economic development and prosperity (economic security) lies in closer economic and financial ties with China, Japan, and South Korea. This clearly begs the question: what value does a subregional association have if the answers to Southeast Asia's problems lie in an East Asian forum? If the APT process begins to establish mechanisms or meetings that either do not include ASEAN members or appear to give the APT an institutional basis separate from ASEAN, this would raise further questions about ASEAN's role in this process and thus the association's continuing value. In this sense the 2002 three-way meeting that involved only Chinese, Japanese, and South Korean foreign ministers can be seen as a potential threat to ASEAN. Likewise, the Malaysian proposal for an APT secretariat could undermine ASEAN's own secretariat, and indeed, this is the reason that

Singapore, Thailand, and Indonesia remain opposed to the proposal. Although the Malaysians argue that the secretariat would help alleviate the burden on the ASEAN secretariat, the very argument that the APT needs its own institutional base because its "agenda will no doubt mount in the years ahead," envisions an active process separate from ASEAN.[50] At the Eighth ASEAN Summit held in Cambodia in November 2002, Malaysia attempted to reassure its fellow ASEAN members that the APT secretariat would not undermine ASEAN, by reclassifying it as a bureau and stating it would be "organically linked" to the ASEAN secretariat.[51] However, Malaysia's proposal remained unacceptable, and no mention of the APT secretariat/bureau appeared in the final press statement. The matter has not ended, though, with Malaysian Foreign Minister Hamid Albar stating, "If no decision is made, we will not stop there. We will continue with our efforts to explain our intention."[52]

It could be argued that as with the ARF, ASEAN will coordinate its members' goals so that in a forum with larger powers the combined voice of the smaller ASEAN members can be influential.[53] This will be dependent upon a strong ASEAN, which is currently not the case, as noted in Chapter 5. In addition, the final press statement from the Sixth ASEAN Plus Three Summit noted a "willingness to explore the phased evolution of the ASEAN + 3 summit into an East Asian summit." It also noted the efforts of the three partner states to achieve greater integration "through their own efforts."[54] Such statements do not indicate that ASEAN is likely to remain central to the process of East Asian regionalism.

Of course, whether the APT will eclipse ASEAN depends upon the APT overcoming a number of its own obstacles. Perhaps the greatest of these will center on the Sino-Japanese relationship, in particular, whether the rise in Chinese economic and military capacity will eclipse the Japanese, thus raising the prospect of Beijing challenging Tokyo for the role of regional hegemon. They are, in this sense, possible competitors. ASEAN members may also prefer not to deepen regional integration with China, with whom they compete in low-wage, labor-intensive industries. Finally, the United States might raise the objections it had toward EAEC and regard APT as undermining U.S. economic interests by eclipsing APEC. At present, though, the APT process is emerging as a key forum. In relations with extraregional powers, therefore, how the APT process evolves will be crucial in determining not only how ASEAN members direct the involvement of extraregional powers in the region but also the continuing salience of ASEAN itself.

Conclusion

This chapter has assessed how the ASEAN members have managed the impact of extraregional powers in Southeast Asia. Although ASEAN adopted the ZOPFAN declaration, this should not be seen as an attempt to neutralize the region, but instead, as creating the blueprint for managing extraregional powers: to ensure that ASEAN members are not peripheral to decisions taken by the great powers over Southeast Asia. ZOPFAN sought to achieve this by insulating the region from the maneuverings of the great powers, but because a number of ASEAN members maintained defense ties with Western powers, this did not depict the reality of the 1970s. ZOPFAN remains an ASEAN goal, but since the 1990s, insulating the region from external state involvement has been dropped.

The outcome of the Cambodian crisis during the 1980s pointed to the strengths and limitations of ASEAN. While ASEAN had been able to keep the issue of Vietnam's invasion on the international agenda throughout the 1980s, the solution came from events and actors outside of Southeast Asia. The changes in the USSR during the late 1980s deprived Hanoi of its main benefactor and caused Vietnam to replace confrontation with cooperation toward neighboring states; ultimately, the solution to the Cambodian crisis relied upon the intervention of the UN and the deployment of UNTAC. For ASEAN, it proved that minimizing the involvement of extraregional powers was not a successful way to take the leading role in determining the region's security outcomes.

Hence in the 1990s ASEAN engaged the extraregional powers (notably China, Japan, and the United States) through the establishment of a security forum (ARF) and an economic forum (APEC). ASEAN's aim has been to be the primary driver in setting the security agenda through a cooperative security approach, that is, seeking security through dialogue, an inclusivity of participants and subject matter, and a belief that security is achievable only in concert with others rather than through unilateral action. Essentially, the ARF's aspiration is that China, Japan, and the United States will conduct their relations through norms and rules of diplomacy established in the ARF, rather than through destabilizing arms races, alliance formations, and deterrence policies. In the long term, the goal is to create a security community arrived at as norm compliance breeds trust and socialization. The ARF has thus far, however, proved a disappointment. ASEAN's cautious approach, while welcomed by China, has left Western ARF members frustrated at the slow pace of the ARF's progress. Not until 2001 did the

ARF take the tentative step of implementing a mild form of preventive diplomacy (stage II), and given the obstacles faced in achieving this plus the limited nature of the CBMs agreed to (stage I), it would seem that movement toward conflict resolution (stage III) is unlikely to begin for some time.

The ARF will probably continue to operate since it is the only Asia-Pacific forum that discusses security issues. Indeed, it has enabled the ASEAN members to continue their military cooperation with the United States while also developing cooperative relations with China. Fears that the great powers might use the ARF as a concert of powers and marginalize the ASEAN members have also proven unsubstantiated. The ARF thus maintains the blueprint of managing extraregional powers and ensuring that ASEAN members are not peripheral to decisions that impact Southeast Asia. Unlike ZOPFAN, though, this is accomplished by engaging the extraregional powers.

Since 1997, a new grouping has materialized—the ASEAN Plus Three. For ASEAN, the APT has emerged as a key process in East Asian regionalism. However, while it continues the goal of engaging extraregional powers (in this case China, South Korea, and Japan), the cooperative approach adopted is considerably more intrusive than that of the ARF. This is captured in the Chiang Mai Initiative, which provides for the APT members to review and exchange information on each other's financial positions. The issue for ASEAN is whether the association can remain the primary driver in an economic forum that includes East Asia's largest economy and the one with the highest levels of growth. While the APT is still in an early stage of development, and the evolving Sino-Japanese relationship will be an important element in the APT's future, it does raise questions regarding ASEAN's continuing importance. Put quite simply, if Southeast Asian problems can be best resolved through an East Asian forum, then this suggests that East Asian and not Southeast Asian regionalism can provide the solutions to Southeast Asia's problems. If ASEAN is sidelined in the process, such a circumstance begs the question: what role/future does ASEAN have?

Outside the APT process, the interest in establishing free trade agreements (FTAs) with ASEAN, as epitomized by India's interest at the November 2002 summit, might suggest that ASEAN's future prospects are good; it is, so the argument goes, still courted by major powers. But is India courting ASEAN? When ASEAN was wooed in the economic miracle years of the 1990s, it was because the suitors wanted to learn the supposedly Asian way of doing business. The current interest in FTAs is simply recognizing the purchasing power of the

Southeast Asian market. Nevertheless, if an FTA is signed with ASEAN, this is a positive development for the association; however, if FTAs are arranged on bilateral bases or outside ASEAN, then the question of ASEAN being sidelined re-emerges.

Notes

1. Michael Leifer, *ASEAN and the Security of South-East Asia* (London: Routledge, 1990), p. 56.
2. Ibid., p. 57.
3. Adam Malik, "Southeast Asia: Towards an Asian Asia," *Far Eastern Economic Review*, 25 September 1971, p. 31; hereafter the *Far Eastern Economic Review* is referred to as *FEER*.
4. David Dewitt, "Common, Comprehensive and Cooperative Security," *The Pacific Review* 7/1 (1994), pp. 1–15.
5. Ralf Emmers, "The Influence of the Balance of Power Factor Within the ASEAN Regional Forum," *Contemporary Southeast Asia* 23/2 (August 2001), pp. 276–277.
6. "Making Waves," *FEER*, 2 March 2000, p. 8.
7. Jeannie Henderson, "Reassessing ASEAN," Adelphi Paper 328 (London: International Institute for Strategic Studies, 1999), p. 26.
8. Michael Leifer, "The ASEAN Regional Forum," Adelphi Paper 302 (London: International Institute for Strategic Studies, 1996), p. 20.
9. The current ARF membership includes the original members: Australia, Brunei, Canada, China, the European Union (presidency), Indonesia, Japan, Laos, Malaysia, New Zealand, Papua New Guinea, the Philippines, the Republic of Korea, Russia, Singapore, Thailand, United States, and Vietnam. Cambodia was admitted at the second ARF in 1995, India and Burma at the third in 1996, Mongolia at the fifth in 1998, and North Korea at the seventh in 2000. The third ARF agreed on the following criteria for future membership: commitment to key ARF goals and previous ARF decisions and statements; relevance to the peace and security of the ARF "geographical footprint" (Northeast and Southeast Asia and Oceania); gradual expansion; and consultation and consensus by all ARF members on all future membership decisions.
10. Leszek Buszynski, "ASEAN's New Challenges," *Pacific Affairs* 70/4 (Winter 1997–1998), p. 571.
11. Quoted in Amitav Acharya, "A New Regional Order in South-East Asia: ASEAN in the Post–Cold War Era," Adelphi Paper 279 (London: International Institute for Strategic Studies, 1993), p. 59.
12. Ibid.
13. Liefer, "The ASEAN Regional Forum," p. 8.
14. Emmers, "The Influence of the Balance of Power Factor Within the ASEAN Regional Forum," p. 280.
15. Acharya, "A New Regional Order in South-East Asia," p. 61. For details of why Japan proposed a multilateral dialogue on security matters, see Paul Midford, "Japan's Leadership Role in East Asian Security Multilateralism:

The Nakayama Proposal and the Logic of Reassurance," *The Pacific Review* 13/3 (2000), pp. 367–397.

16. In 1974, Australia became the first dialogue partner; by 1993, there were seven partners (Australia, Canada, the European Union, Japan, South Korea, New Zealand, and the United States); and by 1996, there were ten with the addition of India, China, and Russia.

17. Buszynski, "ASEAN's New Challenges," pp. 571–572.

18. At the 1996 meeting, China's foreign minister stated that the ARF would continue to play an important role provided it gives "full consideration to the region's diversity, [and] maintains its nature and rules of procedure and develops incrementally on the basis of shared interests and needs of its members in the spirit of consensus." Rosemary Foot, "China in the ASEAN Regional Forum: Organizational Processes and Domestic Modes of Thought," *Asian Survey* 38/5 (May 1998), p. 432.

19. Simon S. C. Tay with Obood Talib, "The ASEAN Regional Forum: Preparing for Preventive Diplomacy," *Contemporary Southeast Asia* 19/3 (December 1997), pp. 252–268.

20. See Leifer, "ASEAN Regional Forum," p. 42.

21. Foot, "China in the ASEAN Regional Forum," p. 437.

22. For details of the ARF track-II process, see Sheldon W. Simon, "Evaluating Track II Approaches to Security Diplomacy in the Asia-Pacific: The CSCAP Experience," *The Pacific Review* 15/2 (2002), pp. 167–200.

23. In the aftermath of the September 11, 2001 terrorist attacks, the chair of the ARF (Brunei) convened two workshops, "Financial Measures Against Terrorism" and "Prevention of Terrorism," and issued a statement on joint action to counter terrorism. For the statement see "2001 ASEAN Declaration on Joint Action to Counter Terrorism" at the Internet site: http://www.aseansec. org/3638.htm.

24. For details see the "Co-Chairmen's Summary Report of the Meeting of the ARF Intersessional Support Group (ISG) on Confidence Building Measures (CBMs), held in Seoul, Republic of Korea, 3 November 2000, and in Kuala Lumpur, Malaysia, 18–20 April 2001" at the Internet site: http://www.dfat. gov.au/arf/report_interses_00_01.html. Also see the "Chairman's Statement, The Eighth Meeting of the ASEAN Regional Forum, Hanoi, 25 July 2001" at the Internet site: http://www.dfat.gov.au/arf/arf8_chairman.html. The *Annual Security Outlook* is available at the Internet site: http://www.aseansec.org/ 12009.htm. For disappointing progress with the *Annual Security Outlook,* see "ARF Insecure About Security," *FEER,* 12 September 2002, p. 11.

25. Simon, "Evaluating Track II Approaches to Security Diplomacy in the Asia-Pacific," p. 188.

26. Gerald Segal, "East Asia and the 'Constrainment' of China," *International Security* 20/4 (Spring 1996), pp. 107–135.

27. Quoted in Amitav Acharya, *Constructing a Security Community in Southeast Asia: ASEAN and the Problem of Regional Order* (London: Routledge, 2001), p. 183.

28. Ibid., p. 184.

29. Foot, "China in the ASEAN Regional Forum," p. 430.

30. For a thoughtful account that measures the progress of the ARF, see John Garofano, "Power, Institutionalism, and the ASEAN Regional Forum: A

Security Community for Asia?" *Asian Survey* 42/3 (May/June 2002), pp. 502–521.

31. Robyn Lim, "The ASEAN Regional Forum: Building on Sand," *Contemporary Southeast Asia* 20/2 (August 1998), p. 117.

32. Shaun Narine, "ASEAN and the ARF: The Limits of the 'ASEAN Way,'" *Asian Survey* 37/10 (October 1997), p. 975.

33. Emmers, "The Influence of the Balance of Power Factor Within the ASEAN Regional Forum," p. 285.

34. Concept and Principles of Preventive Diplomacy, ASEAN Regional Forum Annex D, 2001. Internet site: http://www.dfat.gov.au/arf/arf8_ annexes.html.

35. Simon, "Evaluating Track II Approaches to Security Diplomacy in the Asia-Pacific," p. 190.

36. Kim Sung-Han, "The Role of the ARF and the Korean Peninsula," *Journal of East Asian Affairs* 12/2 (Summer/Fall 1998), pp. 506–528.

37. John Garofano, "Flexibility or Irrelevance: Ways Forward for the ARF," *Contemporary Southeast Asia* 21/1 (April 1999), p. 88.

38. Irene Ngoo, "S'pore-Aussie talks focus on security," *The Straits Times*, 23 February 1999.

39. Richard Borsuk, "Southeast Asia: Singapore, U.S. Welcome Dock Deal—Berthing Facility Is First for American Carriers in Southeast Asia Since 1992—Keeping a Key Factor in Regional Security," *The Asian Wall Street Journal*, 23 March 2001.

40. "Three-way meeting," *The Straits Times–interactive*, 31 July 2002.

41. In 1999 the Singaporean prime minister, Goh Chok Tong, said, "[Y]ou cannot talk about North-east Asia and South-east Asia. What happens in South-east Asia will have an impact on North-east Asia . . . So now we are thinking in terms of evolving an East Asian community." See Luz Baguioro, "ASEAN to push free-trade plan as part of recovery," *The Straits Times*, 29 November 1999.

42. Quoted in Maria Anna Rowena Luz G. Layador, "The Emerging ASEAN Plus Three Process: Another Building Block for Community Building in the Asia Pacific?" *Indonesian Quarterly* 28/4 (2000), p. 439.

43. "The Joint Ministerial Statement of the ASEAN+3 Finance Ministers Meeting," 10 May 2002. Internet site: http://www.aseansec.org/5473.htm.

44. Susan V. Lawrence, "Enough for Everyone," *FEER*, 13 June 2002, pp. 14–18. "Framework Agreement on Comprehensive Economic Co-operation Between the Association of South East Asian Nations and the People's Republic Of China"; Internet site: http://www.aseansec.org/13196.htm.

45. "Joint Declaration of the Leaders of ASEAN and Japan on the Comprehensive Economic Partnership," ASEAN-Japan Summit, 5 November 2002. For details see the Internet site: http://www.aseansec.org/13190.htm.

46. David Kruger, "The Thought of a China-ASEAN Free-Trade Area Galvanises Japan," *FEER*, 13 June 2002, pp. 16–18. In September 2002, ASEAN signed an economic partnership declaration with Australia and New Zealand and was also in talks over a free trade agreement with South Korea and India. See "Narendra Aggarwal, "ASEAN signs trade pact with NZ and Australia," *The Straits Times*, 15 September 2002; "S Korea mulls over FTA

with ASEAN," *The Straits Times*, 15 September 2002; Narendra Aggarwal, "India wants to join AFTA, task force set up," *The Straits Times*, 16 September 2002; Nirmal Ghosh, "India-ASEAN trade pact in the cards," *The Straits Times*, 3 October 2002; and Chua Lee Hoong, "India makes trade offer to ASEAN," *The Straits Times*, 6 November 2002.

47. Layador, "The Emerging ASEAN Plus Three Process," pp. 441–442.

48. Brendan Pereira, "ASEAN+Three takes on security," *The Straits Times–interactive*, 31 July 2002.

49. For details of the APT process and its relationship to APEC and ASEAN, and different opinions as to its likely success, see Douglas Webber, "Two Funerals and a Wedding? The Ups and Downs of Regionalism in East Asia and Asia-Pacific After the Asian crisis," *The Pacific Review* 14/3 (2001), pp. 339–372. See also Richard Stubbs, "ASEAN Plus Three: Emerging East Asian Regionalism?" *Asian Survey* 42/3 (May/June 2002), pp. 440–455.

50. "Malaysia pushes for ASEAN-plus-three secretariat," *Agence France Presse*, 6 October 2002.

51. "KL proposes ASEAN bureau with link to 3 N. Asian states," *The Straits Times*, 2 November 2002.

52. Roziana Hamsawi, "KL seeks to set up ASEAN+3 bureau," *New Straits Times (Malaysia)*, 4 November 2002.

53. Hadi Soesastro, "ASEAN in 2030: The Long View," in Simon S. C. Tay, Jesus P. Estanislao, and Hadi Soesastro (eds.), *Reinventing ASEAN* (Singapore: ISEAS, 2001), p. 307.

54. "Press statement by the Chairman of the 8th ASEAN Summit, the 6th ASEAN + 3 Summit and the ASEAN-China Summit. Internet site: http://www.aseansec.org/13188.htm.

7

Security Broadly Cast:
From the South China Sea
to the War on Terrorism

I t will be evident from the preceding chapters that the study of security has broadened to encompass a wide variety of issues and to address questions and assumptions regarding what or who is to be secured. In this chapter, the cases of the South China Sea dispute and the region's involvement in the war on terrorism concretely illustrate the broadening and deepening of security issues. The South China Sea case highlights the interaction of economic, environmental, and military issues with regard to both state and human security. The study of the war on terrorism focuses on the dangers it poses to state security, human security, and the viability of ASEAN.

The South China Sea Dispute

The South China Sea is a semienclosed body of water surrounded by nine states with conflicting claims to the sea's maritime zones and its many islands, islets, and reefs. There are two main island chains, the Paracel Islands and the Spratly Islands. The Paracels are claimed by both Vietnam and China, while there are conflicting claims to the Spratlys from both these states as well as the Philippines, Malaysia, Brunei, and Taiwan. The Chinese and the Vietnamese claim considerable areas of the South China Sea on historic grounds, while the Philippines justifies its smaller claim through geographical proximity. The Malaysian claim is based on a number of reefs falling within its continental shelf, while the claim from Brunei is based on its exclusive economic zone (EEZ), which became active with the ratification of the 1982 International Law of the Sea on November 16, 1994. In order to strengthen their claims, these states have engaged in a number of activities, which include publicizing maps showing their claims, allowing tourists and journalists to visit their islands, granting concessions to oil companies in their claimed areas, and building structures on the islands they claim. In addition, all participants, with the exception of Brunei, have sought to strengthen their claims by stationing troops on some of the reefs. The Philippines and China also have a dispute over Scarborough Shoal, which is northeast of the Spratlys, and Indonesia maintains a watching brief on Chinese claims to the area around the Natunas, a chain of three hundred islands and atolls southwest of the Spratlys.

The dispute is regarded as a potential flashpoint in Southeast Asia because not only does it encompass an amalgamation of security problems, but it could also impact such extraregional powers as Japan and the United States and thus spill over into a much wider conflict. In this case study, we are interested in the different types of security problems in the South China Sea, how they interact, and their potential for conflict.

In Chapter 4 I noted that both environmental and economic security issues could be regarded as secondary causes of conflict. Conflicts can arise where states seek to protect their resources, whether from other state actors or nongovernmental actors such as pirates, and where environmental conditions force people to migrate to other areas to sustain their livelihoods. In these cases the environmental and economic concerns manifest to the state as security problems in the military field. This has certainly been evident in the South China Sea, where these concerns join such traditional security issues as conflicting territorial claims.

One of the key environmental and economic security issues that has given rise to tensions in the South China Sea is resource scarcity. The resources in question are both nonrenewable (oil and gas) and renewable (fish). Economic development in Asia has increased demands for oil and gas in many Asian states. Despite substantial oil reserves, China became a net importer of oil in 1993, and although it has increased oil production from 138.3 million tonnes in 1990 to around 160 million tonnes in 2000, its oil consumption has risen at a rate of 4.9 percent annually since 1991. This has resulted in demand rising from 114.7 million tonnes in 1990 to around 230 million tonnes in 2000.[1] China has now become one of the world's ten largest oil importers.[2] Likewise, China's natural gas consumption has also risen, and this has led to considerable interest in the availability of hydrocarbons in the South China

Sea. In 1989, China's geology and mineral resources ministry estimated that the Spratlys area had some 130 billion barrels of oil as well as natural gas reserves; this figure, though, is almost certainly overly optimistic and independent sources put the figure much lower.[3] The estimates differ simply because there is a lack of data, although discrepancies also occur because governments make bold statements to attract international interest and investment, while oil companies talk down the figures to secure more commercially favorable contracts. Nevertheless, despite questions over the amount of oil and gas available, it appears quantities are sufficient for commercial exploitation, especially in the Vanguard Bank and to a lesser extent, the Reed Bank.

In addition to oil and gas deposits, the South China Sea has a considerable stock of renewable resources, of which fish are particularly important. The South China Sea provides protein for five hundred million people who live in the coastal areas, and it is estimated that fish is the main source of protein for one billion Asians.[4] Of the total Asian fish catch, the fisheries of Southeast Asia account for 23 percent. The South China Sea is thus of great importance to the welfare of the region's populations, and it is coming under increasing threat from human activity. The most direct problem is overfishing in the region, but just as important are the increase in soil erosion, sewage discharge, destruction of coral reefs, and the depletion of mangrove forests, sea grass, estuaries, and wetlands, which are all placing pressure on the region's ability to recover from overfishing.[5] This has two immediate security effects. First, overfishing represents a threat to the people's welfare and livelihoods (human security), since fishing is a source not only of protein but also employment. Second, the reduction in fish numbers is encouraging fishermen either to fish illegally in other states' maritime zones, or to fish in areas subject to competing claims. Illegal fishing has caused a number of clashes between the fleets of one state and the naval patrol vessels of another, which has led Alan Dupont to claim that "[f]ish [are] central to the Spratlys dispute."[6] The most recent and serious clashes have occurred between the Philippines and China, and these are detailed below.

In addition to resource issues, the South China Sea also holds another economic security problem: a potential disruption to transportation. It is estimated that more than 41,000 ships a year pass through the South China Sea, more than double the number through the Suez Canal, and nearly triple the total for the Panama Canal.[7] To the south, the Strait of Malacca connects the South China Sea to the Indian Ocean, while to the north the Taiwan Strait connects the South China Sea to the Pacific.

This makes freedom of movement along the sea lines of communication (SLOC) imperative to the economic survival and prosperity of a number of Asian states, including Japan. For Japan, unfettered access to the SLOC are vital for its oil imports from the Middle East and its exports of manufactured goods to Asia and Europe. The freedom of navigation thus becomes an important economic security issue for Japan. It is also an important military security issue for the United States, since the freedom of navigation principle implies that U.S. warships have "innocent passage"—they do not need to inform governments of countries bordering the ocean of their warships' passage through the sea. The South China Sea thus has important security implications for extraregional powers such as the United States and Japan.

Indeed, the issue of legal ownership of and rights to use the South China Sea—in essence, contention of sovereign rights—has made this one of Southeast Asia's potential areas of military conflict. Before examining the various incidents and the means claimants have used to resolve the crisis, it is necessary to reveal why and when claims were made over who owns what in the South China Sea.

Prior to World War II, there was very little interest in claiming sovereignty over the islands and reefs of either the Paracels or the Spratlys.[8] Indeed, the main concern was to warn shipping that these areas were dangerous and should be avoided. The claims in place included Britain's 1877 claim to Spratly Island and Amboyna Cay and a Chinese claim of 1909 to the Paracels; in the 1930s the French claimed the Spratlys and Paracels and, unlike the UK and China, even occupied the latter. However in 1939, when the Japanese established a military presence in the Spratlys, the French withdrew. Japan then built a submarine base on Itu Aba (the largest of the Spratly Islands) and used it in 1942 as one of the vantage points for the Japanese invasion of the Philippines. This invasion has been used more recently by Manila to claim the Spratlys have strategic importance for their security.[9] In the aftermath of World War II, the main claimants were the Chinese and the French, who established sovereignty markers, with the Philippines taking an active interest from 1956 by claiming a number of islands and calling the area Kalayaan (Freedomland).

The surge of claims for the islands only began in the 1970s with the concurrence of two factors. First, although British and U.S. oil companies had been interested in locating oil in the area since the 1950s, it was only in 1969, after a geological survey revealed oil in the South China Sea, that exploiting oil and claiming sovereignty by the local states became an issue.[10] Second, the Third United Nations Conference on the Law of the Sea (UNCLOS III), which met between 1973 and 1982, although its decisions did not come into effect until 1994, decided that every coastal state could claim a continental shelf (out to a maximum of 350 nautical miles if the shelf was naturally prolonged that far) and an exclusive economic zone of 200 nautical miles. The EEZ not only applied to exploiting resources in the sea (fish, for example) but the seabed as well. With oil to exploit and the possible extension of continental shelf claims, the states around the South China Sea began to position themselves to take advantage of this new legal regime. The Philippines were the first to stake a claim in 1971 by officially declaring the Kalayaan to be part of the country, and in 1974, Manila awarded a concession to a consortium of oil companies to explore the Reed Bank, where the Philippines occupied eight islets. In 1973, South Vietnam awarded a number of oil exploration contracts to U.S. companies. When in 1974 China attacked and drove out the South Vietnamese from the western Paracels (since then, China has been in sole control of the islands), Saigon used the evicted troops to occupy several islands in the Spratlys. With the reunification of Vietnam, Hanoi took command of these garrisons and has since steadily expanded its control. Vietnam occupies more reefs and islands than any other claimant. With Sabah and Sarawak joining Malaya to form the Malaysian Federation in 1963, this enabled Kuala Lumpur to claim areas of the South China Sea near Borneo. In 1979, it published a map showing an extensive continental shelf claim north of Borneo, and in 1983 and 1986, it sent troops to occupy islands on the shelf. By the mid-1980s, the Philippines, Malaysia, Vietnam, and Taiwan (which occupies Itu Aba) had occupied virtually all the features in the Spratlys that were above the sea at high tide, which is a legal requirement for a feature to be an island.

In the late 1980s, China became the last claimant to enter the scramble for features in the Spratlys. With Vietnam issuing oil concessions to areas that China claimed, it became imperative in Beijing that China have a presence there. The opportunity presented itself when Hanoi's ally, the Soviet Union, began, as part of Mikhail Gorbachev's reforms, to scale back its deployments in the area. In 1988, the Chinese began to occupy several reefs, including Fiery Cross Reef. Vietnamese forces were in the vicinity, and in March a naval exchange occurred near Johnson Reef. Although Chinese forces did not attempt to dislodge the Vietnamese from their garrisons, the naval clash sank three Vietnamese vessels and seventy-seven sailors lost their lives. Despite some recent minor skirmishes, the 1974 and 1988 incidents remain the only examples of force being used over rival claims in the Spratlys.[11]

China's assertive actions led in the 1990s to concern over its intentions in the South China Sea. The adoption by China in 1992 of the Law on the Territorial Waters and their Contiguous Areas, through which Beijing "essentially claimed suzerainty over the whole of the South China Sea," appeared to confirm that the claimant with the greatest military clout was embarking upon a revisionist policy in the South China Sea.[12] Then in 1995, the Philippines discovered that China had been building structures on one of its claims, the aptly named Mischief Reef; they appeared to be guard posts with satellite antennas and a helipad. Three Chinese naval vessels with five support boats were also observed. The Chinese claim that the structures were shelters for fishermen was widely regarded as duplicitous and only confirmed worst-case thinking about Chinese intentions. Coupled to the airbase China had constructed on Woody Island in the Paracels, the Mischief Reef structures appeared to be another stepping-stone toward Chinese military dominance in the South China Sea.[13]

It is immediately evident that the South China Sea is a potential region of conflict first and foremost because of competing territorial claims. It is also evident that the claimant causing the most concern is China. This is for two reasons. First, China's claim to the South China Sea is not entirely clear; at times China appears to consider the South China Sea as its own territorial waters[14]—in other words to treat it as Chinese land, with all the implications that would have for other claimants' EEZs, SLOC, and freedom of navigation. Second, China has by far the greatest military capability of all claimants and is strengthening its naval and air capabilities. In April 2000, the Chinese successfully carried out mid-flight refueling, an essential step to achieve power projection in the South China Sea.[15] While it is not yet capable of resolving the South China Sea dispute through military force—and given that Beijing wishes to cultivate economic ties in Southeast Asia, there are good reasons to believe it would not seek this outcome—in the future, China is the only claimant that could pursue this solution. How likely, though, is conflict in the South China Sea?

Although competing sovereignty claims lie at the heart of the conflict in the South China Sea, the economic and environmental issues noted above explain why tension occurs in the claimants' relations. For example, competing oil and fishing rights help explain the difficulties in the Sino-Vietnamese relationship.[16] The availability of oil in Vanguard Bank and the question of who has the right to award exploration concessions has led to Sino-Vietnamese rivalry in the South China Sea. In May 1992, the Chinese awarded a concession to the American Crestone

Energy Corporation, and in April 1994, the Vietnamese awarded a concession to the Mobil Corporation in waters west of the Crestone concession. In April 1996, Vietnam gave another concession to Conoco of the United States in an area that encompassed half the area the Chinese had awarded to Crestone. Both sides have denounced these actions as illegal. In July 1994, China deployed two warships to blockade a Vietnamese rig, preventing the delivery of food and water.[17] Controversy over sovereign ownership also has arisen in the Gulf of Tonkin where Vietnam has accused China of violating its territorial waters; in 1994, it seized two Chinese vessels, claiming that during this incident Chinese boats used weapons fire. In March 1997, another heated exchange took place between Hanoi and Beijing when the Vietnamese discovered the Chinese were conducting exploratory oil drilling fifty-five nautical miles from Vietnam's baseline.[18] Although relations have improved between the two claimants—in December 2000, they signed a treaty agreement demarcating territorial waters and EEZs in the Gulf of Tonkin—by 2002, it still had not been ratified because of differences over fishing rights.[19] Indeed, in July Vietnam seized nine Chinese boats and detained 179 crewmembers for illegal fishing; they also protested about a Chinese live-fire exercise conducted in their claimed EEZ in June.[20]

How fishing has exacerbated conflicting territorial claims in the South China Sea can also be seen in the Philippines' relationship with China. In this instance, the problems center not only in the Spratlys but also Scarborough Shoal; the latter in particular has witnessed numerous incidents of Philippine naval vessels seizing Chinese fishing boats and detaining their crew. In the first three months of 2001, the Philippine navy boarded 14 Chinese fishing boats off Scarborough Shoal,[21] and in May, 34 fishermen were arrested.[22] In the first two months of 2002, the Philippines detained over 100 Chinese fishermen,[23] and in September, a further 38, but pending the payment of a fine, Manila agreed to return 122 fishermen who had been arrested earlier that year.[24] In May 2000, when the Philippine coast guard intercepted Chinese fishing boats within Philippine territorial waters, a Chinese fisherman was killed.[25] However, deaths are rare; instead, these incidents should be seen as a hindrance to better Sino-Philippine relations. The squabble over returning the 122 fishermen in September 2002 is a case in point; after the Chinese ambassador had "exploded in rage" over the fine levied by Manila, the Philippines justice secretary, Hernando Perez, wanted him declared persona non grata.[26] Needless to say, it soon blew over.[27] Of course, while these incidents are a nuisance to state security, they are very serious for the human security of the fishermen. The issue of human security is discussed below.

In order to prevent the competing sovereignty claims from escalating into conflict, ASEAN members issued in 1992 a declaration on the South China Sea. In essence, it urges all claimants to resolve their competing sovereignty claims through peaceful measures, to refrain from the use of force, and to exercise restraint. It also called upon claimants to cooperate over issues of maritime pollution and combating piracy. Although adopted by the ASEAN members, China, preferring bilateral negotiations, did not subscribe. Indeed, attempts to restrain claimants' actions through declarations or codes of conduct have proved disappointing. Although the Mischief Reef incident in 1995 paved the way for a bilateral code of conduct between the Philippines and China, agreed on in 1995, this has not prevented a series of incidents. The code includes such provisions as no upgrading or expanding of facilities on disputed islands by either side, and each is to inform the other of all naval movements around the islands. Nevertheless, the Chinese continued construction at Mischief Reef in March and May 1996. In April 1997, tensions rose over the presence of Chinese warships near the reef, the establishment of structures on another one, and the Philippine navy's interception of two Chinese vessels near Scarborough Shoal. In late 1998, the Chinese were continuing construction on Mischief Reef, which was completed in early 1999. Despite Chinese claims they were repairing shelters for their fishermen, closer inspection revealed China had expanded the structure and appeared to be adapting the reef for military use. The Philippines claim the new concrete structures are garrisons with provisions for a helipad, gun embankments, and berths for ships.[28] Coupled to the fishing incidents noted earlier, it is not surprising that in 2002, China was still seen as an economic and security threat by the Philippines.[29]

The Chinese action at Mischief Reef did spur the Philippines, Vietnam, and Thailand in 1999 to argue for a code of conduct on the South China Sea to be discussed at the ASEAN Regional Forum. This was rejected by China, but under pressure from the United States, Beijing agreed to consider a draft at an ARF intersessional support group (ISG) on confidence-building measures. Although the South China Sea did appear in ARF reports, including the ISG in November 1999, there was no specific mention of China's actions.[30] In November 1999, the ASEAN members did agree to a draft regional code of conduct in the South China Sea; however, the Chinese rejected it. In March, April, May, August, and October 2000, discussions were held between

ASEAN members and China, but no agreement could be reached. In 2002, a new approach was begun to gain a nonbinding political declaration with China instead. This produced the Declaration on the Conduct of Parties in the South China Sea at the Eighth ASEAN Summit held in Cambodia on November 4, 2002.[31] Although the declaration has Chinese assent and does note that the parties resolve to settle the dispute without resorting to the use of force, it is not a code of conduct, and even though this remains the eventual goal, there is little cause for optimism that it will soon be realized since there are a number of points of difference between China and the ASEAN members (and indeed, among ASEAN members themselves).[32] China does not want the code to be binding; it wants it to apply to nonclaimant states, in other words Japan and the United States; and it wants the code to ban military exercises, which is clearly aimed at U.S. exercises conducted with ASEAN members, most notably the Philippines. Finally, China does not want the Paracels included in a code of conduct, a requirement unacceptable to Vietnam, which maintains its claim to the Paracels.[33]

Although lack of Chinese acquiescence is the main obstacle to implementing a code of conduct, the actions of ASEAN members, notably Malaysia, have also cast doubt as to its usefulness. In May 1999, Malaysia, disregarding ASEAN's 1992 declaration, occupied two more islands in the South China Sea (Investigator Shoal and Erica Reef), drawing protests from the Philippines, China, and Vietnam. However, it was widely suspected in Manila that Malaysian Foreign Minister Syed Albar's visit to Beijing at the time had been to obtain China's acquiescence.[34] Indeed, Malaysia's subsequent view that negotiations should be bilateral rather than multilateral clearly dovetails with China's opinion; in April 2002, Malaysia and China began working on a bilateral code of conduct for the South China Sea.[35] In another incident during October 1999, which breaks the 1992 ASEAN declaration as well as the 1995 bilateral code of conduct between the Philippines and Vietnam, Vietnamese troops on Tennet Reef shot at a Philippine armed forces aircraft that had flown over the reef at a low altitude. The Vietnamese claimed the aircraft had breached their sovereignty and their troops had fired warning shots. Neither side therefore had refrained from an action that would affect their friendship, as they were required to do by their own bilateral code. Such incidents imply that even if a code of conduct can be achieved among the claimants, its restraining effect is likely to be minimal.

Does this mean conflict is likely? Although there has been little headway in tying the claimants into binding norms of agreements through a code of conduct, both Leszek Buszynski and Liselotte Odgaard argue that balance-of-power considerations have had a restraining effect on China.[36] The response by some ASEAN members, especially the Philippines, to China's assertive behavior has been to strengthen the U.S. military's presence in the region. The various exercises the United States has been conducting were discussed in Chapter 6. It is sufficient to note here that the visiting forces agreement (VFA) with the Philippines is seen as strengthening the United States Mutual Defense Treaty commitment to defend the Philippines from attack, including attacks that occur in the South China Sea.[37] While it is certainly true that China has no wish for a U.S. military presence in the area, the reason why the prospect of conflict is low is because China is seeking better relations with the states of Southeast Asia for commercial reasons.[38] At the second informal summit hosted by ASEAN at Kuala Lumpur in December 1997, Chinese President Jiang Zemin reiterated China's position on East Asian cooperation. He highlighted the importance of prioritizing economic, trade, scientific, and technological cooperation while handling disputes and differences through friendly consultations. Echoing the ASEAN Way of managing rather than resolving problems, he noted that if differences could not be resolved, they should be temporarily shelved. The statement issued on December 16, 1997 on ASEAN-China Cooperation Towards the 21st Century declared that both sides "agreed not to allow existing differences to hamper the development of friendly relations and cooperation."[39] The development of the ASEAN Plus Three talks noted in Chapter 6 are therefore much more reflective of ASEAN-China relations than the differences over the South China Sea. Indeed, while balance-of-power considerations may have an impact on Chinese decisionmakers, they did not prevent the Chinese from deploying two warships to Scarborough Shoal in May 2001 and twelve warships to the Spratlys the following month.[40]

The implication for state security of the disputes in the South China Sea is not, at least for the present, particularly grave. Although negotiations on a code of conduct have stalled, and incidents of fishing vessels being seized and the crews detained will grab headlines and complicate relations, ultimately the claimants are seeking better relations with one another for economic gain. The disputes will not disappear since territorial and sovereign rights are at their core, but changing the current status quo is not a goal for any claimant. Although this is a positive conclusion for Southeast Asian state security, it would be erroneous to claim there are not serious security problems in the South China Sea. These problems relate to human security.

It was noted above how important the South China Sea is to the welfare and livelihoods of the millions of people living in Asia's coastal zone. A combination of overfishing and environmental damage to breeding and nursing grounds has seriously depleted traditional fishing grounds. The long-term consequences of this for human security are patent, and they are joined by the more immediate security threats to fishermen that arise from naval patrols defending contentious maritime zones. As Daojiong Zha comments, on "a daily basis, the South China Sea is a security threat first and foremost to the fishermen who rely on the ocean waters as a means of living."[41] Since the fishermen regard the South China Sea as historic fishing grounds used by generations of fishermen, the solution to the South China Sea's human security problem revolves around environmental protocols and cooperation. The answer lies less in formal negotiations to establish a code of conduct for the South China Sea, and more in the informal process of dialogue held under the auspices of the workshops on managing potential conflicts in the South China Sea.

These workshops have been held annually since 1990 and are the brainchild of Hasjim Djalal of the Indonesian Foreign Ministry and Canadian law professor, Ian Townsend-Gault. The workshops concentrate on scientific and technical aspects and have formed technical working groups (TWG), which in turn have a group of expert meetings (GEM) that examine, among other things, marine environmental protection. In addition to the ASEAN members, China and Taiwan also participate. In essence, these workshops have two goals, although the second is not explicitly stated, just implied.[42] First, by implementing cooperative undertakings between the parties involved, a regime can be established to manage, for example, fisheries regulation, environmental protection, and marine scientific research. Work on the first project of the entire workshop process—biodiversity—began in 1998.[43] Second, generating cooperation among claimant states over issues of common concern, such as the environment, may pave the way for cooperation on more politically sensitive issues. The latter goal then is to assist progress toward resolving territorial claims. In terms of human security, while the second goal is important, the first is of more immediate concern.

Unfortunately the workshops' achievements have been marginal. For example, the proposals of the biodiversity project, which brought marine environment–related issues to the attention of decisionmakers, have not been implemented because the parties cannot agree on procedures. Members such as China label the procedures as "too pushy,"[44] although it is more probable that China remains wary of, if not actually opposed to multilateral endeavors. It is difficult to disagree with Mark Valencia, who argues that the "process has yielded few concrete results"; the lack of funding means that "it is but a fragile house of cards ready to crumble if the foundation is shaken," and with members placing restrictions on what can and cannot be discussed, it is not surprising the workshops project has been referred to as a "talking shop."[45] As for human security there remain optimistic, even utopian ideas of turning the Spratlys into a marine park.[46] Ultimately, though, Tom Næss's conclusion is probably right. He writes that in "developing countries the growth of the economy and the welfare of the people are normally seen as more important than protecting the environment. This region is no exception." Of course, protecting the environment and the people's welfare are not mutually exclusive. Næss concludes that in addition, "[T]here has been concern that environmental cooperation could, in some way, infringe or impede actions to defend national security and sustain claims to sovereignty and maritime zones."[47] Thus, while state security in the South China Sea may be reasonably secure, the same cannot be said for human security, in both the long-term effects of environmental degradation and the immediate threat to the livelihoods of the region's fishermen.

The War on Terrorism: Southeast Asia as the "Second Front"

The terrorist attacks on the World Trade Center and the Pentagon in the United States on September 11, 2001 (9/11), have had a variety of security effects on the states and people of Southeast Asia. It has raised further questions about the viability of ASEAN, the preservation of territorial integrity for some of the regional states, and regime threats to their own people's human security. Although the atrocities of 9/11 were in themselves remote to the region (the attacks were conducted by al-Qaeda terrorists headquartered in Afghanistan), it has since emerged that links exist between al-Qaeda and a variety of indigenous Southeast Asian terrorist groups.[48] These links have been so prevalent that Southeast Asia has been referred to as the "second front" in the war on terrorism.[49] The description was even more salient after the terrorist attack in Bali on October 12, 2002, that killed over 180 people; it was the worst attack since 9/11. Before analyzing the security effects of the war on terrorism, it is necessary to note why Southeast Asia is regarded as the second front and to review what has happened since 9/11.

Southeast Asia has been regarded as important in the war on terrorism because it is home to a number of groups that resort to violence to further their cause and because Islam is the main religion in the region. This has led to an overly simplistic assumption that Southeast Asia is a hotbed of Islamic radicalism, where a number of al-Qaeda operatives can function in such weak states as Indonesia and the southern Philippine island of Mindanao. Indeed, the U.S. Federal Bureau of Investigation (FBI) even presumed that Malaysia had links to terrorism because two of the hijackers aboard the plane that hit the Pentagon had attended a meeting with a Jemaah Islamiah (JI) operative, Yazid Sufaat, in Kuala Lumpur two years before the attack.[50] The Bali bombing, coupled to the detention of fifteen terrorists in Singapore in December 2001 and another twenty-one in August 2002, does confirm, however, that terrorists with links to al-Qaeda are active in the region and continue to wage their global terrorist campaign.

Nevertheless, the assumption that the region is one of Islamic radicalism is erroneous. In the largest, predominantly Islamic states in the region—Indonesia and Malaysia—the Muslim population practices an essentially moderate and tolerant form of Islam. In Indonesia, the two main Islamic organizations, Muhammadiyah and Nahdlatul Ulama, advocate a division between religion and politics; their memberships account for one-fourth of the population. Both organizations have denounced extremism and violence by radical Islamic groups, with the Nahdlatul Ulama joining the Indonesian military in encouraging the government to enact antiterrorist legislation.[51] The leaders in both states are also moderates, with Malaysia's prime minister, Mahathir Mohamad, considered a prime example of a modern Muslim leader meshing traditional Islamic ideas with the requirements of a multiracial, globalized society. Indeed, Mahathir has used events since 9/11 to criticize the main opposition party—Parti Islam se-Malaysia (PAS)—for its fundamentalist Islamic stance. In August 2002, Mahathir likened PAS to Al-Arqam, and the National Front (BN) coalition government had earlier referred to them as the "Taliban of Malaysia."[52] In Indonesia, which has a secular regime, the Muslim president, Megawati Sukarnoputri, has been the target of two assassination attempts by Omar al-Faruq, a top al-Qaeda representative in Southeast Asia arrested in June 2002.[53] In other words, while extremists do exist, the vast majority of the region's Muslim population and the regimes in power practice a more moderate form of Islam.

However, Southeast Asia is also home to a variety of groups willing to resort to violence to further their cause. In previous chapters it was noted that a number of guerrilla organizations in Southeast Asia are seeking to gain independence/autonomy for their regions. In Indonesia, these include the Free Aceh Movement (GAM) and the Free Papua Movement (OPM). In the Philippines, the Moro Islamic Liberation Front (MILF) has sought independence/autonomy in Mindanao, and in Southern Thailand a variety of militant organizations have sought the same for the Patani Malay. While Islam, with the exception of the OPM, is an important element in their identities, it relates to their "demands for autonomy or secession, not as an end in and of itself."[54] These are not the militant groups that have emerged since 9/11 that threaten to wreak havoc on the region, although a caveat needs to be added regarding the MILF, where evidence of collusion with the JI has been found.[55]

In addition to these nationalist groups, other groups that are little more than criminal gangs have engaged in hostage taking, extortion, and murder. The best known is probably the Abu Sayyaf that operates in the southern islands of the Philippines. While there is some evidence of early links to al-Qaeda, Abu Sayyaf has no coherent political agenda and has not targeted the United States. In Indonesia, such criminal gangs include the Islamic Defenders Front (IDF, also known by its Bahasa Indonesia acronym, FPI) and Laskar Jihad, the latter being responsible for the upsurge of communal violence in the Moluccas in recent years. Although there is an ideological affinity between the leader of Laskar Jihad, Jafar Umar Thalib, and Osama bin Laden, Jafar has distanced himself from the al-Qaeda leader. Likewise, the IDF has received some financial support from al-Qaeda, but its actions are localized. As with the nationalist groups, these criminal gangs may initiate terrorist activities, but they are not the terrorists that have emerged as post–9/11 regional threats. Indeed, after the Bali terrorist attack Laskar Jihad announced it would disband and the FPI was publicly criticized.[56] As the Bali bomb revealed, however, some terrorists groups represent a regional threat, and we now turn to these.

The groups that have caused concern within the region are the Jemaah Islamiah (JI) and, closely linked to it, the Kumpulan Mujahideen Malaysia (KMM).[57] The JI was established in the mid-1970s, although recent reports refer to it being founded in the mid-1990s. It is led by Abu Bakar Bashir (also spelled Baasyir), an Indonesian cleric who runs a religious boarding school in Indonesia. Bashir, who returned to Indonesia after the fall of Suharto, denies involvement in terrorist activities, although he is a supporter of Osama bin Laden. According to confessions from Omar al-Faruq, Bashir "authorised al-Faruq" to bomb U.S. embassies, including the one in Malaysia,[58] and he has claimed that Bashir had a role in the Bali bombing.[59] The United States, Singapore, and Malaysia wanted Indonesia to arrest Bashir, but Jakarta claimed they did not have the evidence. However, he was detained after the Bali terrorist attack and has been put on trial for trying to overthrow the Indonesian government and establish a region-wide Islamic state.[60]

Between December 2001 and September 2002, Malaysian authorities detained sixty KMM members under the Internal Security Act (ISA) for trying to use force to topple the government and establish an Islamic state.[61] Of the twenty-one terrorists arrested in Singapore in August 2002, the eighteen detained under Singapore's ISA were members of the JI. Apparently they were directed by the JI's second in command, Nurjaman Riduan Isamuddin (also known as Hambali).[62] Hambali is suspected of masterminding the December 2000 attacks, in which twenty bombs exploded simultaneously in nine Indonesian cities; he is also thought to be behind the Bali bombing.[63] The foiled Singapore plan entailed JI members launching a series of attacks against water pipelines, the Singaporean Ministry of Defense, Changi International Airport, and facilities on Jurong Island. The aim was to stir up ethnic strife in Singapore, akin to the communal violence in Ambon, Indonesia. This in turn would lead to Malays from Malaysia intervening and thus initiate a war between Singapore and Malaysia.[64] Ultimately, part of the JI's political ambition was to establish an Islamic caliphate in Southeast Asia that would encompass Malaysia, Indonesia, Mindanao, and eventually Singapore and Brunei. This was the state of affairs at the time of writing, but what does it mean for the security of Southeast Asia?

The political ambition to establish an Islamic caliphate clearly represents a security threat to the states of Malaysia, Indonesia, the Philippines, Singapore, and Brunei. The JI hope to achieve this through an alliance known as the Rabitatul Mujahideen alliance, created in 1999 with the MILF and terrorist groups in southern Thailand. Hambali's plot to stir up ethnic strife in Singapore, however, reveals a degree of naïveté on the part of the JI. While Singapore's racial harmony is not as great as the People's Action Party (PAP) likes to claim, as evidenced by the ethnic mix of the JI Singaporeans, it is simply not comparable to the communal tension in the Moluccas.[65] Thus while David Jones and Mike Smith are right to question the degree of racial harmony claimed by the PAP, the heightened tension necessary to initiate the type of conflict, including interstate conflict, the JI sought simply does not in exist.[66] Likewise, as noted above, the vast majority of Muslims in Southeast Asia are moderates, and thus the Rabitatul Mujahideen alliance is unlikely to create the groundswell of support necessary to establish an

Islamic caliphate. The collapse of the Barisan Alternatif in Malaysia over PAS's goal of founding an Islamic state also indicates the lack of support for such a goal. If the threat posed by terrorism to state security is slight, however, the same cannot be said for its impact on economic security, ASEAN, or human security.

In the immediate aftermath of the Bali bombing on October 12, 2002, it was evident that concern for the safety of foreign holidaymakers and business people was not restricted to Indonesia. The magnitude of the attack tainted the entire region. Australia warned its citizens not to travel to Southeast Asia, and tourist operators in other Western countries reported cancellations for holidays in Thailand and the Philippines. More than thirty-seven million tourists visited Singapore, Malaysia, Thailand, Indonesia, and the Philippines in 2001. The five million that went to Indonesia generated between U.S.$5.4 billion and $5.7 billion, equivalent to 2–3 percent of GDP. The tourist industry is worth even more in Thailand.[67] The loss of tourist revenue, although felt most acutely in the short term, is likely to recover.[68] The larger economic impact will be the negative image terrorism has created for foreign investors. The region is already suffering from foreign direct investment (FDI) competition from China and suspicion that the region's structural deficiencies exposed in the 1997–1998 economic crisis have not been resolved. At best, the picture of further instability in Southeast Asia will merely confirm the need for foreign investors to adopt a wait-and-see attitude; at worst, they will look to other regions in the world. While it is too soon to know its full impact on the region's economic security, terrorism has clearly dealt a fragile recovery a blow. What, though, of ASEAN? Has the region's organization roused itself to meet the challenge posed by terrorism?

As noted in Chapter 5, ASEAN has faced a number of challenges since 1997, ranging from the economic/financial crisis to transnational problems such as pollution and drug trafficking. In the political/security field, ASEAN members rejected the opportunity presented by the Thai foreign minister, Surin Pitsuwan, to embrace flexible engagement, instead establishing the foreign ministers' retreat, procedures for the ASEAN High Council, and the troika in order to reassert the noninterference principle. To what extent, therefore, has the terrorist threat posed yet another challenge to ASEAN?

Within a year of 9/11, ASEAN had made four public declarations. In November 2001 at ASEAN's seventh summit in Brunei, a Declaration on Joint Action to Counter Terrorism was issued. In May 2002 in Kuala Lumpur, ASEAN adopted an action plan to combat transnational crime and terrorism, and in July at the Ninth ASEAN Regional Forum held in Brunei, a Statement on Measures Against Terrorist Financing was issued. Also at that forum an Intersessional Meeting on Counter-Terrorism and Transnational Crime (ISM on CT-TC), to be co-hosted by Malaysia and the United States, was established. Finally, in August 2002, an ASEAN-U.S. Joint Declaration for Cooperation to Combat International Terrorism was agreed. At the Eighth ASEAN Summit held in November that year in Cambodia, ASEAN announced a fifth declaration on terrorism.[69] Are these developments evidence of a revitalized ASEAN?

Although Barry Wain has written that ASEAN's response to terrorism indicates a "comeback" for the association, reasons for caution remain.[70] One such reason relates to how far ASEAN as a group is acting in concert. It was notable, for instance, that the 2001 November declaration failed to support the U.S. military action in Afghanistan; instead, ASEAN issued a statement that the terrorist attacks against the United States were "an attack against humanity and an assault on all of us."[71] The decision not to refer to the U.S. attack on Afghanistan was due to differences among the members over whether to condone or condemn the action. For instance, Mahathir not only opposed any resolution backing the United States, he also wanted ASEAN to go on record against the U.S. action in Afghanistan.[72]

This divergence in opinion is also evident in differences over the actions members have taken against terrorists. Although bilateral action has proved more successful than regional action, as noted below, terrorism has also revealed the primacy of domestic concerns above all else. For example, it was noted earlier that Abu Bakar Bashir, the JI leader, is wanted by Malaysia and Singapore in connection with JI activities in their countries. The Indonesians, prior to the Bali terrorist attack, had not detained him since they claimed there was no evidence to hold him.[73] However, when he was detained on October 19, 2002, after the attack, it was not in connection with this terrorist incident but the December 2000 bombings. This suggests that the Indonesian authorities' reluctance to crack down on Bashir and other militant Muslims was more likely for domestic political reasons than lack of evidence. Megawati requires the coalition support of Muslim parties, and before the Bali attack, it was thought her ability to rule would be seriously imperiled if she buckled under pressure from neighbors such as Singapore, or foreign powers such as the United States. Hence Andrew Tan's comment that "regional cooperation in countering terrorism has not been well coordinated and has continued to be ad hoc, due to constraints of conflicting national interests and mutual suspicions. Whilst Singapore, Malaysia and the Philippines are actively pushing for a regional mechanism to deal with the new terrorism, there is palpable resistance from Indonesia."[74] In the aftermath of the Bali attack, pressure on the Indonesian government to take decisive action mounted, and the initial signs were that the Megawati administration had begun a crackdown—not only was Bashir detained but on the same day, authorities proclaimed two antiterrorist executive presidential decrees. Yet circumspection is still required. With presidential elections to be held in 2004, the leadership appears reluctant to alienate the electorate by being too critical of extremist elements.[75] It is too soon to know what this will mean for Jakarta's relations with its neighbors and whether it is willing adopt a more cooperative and coordinated approach with them.

A further reason to be skeptical that terrorism will resuscitate ASEAN relates to the noninterference principle. It has enabled members to manage problems within their national boundaries, but when transnational problems arose, it has proven to be a hindrance, hence Surin's call for flexible engagement. Terrorism is yet another transnational problem, and solutions to such problems require active cooperation. In the case of terrorism this means, at the very least, exchanging information on suspected terrorists, coordinating surveillance of their actions, and establishing extradition agreements. At the regional level, ASEAN's response has been limited, hamstrung by the noninterference principle. For example, the May 2002 action plan, rather than initiating a regional response, essentially endorsed each member's right to take its own actions against terrorists—effectively sanctioning the use of the ISA by Malaysia and Singapore.[76] Despite claiming that what "has emerged from this meeting is . . . a realisation that there are a lot of things we can do together," the Malaysian deputy prime minister, Abdullah Ahmad Badawi, also indicated that noninterference very much remained the overriding principle. Referring to Singapore's frustration over Indonesia's reluctance to arrest alleged terrorists it wants to question, Abdullah reaffirmed it was a problem to be resolved by the two states themselves. He even affirmed that "we cannot have an extradition arrangement on a regional basis"; this is therefore presumably not an area in which ASEAN members realized they could act together.[77] Another area in which cooperation was missing concerned the definition of terrorism. Although a Malaysian proposal for an ASEAN definition of terrorism was discussed, ASEAN ministers failed to reach an agreement. Abdullah's assertion that the absence of a definition is not an obstacle to ASEAN cooperation should not obscure the fact that

ASEAN members' collective reaction to the threat posed by and the appropriate response to terrorism is highly equivocal.[78] Hence Jones and Smith's assertion that the "reality is that ASEAN cannot agree [upon] a collective position and individual member states will be left to their own devices to deal with the threat as they see it."[79] In other words, a similar "ASEAN" response to past security challenges, such as communism.

The continuing importance of noninterference can also be seen in the ASEAN-U.S. Joint Declaration for Cooperation to Combat International Terrorism. The declaration pledges greater cooperation on exchanging information and intelligence, but at the insistence of Vietnam and Indonesia, it also reaffirms the noninterference principle. Although the United States had initially rejected including the statement, "Recognizing the principles of sovereign equality, territorial integrity and non-intervention in the domestic affairs of other states," it relented when it became clear that Hanoi and Jakarta were concerned the declaration would allow U.S. force deployments.[80] It does not therefore contain such provisions. Where U.S. deployments have occurred, they have been on a bilateral basis, such as the Balikatan military exercise with the Philippines and the Cobra Gold exercise with Thailand, both of which focused on counterterrorism operations in 2002.

Indeed, the regional states' cooperative response to terrorism has occurred below the level of ASEAN. The best example of a multilateral response is the Agreement on Information Exchange and Establishment of Communication Procedures signed by Indonesia, Malaysia, and the Philippines on May 7, 2002. Cambodia acceded to it on July 30, Thailand in November, and Brunei was expected to join by the end of 2003. The existence of such a multilateral arrangement outside ASEAN is an indication that the association is unable to achieve a coordinated response among its entire membership. In addition to this agreement, a number of bilateral agreements have had some success. For example, in January 2002 Malaysia sent renegade Moro National Liberation Front leader, Nur Misuari, back to Manila, while Indonesia sent police specialists to the Philippines to assist in the investigation of Fathur Rohman Al-Ghozi, an Indonesian with links to JI.[81] In April he was sentenced to twelve years in jail for illegal possession of explosives; evidence used to convict him came from Singapore.[82]

Thus it appears that since 9/11, Southeast Asian elites are undertaking some cooperative action to counter terrorism, but at the regional level there remain too many differences in their approaches to make ASEAN an effective tool in the war on terrorism. The fact that after the

Bali attack ASEAN was still calling for stronger cooperation against terrorism and a greater commitment to regionalism reveals the limited action taken between 9/11 and October 12.[83] Simon Sheldon rightly notes that for all of ASEAN's declarations and action plans, there is no "operational coordination to seek out and hunt down terrorists operating cross-nationally, revealing once again ASEAN's limitations as a security mechanism."[84] The war on terrorism thus confirms our previous findings that ASEAN is struggling to remain a useful tool for its members.

The final implication of the war on terrorism for security in Southeast Asia concerns human security.[85] In the South China Sea case, the challenge to human security related to the welfare and livelihoods of the fishermen specifically and, in the long term, the five hundred million Asians who rely on the South China Sea for their food security. In the case of the war on terrorism, human security involves political matters, in particular, civil liberties and human rights. In Chapter 1 I noted that this aspect of human security correlates with the critical security studies' emphasis on emancipation from political oppression. In this final section, therefore, it is the implementation of antiterrorist laws and their implication for civil liberties and human rights that concerns human security. This is not to suggest that terrorists themselves do not represent a threat to human security; they obviously do. Rather, human security can best be secured through the rule of law and not through draconian measures that could be used indiscriminately to deny people their basic rights and civil liberties.

In the introduction it was argued that while nation building in the European experience was a violent one, circumstances have changed, and the European model is not applicable to the third world. Instead, enabling the population to fully participate in the state's political processes—that is, making them citizens of the state—would enable the regime to achieve legitimacy. Such participation can be accomplished only in a democratic environment where people's civil liberties and human rights are respected and protected. Hence Mohammed Ayoob's assertion:

> In the climate of these changed domestic and international attitudes, the move toward democratization is no longer merely a laudable goal for states in the Third World; it has become a political precondition for establishing legitimate state structures and regimes that enjoy the acquiescence, if not the enthusiastic support, of their populations.[86]

However, the pursuit of nation building has often come at the expense of civil liberties, and the process has been achieved at the expense of human security. The 9/11 terrorist attacks have further entrenched this approach.

The impact of 9/11 on human security can be seen with the adoption of new antiterrorist measures, which can be divided into two categories. The first relates to the increase in U.S. military assistance to Southeast Asia's armed forces, in particular to the Philippines and Indonesia, whose armed forces have routinely engaged in extrajudicial killings, torture, forced disappearances, and arbitrary arrest and detention. The Philippines not only received U.S.$100 million in military aid from the United States in November 2001, but U.S. troops have also been deployed in the Philippines to assist Manila in its fight against the Abu Sayyaf. In Indonesia, Washington pledged $50 million to help combat terrorism in August 2002. Although full military ties were not resumed because of the military's human rights record, U.S. Secretary of State Colin Powell noted that while "we are not there yet," the pledge was designed to start "down a path to a normal relationship with respect to military-to-military ties."[87]

The second category of the new antiterrorist measures that is a cause of concern relates to administrative detention. In Malaysia, Singapore, and Burma, the ability to hold suspects without trial was already possible before 9/11. In these states the Internal Security Act enables the ruling elite to bypass the due process of law. There is no trial, those detained are presumed guilty, and they can be held for an indefinite period. Since 9/11, both Malaysia and Singapore, as noted above, have resorted to the ISA. In the latter, prior to September 11, there were moves to abolish it, but this possibility has now been lost. There are worries the ISA will be used to silence government critics. In Malaysia, members of PAS have been detained under the ISA for suspected terrorist activities. Of the 113 ISA detainees at the Kamunting Detention Center, six are reformasi activists who are regarded as prisoners of conscience by Amnesty International.[88] During 2002, antiterrorism bills that are in effect ISAs were being prepared in the Philippines and Indonesia. In the former, there are grave concerns that rights to freedom of speech and freedom of assembly provided in the 1987 constitution will be undermined. In the latter, having repealed the antisubversion law used for decades by Suharto to muzzle critics, concerns were voiced that such a bill would be reintroduced albeit in a different form.[89] The immediate effect of the Bali bombing was to enable Indonesian authorities to pass two presidential decrees that allow for arrest of terrorist suspects without a police warrant and detention without trial. The decrees also provide wide evidentiary powers for investigating authorities by suspending existing legislation against phone tapping, intercepting mail, and other forms of communication intervention. These will remain in place until the antiterrorist bill has been approved by the Indonesian parliament.   .

In Southeast Asia mechanisms for protecting human rights are largely absent, public accountability and constitutional checks and balances are either nonexistent or in their infancy, and there is a history of national security laws being misused. Safeguarding human security was already perilous there, and the situation has been exacerbated since 9/11.

In conclusion, the value of broadening and deepening the study of security can be seen in these two case studies. In both, by looking at the impact of state policies on people, it was possible to show how their security was endangered. The South China Sea case concerns access to fishing grounds in the short term and environmental degradation in the long term—or freedom from want, in the terminology of human security. The war on terrorism has highlighted the other freedom that human security emphasizes—the freedom from fear or oppression. In this instance such fear is exacerbated as state elites adopt and implement counterterrorism measures to silence government critics. The war on terrorism, it is feared, might be used as a cover for a war on the freedom of expression, a freedom already constrained before 9/11.

In the introduction I noted that William Tow and Russell Trood have sought reconciliation between the thinking on human security and traditional security thinking. The former can best be viewed as seeking security through emancipation, while the latter conceives of security emanating from stability and order. Can such contrasting positions be reconciled? The violence and suffering that has marked much of the nation building in Southeast Asia would indicate that reconciliation is greatly needed. The continuing ethnic tensions in the region and the elites' preoccupation with regime security also indicate that their nation-building approach has failed. It was suggested in the introduction that reconciliation lay in ensuring the people formed the security policies of the state, which would occur when the elite were accountable to their populations (democratic governance) and respected their human rights. In essence, problems can be resolved within the regime's political framework, rather than by securitizing the problem in order to solve it through extraordinary measures. Events since 9/11 have not helped to bridge the gap between these differing conceptions of security.

In this regard the problems facing the floundering Association of

South East Asian Nations should provide a salutary lesson. The transnational character of these problems require ASEAN members to coordinate their actions and adopt the more engaged and constructive approach suggested by Surin Pitsuwan in 1998. Yet despite official statements, the members, rather than seeing their security inextricably tied to one another and pooling their sovereignty, have reinforced the noninterference principle that keeps sovereignty firmly in the hands of national elites. There is little indication, with the notable exception of its Vision 2020, that ASEAN elites believe their security would be enhanced by expanding the remit of those who may talk the language of security, whether it be neighboring elites or domestic groups representing their own people.

Notes

1. Figures from Clive Schofield, "Sea of Plenty? The 'Oil Factor' in the South China Sea and Prospects for Joint Development," paper presented at the Panel on the South China Sea, Third International Conference of the European Association of Southeast Asian Studies, London, 6–8 September 2001.

2. Stein Tønnesson, "China and the South China Sea: A Peace Proposal," *Security Dialogue*, 31/3 (September 2000), p. 313.

3. By way of comparison, Iraq, which has the world's second largest oil reserve after Saudi Arabia, is estimated to have 112 billion barrels. See Mamdouh G. Salameh, "China, Oil and the Risk of Regional Conflict," *Survival* 37/4 (Winter 1995–1996), p. 134. Also see Mark J. Valencia, Jon M. Van Dyke, and Noel A. Ludwig, *Sharing Resources of the South China Sea* (The Hague: Kluwer Law International, 1997), pp. 9–11.

4. For details of fishery resources, see Kuan-Hsiung Wang, "Bridge over Troubled Waters: Fisheries Cooperation as a Resolution to the South China Sea Conflicts," *The Pacific Review* 14/4 (2001), pp. 534–536. For figures see Karin Dokken, "Environment, Security and Regionalism in the Asia-Pacific: Is Environmental Security a Useful Concept?" *The Pacific Review* 14/4 (2001), p. 516.

5. Coral reefs, mangrove forests, sea grass, estuaries, and wetlands are all important breeding and nursing grounds for marine life. See Tom Næss, "Environmental Cooperation Around the South China Sea: The Experience of the South China Sea Workshops and the United Nations Environment Programme's Strategic Action Programme," *The Pacific Review* 14/4 (2001), pp. 556–558.

6. Alan Dupont, "The Environment and Security in Pacific Asia," Adelphi Paper 319 (London: International Institute for Strategic Studies, 1998), p. 53.

7. Richard Halloran, "Now an Effort to Stop the Rot in U.S.-Japan Relations," *International Herald Tribune*, 3 May 1999.

8. For details of the claims, see Greg Austin, *China's Ocean Frontier:*

International Law, Military Force and National Development (St. Leonards, Australia: Allen & Unwin, 1998). Also see Stein Tønnesson, "An International History of the Dispute in the South China Sea," EAI Working Paper No. 71 (Singapore: East Asian Institute, 2001).

9. Mark J. Valencia, "China and the South China Sea Disputes," Adelphi Paper 298 (London: International Institute for Strategic Studies, 1995), p. 8.

10. Tønnesson, "An International History of the Dispute in the South China Sea," p. 15.

11. However, the Chinese did send nine navy vessels to Mischief Reef in 1995; they arrested Philippine fishermen and left troops to guard the reef. Whether this could be described as a use of force is questionable—Gerald Segal argues "China clearly did 'use force' to eject the Philippine fisherman"— but it was clearly not equivalent to that used against Vietnam in 1988. See Gerald Segal, "East Asia and the 'Constrainment' of China," *International Security* 20/4 (Spring 1996), p. 121n34.

12. Ang Cheng Guan, "The South China Sea Dispute Revisited," *Australian Journal of International Affairs* 54/2 (2000), p. 205.

13. Rigoberto Tiglao, Andrew Sherry, Nate Thayer, and Michael Vatikiotis, "Tis the Season," *Far Eastern Economic Review*, 24 December 1998, pp. 18–20; hereafter the *Far Eastern Economic Review* is referred to as *FEER*.

14. Tønnesson, "China and the South China Sea: A Peace Proposal," p. 312.

15. "China refuels, mid-flight," *FEER*, 11 May 2000.

16. For details of why oil is not so important as is often thought, see Daojiong Zha, "Security in the South China Sea," *Alternatives* 26/1 (January–March 2001), p. 40.

17. Although there was some initial confusion over whether the Chinese had blockaded the rig, the evidence now suggests the incident did occur. See Esmond D. Smith, Jr. "China's Aspirations in the Spratly Islands," *Contemporary Southeast Asia* 16/3 (December 1994), p. 275.

18. See Michael Vatikiotis, Murray Hiebert, Nigel Holloway, and Matt Forney, "Drawn to the Fray," *FEER*, 3 April 1997, pp. 14–16.

19. "Vietnam, China reach no agreement in border talks," *Agence France Presse*, 28 February 2002.

20. "Vietnam detains 179 Chinese fishermen for illegal fishing," *Agence France Presse*, 22 July 2002; "Vietnam protests Chinese firing exercises," *Agence France Presse*, 11 June 2002.

21. "Philippines send gunboat to keep China from shoal," *Agence France Presse*, 28 March 2001.

22. "China Wants 34 Fishermen Freed," *Manila Standard*, 2 June 2001.

23. "Philippine troops board Chinese fishing vessels off Luzon island," *Agence France Presse*, 11 February 2002.

24. "122 Chinese poachers to be freed in Philippines, as 38 more arrested," *Agence France Presse*, 13 September 2002.

25. "Chinese fisherman killed in shoot-out with Philippine coast guard," *Agence France Presse*, 27 May 2000.

26. Luz Baguioro, "Filipino minister wants furious China envoy out," *The Straits Times*, 21 September 2002.

27. "Filipino minister, Chinese envoy make up," *The Straits Times*, 26 September 2002.

28. For more details see Ian James Storey, "Creeping Assertiveness: China, the Philippines and the South China Sea," *Contemporary Southeast Asia* 21/1 (April 1999), pp. 95–118.

29. In July 2002, former President Fidel Ramos said that "China poses both a security and economic challenge" to the Philippines. His views echoed those of the vice-president and former foreign minister, Teofisto Guingona. See "South China Sea is crucial test of China's relations: Philippines," *Agence France Presse*, 3 July 2002.

30. Leszek Buszynski, "Realism, Institutionalism, and Philippine Security," *Asian Survey* 42/3 (May/June 2002), p. 495.

31. "Declaration on the Conduct of Parties in the South China Sea." Internet site: http://www.aseansec.org/13165.htm.

32. Barry Wain, "Taking Charge," *FEER*, 14 November 2002, p. 26.

33. For a clear account of the problems of achieving a code of conduct, see Mark J. Valencia, "Building Confidence and Security in the South China Sea: The Way Forward," in Andrew T. H. Tan and J. D. Kenneth Boutin (eds.), *Non-Traditional Security Issues in Southeast Asia* (Singapore: Institute of Defence and Strategic Studies, 2001), pp. 527–535.

34. Buszynski, "Realism, Institutionalism, and Philippine Security," p. 493.

35. "Malaysia and China Agree on Code of Conduct in South China Sea," *BERNAMA (Malaysian National News Agency)*, 24 April 2002.

36. Buszynski, "Realism, Institutionalism, and Philippine Security," pp. 483–501. Liselotte Odgaard, "Deterrence and Co-operation in the South China Sea," *Contemporary Southeast Asia* 23/2 (August 2001), pp. 292–306.

37. Buszynski, "Realism, Institutionalism, and Philippine Security," p. 498.

38. Sheng Lijun, "FTA with ASEAN a safety cushion for China," *The Straits Times*, 8 November 2002.

39. Lee Lai To, *China and the South China Sea Dialogues* (Westport, CT: Praeger, 1999), pp. 50–52.

40. Bill Gertz, "Chinese navy deploys warships to disputed Spratly island chain," *The Washington Times*, 25 June 2001.

41. Daojiong Zha, "Localizing the South China Sea Problem: The Case of China's Hainan," *The Pacific Review* 14/4 (2001), p. 577.

42. At the outset the organizers stated the workshops were aimed at "encouraging confidence building measures between the states of the South China Sea region, thus easing tensions arising from sovereignty and jurisdictional disputes over the Spratly and Paracel island groups." Næss, "Environmental Cooperation Around the South China Sea," p. 560.

43. Ian Townsend-Gault, "Preventive Diplomacy and Pro-Activity in the South China Sea," *Contemporary Southeast Asia* 20/2 (August 1998), p. 186.

44. Næss, "Environmental Cooperation Around the South China Sea," p. 565.

45. Valencia, "Building Confidence and Security in the South China Sea," pp. 536–537. The talking shop comment is from Lee Lai To, "The South China Sea: China and Multilateral Dialogues," *Security Dialogue* 30/2 (June 1999), p. 167.

46. See Edgardo D. Gomez, "Marine Scientific Research in the South China Sea and Environmental Security," *Ocean Development & International Law* 32/2 (April–June 2001), p. 210. Also see Tønnesson, "China and the South China Sea," p. 322.

47. Næss, "Environmental Cooperation Around the South China Sea," p. 570.

48. Questions concerning the type of links and their significance are controversial. See Rohan Gunaratna, *Inside Al Qaeda: Global Network of Terror* (London: Hurst & Company, 2002). Also see Shefali Rekhi, "The walking-talking dictionary on terrorism," *The Straits Times*, 28 October 2002.

49. For reference to the second front, see John Aglionby, "Powell shores up south-east Asia support," *The Guardian*, 30 July 2002; and Giles Tremiett et al., "Al-Qaida units in world's lawless zones," *The Guardian*, 4 September 2002. The U.S. State Department has also named the Philippines, Indonesia, and Malaysia as "potential Al Qaeda hubs." See Barry Desker and Kumar Ramakrishna, "Forging an Indirect Strategy in Southeast Asia," *The Washington Quarterly* 25/2 (Spring 2002), p. 162.

50. Brendan Pereira, "KL protests against label," *The Straits Times*, 20 September 2002.

51. Devi Asmarani, "TNI, Islamic body back terror law," *The Straits Times*, 28 September 2002.

52. Al-Arqam was outlawed on August 26, 1994. For details of the movement, see Michael Vatikiotis, "Radical Chic," *FEER*, 26 May 1994, pp. 33–36. For Mahathir's comments, see Brendan Pereira, "Mahathir likens PAS to Al-Arqam," *The Straits Times*, 23 August 2002. For "Taliban of Malaysia," see "I'm only co-ordinator for Umno, says Muhammad," *New Straits Times (Malaysia)*, 29 December 2001.

53. For details of Omar al-Faruq's terrorist activities, including the assassination attempts, see "Confessions of an Al-Qaeda Terrorist," *Time*, 23 September 2002, pp. 34–40.

54. John Gershman, "Is Southeast Asia the Second Front?" *Foreign Affairs* 81/4 (July/August 2002), p. 67.

55. "Web of Terror: Jemaah Islamiah forged links with Regional Groups," *The Straits Times*, 20 September 2002.

56. Robert Go, "Laskar Jihad disbands in face of blast outrage," *The Straits Times*, 16 October 2002.

57. Malaysian authorities refer to it as the "second wing" of the Jemaah Islamiah. Barry Wain, "Moving Target," *FEER*, 26 September 2002, p. 19.

58. Brendan Pereira and Robert Go, "Al-Qaeda operative planned to bomb US embassies," *The Straits Times*, 17 September 2002.

59. Alfred Lee, "Osama 'gave Bashir money for Bali bombs,'" *The Straits Times*, 21 October 2002.

60. John Aglionby, "Indonesia puts emir on trial for bombings." *The Guardian*, 24 April 2003.

61. Reme Ahmad, "Key militant leader linked to JI terror group nabbed," *The Straits Times*, 28 September 2002.

62. For a brief background on Hambali, see Brendan Pereira, "From selling kebabs to dispensing martyrdom," *The Straits Times*, 28 October 2002.

63. Jason Burke, "The secret mastermind behind the Bali horror," *The Observer*, 20 October 2002.

64. Lydia Lim, "Govt reveals plot to spark religious violence here," *The Straits Times*, 20 September 2002.

65. The JI Singaporeans consisted of seven Malays, three each of Indian, Javanese, and Boyanese descent, and one each of Arab and Pakistani descent. For details of the JI members, see "The Face of Terror," *The Straits Times*, 20 September 2002.

66. See David Martin Jones and Mike Lawrence Smith, "Southeast Asia and the War Against Terrorism: The Rise of Islamism and the Challenge to the Surveillance State," in Uwe Johannen, Alan Smith, and James Gomez (eds.), *September 11 & Political Freedom: Asian Perspectives* (Singapore: Select Publishing, 2003), pp. 154–157.

67. Brendan Pereira, "Fair or not, red flag is up for entire region," *The Straits Times*, 21 October 2002.

68. Devi Asmarani, "Devastated tourism industry tries to rise from ashes," *The Straits Times*, 21 October 2002.

69. "Declaration on Terrorism by the 8th ASEAN Summit." Internet site: http://www.aseansec.org/13154.htm.

70. Barry Wain, "Still Relevant," *FEER*, 15 August 2002, p. 22.

71. The declaration is printed in full in Bantarto Bandoro, "Global Coalition Against Terrorism: Security Perspective and ASEAN's Role," *The Indonesian Quarterly* 30/1 (2002), pp. 53–54.

72. Sheldon W. Simon, "Mixed Reactions in Southeast Asia to the US War on Terrorism," *Comparative Connections—A Quarterly E-Journal on East Asian Bilateral Relations* 3/4 (2001), p. 51.

73. Barry Wain and John McBeth, "A Perilous Choice for the Presidents," *FEER*, 3 October 2002, pp. 16–20.

74. Andrew Tan, "The 'New' Terrorism: How Southeast Asia Can Counter It," in Uwe Johannen, Alan Smith, and James Gomez (eds.), *September 11 & Political Freedom: Asian Perspectives* (Singapore: Select, 2003), p. 107.

75. Barry Desker, "After Bali, will Indonesia act?" *The Straits Times*, 31 October 2002. Also see John McBeth, "In Search of Justice," *FEER*, 31 October 2002, pp. 20–22.

76. For details of what was agreed in May 2002, see "Main points of ASEAN security ministers' joint communique," *Agence France Presse*, 21 May 2002. Also see Reme Ahmad, "ASEAN adopts plan to fight terrorism," *The Straits Times*, 22 May 2002.

77. "ASEAN adopts anti-terrorism plan but leaves much to each member," *Deutsche Presse-Agentur*, 21 May 2002.

78. Eileen Ng, "ASEAN endorses preventive laws despite split on terrorism definition," *Agence France Presse*, 21 May 2002.

79. Jones and Smith, "Southeast Asia and the War Against Terrorism," p. 159.

80. "ASEAN, US Sign Joint Anti-terror Declaration," *People's Daily Online*, 1 August 2002.

81. Sheldon W. Simon, "Southeast Asia and the U.S. War on Terrorism," *NBR Analysis* 13/4 (July 2002), p. 36.

82. "Two JI leaders 'funded' explosives buy," *The Straits Times*, 20 September 2002.

83. "ASEAN Secretary-General Calls for Stronger Cooperation Against Terrorism," *BERNAMA (Malaysian National News Agency)*, 15 October 2002.

84. Sheldon, "Southeast Asia and the U.S. War on Terrorism," p. 27.

85. For an early account, see Hadi Soesastro, "Southeast Asia and Global Terrorism: Implications on State Security and Human Security," *The Indonesian Quarterly* 30/1 (2002), pp. 31–37.

86. Mohammed Ayoob, *The Third World Security Predicament: State Making, Regional Conflict, and the International System* (Boulder: Lynne Rienner, 1995), p. 179.

87. Derwin Pereira, "US funds for Indonesia's fight against terror," *The Straits Times*, 3 August 2002.

88. Sinapan Samydorai, "9/11 Anti-Terrorist Measures and Their Impact on Human Rights in Asia," in Uwe Johannen, Alan Smith, and James Gomez (eds.), *September 11 & Political Freedom: Asian Perspectives* (Singapore: Select, 2003), p. 236.

89. Devi Asmarani, "Muslims oppose Jakarta anti-terror bill," *The Straits Times*, 11 May 2002; "Substitute Terrorism Bill Raises Fears of Abuse," *Manila Standard*, 26 May 2002.

Acronyms and Abbreviations

ABIM	Malaysian Youth Movement
ABRI	Armed Forces of the Republic of Indonesia
ADNSC	Anti-Military Dictatorship Solidarity Committee, Burma
AEC	ASEAN Economic Community
AFPFL	Anti-Fascist People's Freedom League, Burma
AFTA	ASEAN Free Trade Area
AIA	ASEAN Investment Area
AMM	ASEAN Ministerial Meeting
ANIE	Asian newly industrialized economy
APA	ASEAN People's Assembly
APEC	Asia-Pacific Economic Cooperation
APT	ASEAN Plus Three
ARF	ASEAN Regional Forum
ASA	Association of South-East Asia
ASEAN	Association of Southeast Asian Nations
ASP	ASEAN Surveillance Process
BA	Barisan Alternatif
BN	Barisan Nasional (National Front), Malaysia
CARAT	Cooperation Afloat Readiness and Training
CBM	Confidence-building measure
CCP	Chinese Communist Party
CEP	Comprehensive Economic Partnership
CGDK	Coalition Government of Democratic Kampuchea
CIQ	Customs, immigration, and quarantine
CMLV	Cambodia, Myanmar, Laos, and Vietnam
CNRM	National Council of Maubere Resistance, East Timor

CPM	Communist Party of Malaya
CPT	Communist Party of Thailand
CRISP	Centre for Remote Imaging, Sensing and Processing
CSBM	Confidence and security-building measure
CSCA	Conference on Security Cooperation in Asia
CSCAP	Councils for Security Cooperation in the Asia-Pacific
CSCE	Conference on Security and Cooperation in Europe
CSCT	Classical Security Complex Theory
CSS	Critical security studies
DAB	Democratic Alliance of Burma
DAP	Democratic Action Party, Malaysia
DOM	Military Operations Area, Indonesia
EAEC	East Asian Economic Caucus
EAEG	East Asian Economic Grouping
EAGA	East ASEAN Growth Area
EEZ	Exclusive economic zone
EPG	ASEAN eminent persons group
FDI	Foreign direct investment
FPDA	Five Power Defence Arrangements
FRETILIN	Revolutionary Front for an Independent East Timor
GAM	Free Aceh Movement, Indonesia
GATT	General Agreement on Tariffs and Trade
GEM	Group of expert meetings
HPA	Hanoi Plan of Action, ASEAN
IAI	Initiative for ASEAN Integration
ICJ	International Court of Justice, The Hague
ICK	International Conference on Kampuchea
IDF	Islamic Defenders Front, Indonesia
IMF	International Monetary Fund
IMT-GT	Indonesia-Malaysia-Thailand growth triangle
INTERFET	International Force for East Timor
ISA	Internal Security Act
ISG	Intersessional support group
ISM	Intersessional meetings
JI	Jemaah Islamiah
KEDO	Korean Peninsula Energy Development Organization
KKN	Korupsi (corruption); Kolusi (collusion); Nepotisme (nepotism)
KMM	Kumpulan Mujahideen Malaysia
KNDO	Karen National Defense Organization, Burma
KNLA	Karen National Liberation Army, Burma

KNPP	Karenni National Progressive Party, Burma
KNU	Karen National Union, Burma
MAPHILINDO	Malaya, the Philippines, and Indonesia
MCA	Malaysian Chinese Association
MIC	Malaysian Indian Congress
MILF	Moro Islamic Liberation Front
MPR	People's Consultative Assembly, Indonesia
NAFTA	North American Free Trade Agreement
NCCC	National Counter Corruption Commission
NCGUB	National Coalition Government of the Union of Burma
NDF	National Democratic Front, Burma
NEP	New Economic Policy, Malaysia
NGO	Nongovernmental organization
NLD	National League for Democracy, Burma
NMP	Nominated member of parliament, Singapore
NMSP	New Mon State Party, Burma
OPM	Free Papua Movement
PAP	People's Action Party, Singapore
PAS	Parti Islam Se-Malaysia
PD	Preventive diplomacy
PDI	Indonesian Democratic Party
PKI	Indonesian Communist Party
PLA	People's Libration Army
PMC	ASEAN Post-Ministerial Conference
PNO	Pa-O National Organization, Burma
POLRI	Indonesian National Police
PPP	United Democratic Party, Indonesia
PRC	People's Republic of China
PRK	People's Republic of Kampuchea
PSLP	Palaung State Liberation Party, Burma
PTA	Preferential trading arrangement
PUB	Public utilities board, Singapore
RIA	Roadmap for Integration of ASEAN
SAF	Singapore Armed Forces
SEANWFZ	South East Asian Nuclear Weapons Free Zone
SEATO	South-East Asian Treaty Organization
SIJORI	Singapore-Johor-Riau growth triangle
SLOC	Sea lines of communication
SLORC	State Law and Order Restoration Council, Burma
SPDC	State Peace and Development Council, Burma

SPSI	All-Indonesian Workers Union
SSA	Shan State Army, Burma
SSPP	Shan State Progress Party, Burma
TAC	Treaty of Amity and Cooperation in Southeast Asia
TNI	Indonesian National Forces
TWG	Technical working groups
UDT	Timorese Democratic Party
UMNO	United Malays National Organization
UNAMET	UN Mission in East Timor
UNCLOS	UN Conference on the Law of the Sea
UNDP	UN Development Program
UNTAC	UN Transitional Authority in Cambodia
UNTAET	UN Transitional Administration in East Timor
UNTEA	UN Temporary Executive Authority
UPM	Unregulated population movement
UWSA	United Wa State Army, Burma
VFA	Visiting forces agreement
WTO	World Trade Organization
ZOPFAN	Zone of Peace, Freedom and Neutrality

Bibliography

This is a selection of the books and articles consulted. In addition to these sources the following were also used: the *Far Eastern Economic Review*; various newspapers including *The Straits Times*, *Agence France Presse*, and *The Guardian*; and the ASEAN website.

Abad, M. C., Jr., "The Challenge of Balancing State Security with Human Security," *Indonesian Quarterly* 28/4 (2000), pp. 403–410.

Abdullah, Kamarulnizam, "National Security and Malay Unity: The Issue of Radical Religious Elements in Malaysia," *Contemporary Southeast Asia* 21/2 (August 1999), pp. 261–282.

Acharya, Amitav, "Regional Military-security Cooperation in the Third World: A Conceptual Analysis of the Relevance and Limitations of ASEAN (Association of Southeast Asian Nations), *Journal of Peace Research* 29/1 (February 1992), pp. 7–21.

———, "A New Regional Order in South-East Asia: ASEAN in the Post–Cold War Era," Adelphi Paper 279 (London: International Institute for Strategic Studies, 1993).

———, "An Arms Race in Post–Cold War Southeast Asia? Prospects for Control," Pacific Strategic Paper 8 (Singapore: Institute of Southeast Asian Studies, 1994).

———, "The Periphery as the Core: The Third World and Security Studies," in Keith Krause and Michael C. Williams (eds.), *Critical Security Studies: Concepts and Cases* (London: University College of London Press, 1997), pp. 299–327.

———, "Ideas, Identity, and Institution-building: From the 'ASEAN Way' to the 'Asian-Pacific Way'?" *The Pacific Review* 10/3 (1997), pp. 319–346.

———, "Southeast Asia's Democratic Moment," *Asian Survey*, 39/3 (May/June 1999), pp. 418–432.

———, *The Quest for Identity: International Relations of Southeast Asia* (Singapore: Oxford University Press, 2000).

————, *Constructing a Security Community in Southeast Asia: ASEAN and the Problem of Regional Order* (London: Routledge, 2001).

————, "Human Security: East Versus West?" IDSS Working Paper 17 (Singapore: Institute of Defence and Strategic Studies, September 2001).

————, "Democratization and the Prospects for Participatory Regionalism in Southeast Asia," *Third World Quarterly* 24/2 (April 2003), pp. 375–390.

Alagappa, Muthiah, "The Dynamics of International Security in Southeast Asia: Change and Continuity," *Australian Journal of International Affairs* 45/1 (May 1991), pp. 1–37.

————, "The Anatomy of Legitimacy," in Muthiah Alagappa (ed.), *Political Legitimacy in Southeast Asia: The Quest for Moral Authority* (Stanford: Stanford University Press, 1995), pp. 11–30.

————, "Contestation and Crisis," in Muthiah Alagappa (ed.), *Political Legitimacy in Southeast Asia: The Quest for Moral Authority* (Stanford: Stanford University Press, 1995), pp. 54–65.

————, "International Politics in Asia: The Historical Context," in Muthiah Alagappa (ed.), *Asian Security Practice: Material and Ideational Influences* (Stanford: Stanford University Press, 1998), pp. 65–111.

Alatas, Ali, "ASEAN in a Globalizing World," *Asia-Pacific Review* 8/2 (2001), pp. 1–9.

————, "'ASEAN Plus Three' Equals Peace Plus Prosperity," *Trends in Southeast Asia*, No. 2 (Singapore: Institute of Southeast Asian Studies, 2001).

Anderson, Benedict, *Imagined Communities,* 2nd ed. (London: Verso, 1991).

Anwar, Dewi Fortuna, "Indonesia: Domestic Priorities Define National Security," in Muthiah Alagappa (ed.), *Asian Security Practice: Material and Ideational Influences* (Stanford: Stanford University Press, 1998), pp. 477–512.

Ariff, Mohamed, "Trade, Investment, and Interdependence," in Simon S. C. Tay, Jesus P. Estanislao, and Hadi Soesastro (eds.), *Reinventing ASEAN* (Singapore: Institute of Southeast Asian Studies, 2001), pp. 45–66.

Askandar, Kamarulzaman, "ASEAN and Conflict Management: The Formative Years of 1967–1976," *Pacifica Review* 6/2 (1994), pp. 57–69.

Austin, Greg, *China's Ocean Frontier: International Law, Military Force and National Development* (St. Leonards, Australia: Allen & Unwin, 1998).

Ayoob, Mohammed, *The Third World Security Predicament: State Making, Regional Conflict, and the International System* (Boulder: Lynne Rienner, 1995).

Baldwin, David, "The Concept of Security," *Review of International Studies* 23/1 (January 1997), pp. 5–26.

Ball, Desmond, "Arms and Affluence: Military Acquisitions in the Asia-Pacific Region," *International Security* 18/3 (Winter 1993/94), pp. 78–112.

Bandoro, Bantarto, "Global Coalition Against Terrorism: Security Perspective and ASEAN's Role," *The Indonesian Quarterly* 30/1 (2002), pp. 44–55.

Barnett, Jon and Stephen Dovers, "Environmental Security, Sustainability and Policy," *Pacifica Review* 13/2 (June 2001), pp. 157–169.

Beeson, Mark, "Southeast Asia and the Politics of Vulnerability," *Third World Quarterly* 23/3 (2002), pp. 549–564.

Bellamy, Alex J. and Matt McDonald, "The Utility of Human Security: Which Humans? What Security? A Reply to Thomas & Tow," *Security Dialogue* 33/3 (September 2002), pp. 373–377.

Beschorner, Natasha, "Water and Instability in the Middle East," Adelphi Paper 273 (London: International Institute for Strategic Studies, 1992).

Booth, Ken, "Security and Emancipation," *Review of International Studies* 17/4 (October 1991), pp. 313–327.

———, "War, Security and Strategy: Towards a Doctrine for Stable Peace," in Ken Booth (ed.), *New Thinking About Strategy and International Security* (London: HarperCollins Academic, 1991), pp. 335–376.

Brown, David, *The State and Ethnic Politics in South-East Asia* (London: Routledge, 1994).

———, *Contemporary Nationalism: Civic, Ethnocultural & Multicultural Politics* (London: Routledge, 2000).

Burke, Anthony, "Caught Between National and Human Security: Knowledge and Power in Post-crisis Asia," *Pacifica Review* 13/3 (October 2001), pp. 215–239.

Busse, Nikolas, "Constructivism and Southeast Asian Security," *The Pacific Review* 12/1 (1999), pp. 39–60.

Buszynski, Leszek, "ASEAN's New Challenges," *Pacific Affairs* 70/4 (Winter 1997–1998), pp. 555–577.

———, "Realism, Institutionalism, and Philippine Security," *Asian Survey* 42/3 (May/June 2002), pp. 483–501.

Buzan, Barry, "The Southeast Asian Security Complex," *Contemporary Southeast Asia* 10/1 (June 1988), pp. 1–16.

———, *People, States and Fear: An Agenda for International Security Studies in the Post–Cold War Era,* 2nd ed. (Boulder: Lynne Rienner and London: Harvester Wheatsheaf, 1991).

———, "Third World Regional Security in Structural and Historical Perspective," in Brian L. Job (ed.), *The Insecurity Dilemma: National Security of Third World States* (Boulder: Lynne Rienner, 1992), pp. 167–189.

———, "Societal Security, State Security and Internationalisation," in Ole Wæver, Barry Buzan, Morten Kelstrup, and Pierre Lemaitre, *Identity, Migration and the New Security Agenda in Europe* (London: Pinter, 1993), pp. 41–58.

Buzan, Barry, Morten Kelstrup, Pierre Lemaitre, Elzbieta Tromer, and Ole Wæver, *The European Security Order Recast* (London: Pinter, 1990).

Buzan, Barry and Ole Wæver, "Slippery? Contradictory? Sociologically Untenable? The Copenhagen School Replies," *Review of International Studies* 23/2 (April 1997), pp. 241–250.

Buzan, Barry, Ole Wæver, and Jaap de Wilde, *Security: A New Framework for Analysis* (Boulder: Lynne Rienner, 1998).

Caballero-Anthony, Mely, "Mechanisms of Dispute Settlement: The ASEAN Experience," *Contemporary Southeast Asia* 20/1 (April 1998), pp. 38–66.

Capie, David and Paul Evans, *The Asia-Pacific Security Lexicon* (Singapore: Institute of Southeast Asian Studies, 2002).

Carey, Peter and Steve Cox, *Generations of Resistance: East Timor* (London: Cassell, 1995).

Carpenter, William M. and David G. Wiencek, "Maritime Piracy in Asia," in William M. Carpenter and David G. Wiencek (eds.), *Asian Security Handbook 2000* (New York: M. E. Sharpe, 2000), pp. 88–98.

Case, William, "Malaysia: Aspects and Audiences of Legitimacy," in Muthiah Alagappa (ed.), *Political Legitimacy in Southeast Asia: The Quest for Moral Authority* (Stanford: Stanford University Press, 1995), pp. 69–107.

Caulfield, Catherine, *In the Rainforest* (London: Heinemann, 1985).

Chalk, Peter, "Contemporary Maritime Piracy in Southeast Asia," *Studies in Conflict & Terrorism* 21 (1998), pp. 87–112.

Chalmers, Malcolm, *Confidence-Building in South-East Asia,* Bradford Arms Register Studies No. 6 (Boulder: Westview, 1996).

———, "The Debate on a Regional Arms Register in Southeast Asia," *The Pacific Review* 10/1 (1997), pp. 104–123.

Cheeseman, Graeme, "Asian-Pacific Security Discourse in the Wake of the Asian Economic Crisis," *The Pacific Review* 12/3 (1999), pp. 333–356.

Cheesman, Nick, "Seeing 'Karen' in the Union of Myanmar," *Asian Ethnicity* 3/2 (September 2002), pp. 199–220.

Chien-pin Li, "Fear, Greed, or Garage Sale? The Analysis of Military Expenditure in East Asia," *Pacifica Review* 10/2 (1997), pp. 274–288.

Cho-Oon Khong, "Singapore: Political Legitimacy Through Managing Conformity," in Muthiah Alagappa (ed.), *Political Legitimacy in Southeast Asia: The Quest for Moral Authority* (Stanford: Stanford University Press, 1995), pp. 108–135.

Chopra, Jarat, "The UN's Kingdom of East Timor," *Survival* 42/3 (Autumn 2000), pp. 27–39.

Christie, Clive J., *A Modern History of South East Asia: Decolonization, Nationalism and Separatism* (London: Tauris Academic Press, 1996).

Cline, Lawrence, "The Islamic Insurgency in the Philippines," *Small Wars and Insurgencies* 11/3 (Winter 2000), pp. 115–138.

Colchester, Marcus, "Banking on Disaster: International Support for Transmigration," *The Ecologist* 16 2/3 (1986), pp. 61–70.

Collins, Alan, *The Security Dilemmas of Southeast Asia* (Basingstoke, UK: Macmillan, 2000).

Cotton, James, "The 'Haze' over Southeast Asia: Challenging the ASEAN Mode of Regional Engagement," *Pacific Affairs* 72/3 (Fall 1999), pp. 331–351.

Crouch, Harold, "Malaysia: Do Elections Make a Difference?" in R. H. Taylor (ed.), *The Politics of Elections in Southeast Asia* (Washington: Woodrow Wilson Center, 1996), pp. 114–135.

Dahm, Bernhard, "Ethnic Groups, Colonial Conquest and Nationalism in Sumatra," in Thomas Engelbert and Andreas Schneider (eds.), *Ethnic Minorities and Nationalism in Southeast Asia* (Frankfurt am Main: Peter Lang, 2000), pp. 13–38.

Davis, Michael, "Laskar Jihad and the Political Position of Conservative Islam in Indonesia," *Contemporary Southeast Asia* 24/1 (April 2002), pp. 12–32.

de Magalhães, A. Barbedo, *East Timor: Indonesian Occupation and Genocide* (Porto Codex: Oporto University, 1992).

Dent, Christopher M., "Singapore's Foreign Economic Policy: The Pursuit of Economic Security," *Contemporary Southeast Asia* 23/1 (April 2001), pp. 1–23.

———, "Reconciling Multiple Economic Multilateralisms: The Case of Singapore," *Contemporary Southeast Asia* 24/1 (April 2002), pp. 146–165.

Desker, Barry and Kumar Ramakrishna, "Forging an Indirect Strategy in Southeast Asia," *The Washington Quarterly* 25/2 (Spring 2002), pp. 161–176.

Deutsch, Karl, *Political Community and the North Atlantic Area: International Organization in the Light of Historic Experience* (Princeton: Princeton University Press, 1957).

Dewitt, David, "Common, Comprehensive and Cooperative Security," *The Pacific Review* 7/1 (1994), pp. 1–15.

Dhanani, Shafiq and Iyanatul Islam, "Poverty, Vulnerability and Social Protection in a Period of Crisis: The Case of Indonesia," *World Development* 30/7 (July 2002), pp. 1211–1231.

Dibb, Paul, "Indonesia: The Key to South-East Asia's Security," *International Affairs* 77/4 (2001), pp. 829–842.

Dokken, Karin, "Environment, Security and Regionalism in the Asia-Pacific: Is Environmental Security a Useful Concept?" *The Pacific Review* 14/4 (2001), pp. 509–530.

Doyle, Michael. "Liberalism and World Politics," *American Political Science Review* 80/4 (December 1986), pp. 1151–1169.

Dupont, Alan, "Indonesian Defence Strategy and Security: Time for a Rethink?" *Contemporary Southeast Asia* 18/3 (December 1996), pp. 275–297.

———, "The Environment and Security in Pacific Asia," Adelphi Paper 319 (London: International Institute for Strategic Studies, 1998).

———, "ASEAN's Response to the East Timor Crisis," *Australian Journal of International Affairs* 54/2 (2000), pp. 163–170.

———, *East Asia Imperilled: Transnational Challenges to Security* (Cambridge, UK: Cambridge University Press, 2001).

Eklöf, Stefan, *Indonesian Politics in Crisis: The Long Fall of Suharto, 1996–98* (Copenhagen: Nordic Institute of Asian Studies, 1999).

Emerson, Donald K., "Will Indonesia Survive?" *Foreign Affairs* 79/3 (May/June 2000), pp. 95–106.

Emmers, Ralf, "The Influence of the Balance of Power Factor Within the ASEAN Regional Forum," *Contemporary Southeast Asia* 23/2 (August 2001), pp. 275–291.

Esche, Annemarie, "Nation, Nation-State and Ethnicity (with Reference to the Union of Myanmar)," in Thomas Engelbert and Andreas Schneider (eds), *Ethnic Minorities and Nationalism in Southeast Asia* (Frankfurt am Main: Peter Lang, 2000), pp. 85–92.

Evans, Gareth, "Cooperative Security and Intrastate Conflict," *Foreign Policy* 96 (Fall 1994), pp. 3–21.

Fifield, Russell H., *National and Regional Interests in ASEAN: Competition and Co-operation in International Politics*, Occasional Paper 57 (Singapore: Institute of Southeast Asian Studies, 1979)

Foot, Rosemary, "China in the ASEAN Regional Forum: Organizational Processes and Domestic Modes of Thought," *Asian Survey* 38/5 (May 1998), pp. 425–440.

Fukuda, Chisako M., "Peace Through Nonviolent Action: The East Timorese Resistance Movement's Strategy for Engagement," *Pacifica Review* 12/1 (February 2000), pp. 17–31.

Funston, N. J., *Malay Politics in Malaysia: A Study of the United Malays National Organisation and Party Islam* (Kuala Lumpur: Heinemann, 1980).

Funston, John, "ASEAN: Out of Its Depth," *Contemporary Southeast Asia* 20/1 (April 1998), pp. 22–37.

———, "Malaysia's Tenth Elections: Status Quo, *Reformasi* or Islamization?" *Contemporary Southeast Asia* 22/1 (April 2000), pp. 23–59.

Ganesan, N., "Bilateral Tensions in Post–Cold War ASEAN," Pacific Strategic Papers 9 (Singapore: Institute of Southeast Asian Studies, 1999).

———, "ASEAN's Relations with Major External Powers," *Contemporary Southeast Asia* 22/2 (August 2000), pp. 258–278.

Garofano, John, "Flexibility or Irrelevance: Ways Forward for the ARF," *Contemporary Southeast Asia* 21/1 (April 1999), pp. 74–94.

———, "Power, Institutionalism, and the ASEAN Regional Forum: A Security Community for Asia?" *Asian Survey* 42/3 (May/June 2002), pp. 502–521.

Gershman, John, "Is Southeast Asia the Second Front?" *Foreign Affairs* 81/4 (July/August 2002), pp. 60–74.

Goh, Evelyn, "The Hydro-politics of the Mekong River Basin: Regional Cooperation and Environmental Security," in Andrew T. H. Tan and J. D. Kenneth Boutin (eds.), *Non-Traditional Security Issues in Southeast Asia* (Singapore: Institute of Defence and Strategic Studies, 2001), pp. 468–506.

Gomez, Edgardo D., "Marine Scientific Research in the South China Sea and Environmental Security," *Ocean Development & International Law* 32/2 (April-June 2001).

Gravers, Mikael, *Nationalism as Political Paranoia in Burma* (Richmond, UK: Curzon Press, 1999).

Gray, Colin S., *Modern Strategy* (Oxford: Oxford University Press, 1999).

Guan, Ang Cheng, "The South China Sea Dispute Revisited," *Australian Journal of International Affairs* 54/2 (2000), pp. 201–215.

Gunaratna, Rohan, *Inside Al Qaeda: Global Network of Terror* (London: Hurst & Company, 2002).

Haacke, Jürgen, "The Concept of Flexible Engagement and the Practice of Enhanced Interaction: Intramural Challenges to the 'ASEAN Way,'" *The Pacific Review* 12/4 (1999), pp. 581–611.

———, *ASEAN's Diplomatic and Security Culture: Origins, Development and Prospects* (London: Routledge/Curzon, 2003).

Haque, M. Shamsul, "Environmental Security in East Asia: A Critical View," *Journal of Strategic Studies* 24/4 (December 2001), pp. 203–234.

Hara, Abubakar E., "The Difficult Journey of Democratization in Indonesia," *Contemporary Southeast Asia* 23/2 (August 2001), pp. 307–326.

Harper, T. N., "New Malays, New Malaysians: Nationalism, Society and History," *Southeast Asian Affairs 1996* (Singapore: Institute of Southeast Asian Studies, 1996).

Hayami, Yoko and Susan M. Darlington, "The Karen of Burma and Thailand," in Leslie E. Sponsel (ed.), *Endangered Peoples of Southeast and East Asia: Struggles to Survive and Thrive* (Westport, CT: Greenwood, 2000), pp. 137–155.

Hechter, Michael, *Internal Colonialism: The Celtic Fringe in British National Development 1536–1966* (London: Routledge & Kegan Paul, 1975).

Henderson, Jeannie, "Reassessing ASEAN," Adelphi Paper 328 (London: International Institute for Strategic Studies, 1999).

Heryanto, Ariel, "Ethnic Identities and Erasure: Chinese Indonesians in Public Culture," in Joel S. Kahn (ed.), *Southeast Asian Identities: Culture and the Politics of Representation in Indonesia, Malaysia, Singapore, and Thailand* (Singapore: Institute of Southeast Asian Studies, 1998), pp. 95–114.

Hoang Anh Tuan, "ASEAN Dispute Management: Implications for Vietnam and an Expanded ASEAN," *Contemporary Southeast Asia* 18/1 (June 1996), pp. 61–80.

Houtman, Gustaaf, *Mental Culture in Burmese Crisis Politics* (Tokyo: Institute for the Study of Languages and Cultures of Asia and Africa, Tokyo University of Foreign Studies, 1999).

Hund, Markus, "From 'Neighbourhood Watch Group' to Community? The Case of ASEAN Institutions and the Pooling of Sovereignty," *Australian Journal of International Affairs* 56/1 (2002), pp. 99–122.

Huntington, Samuel P., *The Third Wave: Democratization in the Late Twentieth Century* (Norman: University of Oklahoma Press, 1991).

Huxley, Tim, "Singapore and Malaysia: A Precarious Balance?" *The Pacific Review* 4/3 (1991), pp. 204–213.

———, *Insecurity in the ASEAN Region* (London: Royal United Services Institute Whitehall Paper, 1993).

———, "Southeast Asia in the Study of International Relations: The Rise and Decline of a Region," *The Pacific Review* 9/2 (1996), pp. 199–228.

———, *Defending the Lion City: The Armed Forces of Singapore* (London: Allen & Unwin, 2000).

———, "Reforming Southeast Asia's Security Sectors," *The Conflict, Security & Development Group Working Papers* (London: Centre for Defence Studies, King's College, 2001).

———, "Singapore in 2001: Political Continuity Despite Deepening Recession," *Asian Survey* 42/1 (January/February 2002), pp. 156–164.

Huxley, Tim and Susan Willett, "Arming East Asia," Adelphi Paper 329 (London: International Institute for Strategic Studies, 1999).

I Ketut Putra Erawan, "Political Reform and Regional Politics in Indonesia," *Asian Survey* 39/4 (July/August 1999), pp. 588–612.

Jackson, Robert H., *Quasi-states: Sovereignty, International Relations and the Third World* (Cambridge: Cambridge University Press, 1993).

Jesudason, James V., "Chinese Business and Ethnic Equilibrium in Malaysia," *Development and Change* 28/1 (1997), pp. 119–141.

Job, Brian L., "The Insecurity Dilemma: National, Regime, and State Securities in the Third World," in Brian L. Job (ed.), *The Insecurity Dilemma: National Security of Third World States* (Boulder: Lynne Rienner, 1992), pp. 11–35.

Johnson, Douglas M., "Anticipating Instability in the Asia-Pacific Region," *The Washington Quarterly* 15/3 (Summer 1992), pp. 103–112.

Johnston, Alastair Iain, "The Myth of the ASEAN Way? Explaining the Evolution of the ASEAN Regional Forum," in Helga Haftendorn, Robert O. Keohane, and Celeste A. Wallander (eds.), *Imperfect Unions: Security Institutions over Time and Space* (New York: Oxford University Press, 1999), pp. 287–324.

Jones, David Martin and Mike Lawrence Smith, "Southeast Asia and the War Against Terrorism: The Rise of Islamism and the Challenge to the Surveillance State," in Uwe Johannen, Alan Smith, and James Gomez (eds.), *September 11 & Political Freedom: Asian Perspectives* (Singapore: Select Publishing, 2003), pp. 142–173.

Jørgensen-Dahl, Arnfinn, "Indonesia as Regional Great Power," in Iver B. Neumann (ed.), *Regional Great Powers in International Politics* (London: St. Martin's, 1992), pp. 70–94.

Keyes, Charles F., *Isan: Regionalism in Northeastern Thailand* Data Paper 65 (Ithaca: Cornell University Southeast Asia Program, 1967).

Kim Sung-Han, "The Role of the ARF and the Korean Peninsula," *Journal of East Asian Affairs* 12/2 (Summer/Fall 1998), pp. 506–528.

King, Gary and Christopher J. L. Murray, "Rethinking Human Security," *Political Science Quarterly* 116/4 (2001–2002), pp. 585–610.

Klare, Michael T., "The Next Great Arms Race," *Foreign Affairs* 72/3 (Summer 1993), pp. 136–152.

Knudsen, Olav F., "Post-Copenhagen Security Studies: Desecuritizing Securitization," *Security Dialogue* 32/3 (September 2001), pp. 355–368.

Kraft, Herman, "ASEAN and Intra-ASEAN Relations: Weathering the Storm?" *The Pacific Review* 13/3 (2000), pp. 453–472.

Krause, Keith and Michael C. Williams, *Critical Security Studies: Concepts and Cases* (London: University College of London Press, 1997).

Lawson, Stephanie, "Sanitizing Ethnicity: The Creation of Singapore's Apolitical Culture," *Nationalism & Ethnic Politics* 7/1 (Spring 2001), pp. 63–84.

Layador, Maria Anna Rowena Luz G., "The Emerging ASEAN Plus Three Process: Another Building Block for Community Building in the Asia Pacific?" *Indonesian Quarterly* 28/4 (2000), pp. 434–443.

Lee Kuan Yew, *The Singapore Story: Memoirs of Lee Kuan Yew* (Singapore: Prentice Hall, 1998).

Lee Lai To, *China and the South China Sea Dialogues* (Westport, CT: Praeger, 1999).

———, "The South China Sea: China and Multilateral Dialogues," *Security Dialogue* 30/2 (June 1999), pp. 165–178.

Leifer, Michael, *ASEAN and the Security of South-East Asia* (London: Routledge, 1990).

————, "Debating Asian Security: Michael Leifer Responds to Geoffrey Wiseman," *The Pacific Review* 5/2 (1992), pp. 167–169.

————, "The ASEAN Regional Forum," Adelphi Paper 302 (London: International Institute for Strategic Studies, 1996).

————, "The ASEAN Peace Process: A Category Mistake," *The Pacific Review* 12/1 (1999), pp. 25–38.

Liddle, R. William, "Coercion, Co-option, and the Management of Ethnic Relations in Indonesia," in Michael E. Brown and Šumit Ganguly (eds.), *Government Policies and Ethnic Relations in Asia and the Pacific* (Cambridge, MA: MIT Press, 1997), pp. 273–319.

Lim, Robyn, "The ASEAN Regional Forum: Building on Sand," *Contemporary Southeast Asia* 20/2 (August 1998), pp. 115–136.

Long, Joey, "Desecuritizing the Water Issue in Singapore-Malaysia Relations," *Contemporary Southeast Asia* 23/3 (December 2001), pp. 504–532.

MacIntyre, Andrew J., "Interpreting Indonesian Foreign Policy: The Case of Kampuchea 1979–1986," *Asian Survey* 27/5 (May 1987), pp. 515–534.

Mak, J. N. and B. A. Hamzah, "The External Maritime Dimension of ASEAN Security," *Journal of Strategic Studies* 18/3 (September 1995), pp. 123–146.

Malley, Michael S., "Indonesia in 2001: Restoring Stability in Jakarta," *Asian Survey* 42/1 (January/February 2002), pp. 124–132.

Mandel, Robert, *The Changing Face of National Security: A Conceptual Analysis* (Westport, CT: Greenwood, 1994).

Martinez, Patricia, "Malaysia in 2001: An Interlude of Consolidation," *Asian Survey* 42/1 (January/February 2002), pp. 133–140.

Mason, T. David and Dale A. Krane, "The Political Economy of Death Squads: Toward a Theory of the Impact of State-Sanctioned Terror," *International Studies Quarterly* 33/2 (June 1989), pp. 175–198.

Matthew, Richard A., "Integrating Environmental Factors into Conventional Security," in Miriam R. Lowi and Brian R. Shaw (eds.), *Environment and Security: Discourses and Practices* (Basingstoke, UK: Macmillan, 2000), pp. 33–48.

Matthews, Bruce, "Ethnic and Religious Diversity," ISEAS Working Paper (Singapore: Institute of Southeast Asian Studies, 2001).

Mauzy, Diane K. and R. S. Milne, *Singapore Politics Under the People's Action Party* (London: Routledge, 2002).

McCargo, Duncan, "Security, Development and Political Participation in Thailand: Alternative Currencies of Legitimacy," *Contemporary Southeast Asia* 24/1 (April 2002), pp. 50–67.

McDougall, Derek, "Asia-Pacific Security Regionalism: The Impact of Post–1997 Developments," *Contemporary Security Policy* 23/2 (August 2002), pp. 113–134.

McSweeny, Bill, "Identity and Security: Buzan and the Copenhagen School," *Review of International Studies* 22/1 (January 1996), pp. 81–93.

Midford, Paul, "Japan's Leadership Role in East Asian Security Multilateralism: The Nakayama Proposal and the Logic of Reassurance," *The Pacific Review* 13/3 (2000), pp. 367–397.

Möller, Kay, "Cambodia and Burma: The ASEAN Way Ends Here," *Asian Survey* 38/12 (December 1998), pp. 1087–1104.

Mutalib, Hussein, "Singapore's Embrace of Globalization—and Its Implications for the Republic's Security," *Contemporary Security Policy* 23/1 (April 2002), pp. 129–148.

Mutimer, David, "Beyond Strategy: Critical Thinking and the New Security Studies," in Craig A. Snyder (ed.), *Contemporary Security and Strategy* (London: Macmillan, 1999), pp. 75–101.

Næss, Tom, "Environmental Cooperation Around the South China Sea: The Experience of the South China Sea Workshops and the United Nations Environment Programme's Strategic Action Programme," *The Pacific Review* 14/4 (2001), pp. 553–573.

Narine, Shaun, "ASEAN and the ARF: The Limits of the "ASEAN Way,'" *Asian Survey* 37/10 (October 1997), pp. 961–978.

———, "ASEAN into the Twenty-first Century," *The Pacific Review* 12/3 (1999), pp. 357–380.

———, "ASEAN in the Aftermath: The Consequences of the East Asian Economic Crisis," *Global Governance* 8/2 (April-June 2002), pp. 179–194.

Nathan, K. S., "Malaysia: Reinventing the Nation," in Muthiah Alagappa (ed.), *Asian Security Practice: Material and Ideational Influences* (Stanford: Stanford University Press, 1998), pp. 513–548.

Nesadurai, Helen E. S., "Cooperation and Institutional Transformation in ASEAN: Insights from the AFTA Project," in Andrew T. H. Tan and J. D. Kenneth Boutin (eds.), *Non-Traditional Security Issues in Southeast Asia* (Singapore: Institute of Defence and Strategic Studies, 2001), pp. 197–226.

———, "Attempting Developmental Regionalism Through AFTA: The Domestic Politics—Domestic Capital Nexus," IDSS Working Paper 31 (Singapore: Institute of Defence and Strategic Studies, August 2002).

Nischalke, Tobias Ingo, "Insights from ASEAN's Foreign Policy Co-operation: The 'ASEAN Way,' a Real Spirit or a Phantom?" *Contemporary Southeast Asia* 22/1 (April 2000), pp. 89–112.

———, "Does ASEAN Measure Up? Post–Cold War Diplomacy and the Idea of Regional Community," *The Pacific Review* 15/1 (2002), pp. 89–117.

Nye, Jospeh S., Jr., and Sean M. Lynn-Jones, "International Security Studies: A Report of a Conference on the State of the Field," *International Security* 12/4 (Spring 1988), pp. 5–27.

O'Rourke, Kevin, *Reformasi: The Struggle for Power in Post-Soeharto Indonesia* (Crows Nest, Australia: Allen & Unwin, 2002).

Odgaard, Liselotte, "Deterrence and Co-operation in the South China Sea," *Contemporary Southeast Asia* 23/2 (August 2001), pp. 292–306.

Ooi Kee Beng, "New Crisis and Old Problems in Malaysia," in Ho Khai Leong and James Chin (eds.), *Mahathir's Administration: Performance and Crisis in Governance* (Singapore: Times Books International, 2001), pp. 100–119.

Osborne, Milton, "The Strategic Significance of the Mekong," *Contemporary Southeast Asia* 22/3 (December 2000), pp. 429–444.

Overholt, William H., "Thailand's Financial and Political Systems: Crisis and Rejuvenation," *Asian Survey* 39/6 (November/December 1999), pp. 1009–1035.

Pabottingi, Mochtar, "Indonesia: Historicizing the New Order's Legitimacy Dilemma," in Muthiah Alagappa (ed.), *Political Legitimacy in Southeast Asia: The Quest for Moral Authority* (Stanford: Stanford University Press, 1995), pp. 224–256.

Palme Commission (Independent Commission on Disarmament and Security Issues), *Common Security: A Programme for Disarmament* (London: Pan Books, 1982).

Paris, Roland, "Human Security: Paradigm Shift or Hot Air?" *International Security* 26/2 (Fall 2001), pp. 87–102.

Pettiford, Lloyd, "When Is a Realist Not a Realist? Stories Knudsen Doesn't Tell," *Security Dialogue* 32/3 (September 2001), pp. 369–374.

Pitsuwan, Surin, "Future Directions for ASEAN," *Trends in Southeast Asia*, No. 10 (Singapore: Institute of Southeast Asian Studies, 2001).

Ramcharan, Robin, "ASEAN and Non-interference: A Principle Maintained," *Contemporary Southeast Asia* 22/1 (April 2000), pp. 60–88.

Reilly, Benjamin, "Internal Conflict and Regional Security in Asia and the Pacific," *Pacifica Review* 14/1 (February 2002), pp. 7–21.

Rothstein, Robert L., "The 'Security Dilemma' and the 'Poverty Trap' in the Third World," *Jerusalem Journal of International Relations* 8/4 (1986), pp. 1–38.

Rüland, Jürgen, "ASEAN and the Asian Crisis: Theoretical Implications and Practical Consequences for Southeast Asian Regionalism," *The Pacific Review* 13/3 (2000), pp. 421–451.

Salameh, Mamdouh G., "China, Oil and the Risk of Regional Conflict," *Survival* 37/4 (Winter 1995–1996), pp. 133–146.

Samydorai, Sinapan, "9/11 Anti-Terrorist Measures and Their Impact on Human Rights in Asia," in Uwe Johannen, Alan Smith, and James Gomez (eds.), *September 11 & Political Freedom: Asian Perspectives* (Singapore: Select, 2003), pp. 216–240.

SarDesai, D. R., *Southeast Asia: Past & Present,* 4th ed. (Boulder: Westview, 1997).

Schiller, Anne and Bambang Garang, "Religion and Inter-ethnic Violence in Indonesia," *Journal of Contemporary Asia* 32/2 (2002), pp. 244–254.

Schofield, Clive, "Sea of Plenty? The 'Oil factor' in the South China Sea and Prospects for Joint Development," paper presented at the Panel on the South China Sea, Third International Conference of the European Association of Southeast Asian Studies, London, 6–8 September 2001.

Schofield, Julian, "War and Punishment: The Implication of Arms Purchases in Maritime Southeast Asia," *Journal of Strategic Studies* 21/2 (June 1998), pp. 75–106.

Schwarz, Adam, *A Nation in Waiting: Indonesia in the 1990s* (Boulder: Westview, 1994).

Searle, Peter, "Ethno-Religious Conflicts: Rise or Decline? Recent Developments in Southeast Asia," *Contemporary Southeast Asia* 24/1 (April 2002), pp. 1–11.

Sebastian, Leonard C., "Values and Governance Issues in the Foreign Policy of Singapore," in Han Sung-Joo (ed.), *Changing Values in Asia: Their Impact on Governance and Development* (Tokyo: Japan Center for International Exchange, 1999), pp. 219–250.

Segal, Gerald, "Managing New Arms Races in the Asia/Pacific," *The Washington Quarterly* 15/3 (Summer 1992), pp. 83–101.

———, "East Asia and the 'Constrainment' of China," *International Security* 20/4 (Spring 1996), pp. 107–135.

Seng, Tan See, "Human Security: Discourse, Statecraft, Emancipation," IDSS Working Paper 11 (Singapore: Institute of Defence and Strategic Studies, May 2001).

Sherlock, Stephen, "Political Economy of the East Timor Conflict," *Asian Survey* 36/9 (September 1996), p. 835–851.

Silverstein, Josef, *Burmese Politics: The Dilemma of National Unity* (New Brunswick, NJ: Rutgers University Press, 1980).

———, "The Civil War, the Minorities and Burma's New Politics," in Peter Carey (ed.), *Burma: The Challenge of Change in a Divided Society* (Basingstoke, UK: Macmillan, 1997), pp. 129–156.

Simon, Sheldon W., "Mixed Reactions in Southeast Asia to the US War on Terrorism," *Comparative Connections—A Quarterly E-Journal on East Asian Bilateral Relations* 3/4 (2001), pp. 47–55.

———, "Evaluating Track II Approaches to Security Diplomacy in the Asia-Pacific: The CSCAP Experience," *The Pacific Review* 15/2 (2002), pp. 167–200.

———, "Southeast Asia and the U.S. War on Terrorism," *NBR Analysis* 13/4 (July 2002), pp. 25–37.

Singh, Bilveer, *Succession Politics in Indonesia: The 1998 Presidential Elections and the Fall of Suharto* (Basingstoke, UK: Macmillan, 2000).

Siow Yue, Chia, "The ASEAN Free Trade Area," *The Pacific Review* 11/2 (1998), pp. 213–232.

———, "Trade, Foreign Direct Investment and Economic Development of Southeast Asia," *The Pacific Review* 12/2 (1999), pp. 249–270.

Smith, Anthony L., "Recent Political Developments in Southeast Asia," *Trends in Southeast Asia*, No. 6 (Singapore: Institute of Southeast Asian Studies, 2002).

Smith, Esmond D., Jr. "China's Aspirations in the Spratly Islands," *Contemporary Southeast Asia* 16/3 (December 1994), pp. 274–294.

Smith, M. L. and D. M. Jones, "ASEAN, Asian Values and Southeast Asian Security in the New World Order," *Contemporary Security Policy* 18/3 (December 1997), pp. 126–156.

Smith, Steve, "The Increasing Insecurity of Security Studies: Conceptualizing Security in the Last Twenty Years," in Stuart Croft and Terry Terriff (eds.), *Critical Reflections on Security and Change* (London: Frank Cass, 2000), pp. 72–101.

Smoke, Richard, "A Theory of Mutual Security," in Richard Smoke and Andrei Kortunov (eds), *Mutual Security: A New Approach to Soviet-American Relations* (Basingstoke, UK: Macmillan: 1991), pp. 59–111.

Snitwongse, Kusuma, "Thai Foreign Policy in the Global Age: Principle or

Profit?" *Contemporary Southeast Asia* 23/2 (August 2001), pp. 189–212.

Soesastro, Hadi, "ASEAN in 2030: The Long View," in Simon S. C. Tay, Jesus P. Estanislao, and Hadi Soesastro (eds.), *Reinventing ASEAN* (Singapore: Institute of Southeast Asian Studies, 2001), pp. 273–310.

——, "Towards an East Asian Regional Trading Arrangement," in Simon S. C. Tay, Jesus P. Estanislao, and Hadi Soesastro (eds.), *Reinventing ASEAN* (Singapore: Institute of Southeast Asian Studies, 2001), pp. 226–242.

——, "Southeast Asia and Global Terrorism: Implications on State Security and Human Security," *Indonesian Quarterly* 30/1 (2002), pp. 31–37.

Solingen, Etel, "ASEAN, Quo Vadis? Domestic Coalitions and Regional Cooperation," *Contemporary Southeast Asia* 21/1 (April 1999), pp. 30–53.

Sorpong Peou, "Realism and Constructivism in Southeast Asian Security Studies Today: A Review Essay," *The Pacific Review* 15/1 (2002), pp. 119–138.

Steinberg, David I., *The Future of Burma: Crisis and Choice in Myanmar* (Lanham, MD: University Press of America, 1990).

Storey, Ian James, "Creeping Assertiveness: China, the Philippines and the South China Sea," *Contemporary Southeast Asia* 21/1 (April 1999), pp. 95–118.

Stubbs, Richard, "ASEAN Plus Three: Emerging East Asian Regionalism?" *Asian Survey* 42/3 (May/June 2002), pp. 440–455.

Sukatipan, Saitip, "Thailand: The Evolution of Legitimacy," in Muthiah Alagappa, (ed.), *Political Legitimacy in Southeast Asia: The Quest for Moral Authority* (Stanford: Stanford University Press, 1995), pp. 193–223.

Sukma, Rizal, *Indonesia and China: The Politics of a Troubled Relationship* (London: Routledge, 1999).

Sulistiyanto, Priyambudi, "Whither Aceh?" *Third World Quarterly* 22/3 (June 2001), pp. 437–452.

Suryadinata, Leo, "Chinese Politics in Post-Suharto's Indonesia," *Asian Survey* 41/3 (May/June 2001), pp. 502–524.

Tan, Andrew, *Intra-ASEAN Tensions*, Discussion Paper 84 (London: Royal Institute of International Affairs, 2000).

——, "The 'New' Terrorism: How Southeast Asia Can Counter It," in Uwe Johannen, Alan Smith, and James Gomez (eds.), *September 11 & Political Freedom: Asian Perspectives* (Singapore: Select Publishing, 2003), pp. 86–113.

Tay, Simon S. C., "What Should Be Done About the Haze," *Indonesian Quarterly* 26/2 (1998), pp. 99–117.

——, "ASEAN and East Asia: A New Regionalism?" in Simon S. C. Tay, Jesus P. Estanislao, and Hadi Soesastro (eds.), *Reinventing ASEAN* (Singapore: Institute of Southeast Asian Studies, 2001), pp. 206–225.

——, "Institutions and Processes: Dilemmas and Possibilities," in Simon S. C. Tay, Jesus P. Estanislao, and Hadi Soesastro (eds.), *Reinventing ASEAN* (Singapore: Institute of Southeast Asian Studies, 2001), pp. 243–272.

Tay, Simon S. C. with Obood Talib, "The ASEAN Regional Forum: Preparing for Preventive Diplomacy," *Contemporary Southeast Asia* 19/3 (December 1997), pp. 252–268.

Taylor, John G., *Indonesia's Forgotten War: The Hidden History of East Timor* (London: Zed Books, 1991).

Taylor, Robert H., "The Constitutional Future of Myanmar in Comparative Perspective," in Peter Carey (ed.), *Burma: The Challenge of Change in a Divided Society* (Basingstoke, UK: Macmillan, 1997), pp. 55–67.

Than, Tin Maung Maung, "Myanmar: The Dilemma of Stalled Reforms," *Trends in Southeast Asia*, No. 10 (Singapore: Institute of Southeast Asian Studies, 2000).

Thomas, Caroline, *In Search of Security: The Third World in International Relations* (Boulder: Lynne Rienner, 1987).

Thomas, Nicholas and William T. Tow, "The Utility of Human Security: Sovereignty and Humanitarian Intervention," *Security Dialogue* 33/2 (June 2002), pp. 177–192.

———, "Gaining Security by Trashing the State? A Reply to Bellamy & McDonald," *Security Dialogue* 33/3 (September 2002), pp. 379–382.

Tilly, Charles, "Reflections on the History of European State-Making," in Charles Tilly (ed.), *The Formation of National States in Western Europe* (Princeton: Princeton University Press, 1975), pp. 3–84.

Tønnesson, Stein, "China and the South China Sea: A Peace Proposal," *Security Dialogue* 31/3 (September 2000), pp. 307–326.

———, "An International History of the Dispute in the South China Sea," EAI Working Paper No. 71 (East Asian Institute, 2001).

Törnquist, Olle, "Dynamics of Indonesian Democratisation," *Third World Quarterly* 21/3 (2000), pp. 383–423.

Tow, William T., "Alternative Security Models: Implications for ASEAN," in Andrew T. H. Tan and J. D. Kenneth Boutin, eds., *Non-Traditional Security Issues in Southeast Asia* (Singapore: Institute of Defence and Strategic Studies, 2001), pp. 257–285.

Tow, William T. and Russell Trood, "Linkages Between Traditional Security and Human Security," in William T. Tow, Ramesh Thakur, and In-Taek Hyun (eds.), *Asia's Emerging Regional Order: Reconciling Traditional and Human Security* (Tokyo: United Nations University Press, 2000), pp. 13–32.

Townsend-Gault, Ian, "Preventive Diplomacy and Pro-Activity in the South China Sea," *Contemporary Southeast Asia* 20/2 (August 1998), pp. 171–190.

Unger, Danny, "A Regional Economic Order in East and Southeast Asia?" *Journal of Strategic Studies* 24/4 (December 2001), pp. 179–202.

United Nations Development Program, *Human Development Report, 1994* (New York: Oxford University Press, 1994)

Vagg, Jon, "Rough Seas? Contemporary Piracy in South East Asia," *British Journal of Criminology* 35/1 (Winter 1995), pp. 63–80.

Valencia, Mark J., "China and the South China Sea Disputes," Adelphi Paper 298 (London: International Institute for Strategic Studies, 1995).

———, "Building Confidence and Security in the South China Sea: The Way Forward," in Andrew T. H. Tan and J. D. Kenneth Boutin (eds.), *Non-Traditional Security Issues in Southeast Asia* (Singapore: Institute of Defence and Strategic Studies, 2001), pp. 528–569.

Valencia, Mark J., Jon M. Van Dyke, and Noel A. Ludwig, *Sharing Resources of the South China Sea* (The Hague: Kluwer Law International, 1997).

Väyrynen, Raimo, "Regional Conflict Formations: An Intractable Problem of International Relations," *Journal of Peace Research* 21/4 (1984), pp. 357–359.

Walt, Stephen M., "The Renaissance of Security Studies," *International Studies Quarterly* 35/2 (1991), pp. 211–239.

Wanandi, Jusuf, "ASEAN's Past and the Challenges Ahead: Aspects of Politics and Security," in Simon S. C. Tay, Jesus P. Estanislao, and Hadi Soesastro (eds.), *Reinventing ASEAN* (Singapore: Institute of Southeast Asian Studies, 2001), pp. 25–34.

Wang, Kuan-Hsiung, "Bridge over Troubled Waters: Fisheries Cooperation as a Resolution to the South China Sea Conflicts," *The Pacific Review* 14/4 (2001), pp. 531–551.

Wattanayagorn, Panitan, "Thailand: The Elite's Shifting Conceptions of Security," in Muthiah Alagappa (ed.), *Asian Security Practice: Material and Ideational Influences* (Stanford: Stanford University Press, 1998), pp. 417–444.

Webber, Douglas, "Two Funerals and a Wedding? The Ups and Downs of Regionalism in East Asia and Asia-Pacific After the Asian Crisis," *The Pacific Review* 14/3 (2001), pp. 339–372.

Weiss, Meredith L., "The 1999 Malaysian General Election: Issues, Insults, and Irregularities," *Asian Survey* 40/3 (May/June 2000), pp. 413–435.

Willet, Susan, "Dragon's Fire and Tiger's Claws: Arms Trade and Production in Far East Asia," *Contemporary Security Policy* 15/2 (August 1994), pp. 112–135.

Wiseman, Geoffrey, "Common Security in the Asia-Pacific Region," *The Pacific Review* 5/1 (1992), pp. 42–59.

Wolfers, Arnold, *Discord and Collaboration: Essays on International Politics* (Baltimore: Johns Hopkins University Press, 1962).

Wyn Jones, Richard, "'Travel Without Maps': Thinking About Security After the Cold War," in M. Jane Davis (ed.), *Security Issues in the Post–Cold War World* (Cheltenham, UK: Edward Elgar, 1996), pp. 196–218.

Zha, Daojiong, "Localizing the South China Sea Problem: The Case of China's Hainan," *The Pacific Review* 14/4 (2001), pp. 575–598.

———, "Security in the South China Sea," *Alternatives* 26/1 (January-March 2001), pp. 33–51.

Index

237

About the Book

From internal oppression in Burma to interstate conflict in the South China Sea, the people of Southeast Asia face a range of threats. This book identifies and explains the security challenges—both traditional and nontraditional—confronting the region.

Collins addresses the full spectrum of security issues, discussing the impact of ethnic tensions and competing political ideologies, the evolving role of ASEAN, and Southeast Asia's interactions with key external actors (China, Japan, and the United States). The final section of the book explores how the region's security issues are reflected in two current cases: the South China Sea dispute and the war on terrorism.

Alan Collins is lecturer in the Department of Politics and International Relations at the University of Wales Swansea. His publications include *The Security Dilemma and the End of the Cold War.*